The Diaconate

THE DIACONATE

A FULL AND EQUAL ORDER

A Comprehensive and Critical Study
of the Origin, Development, and
Decline of the Diaconate in the Context
of the Church's Total Ministry
and A Proposal for Renewal

James Monroe Barnett

SEABURY · NEW YORK

1981
The Seabury Press
New York, N.Y. 10017

Library of Congress Cataloging in Publication Data

Barnett, James Monroe.
The diaconate—a full and equal order.

Revision of thesis (M.S.T.)—University of the South.
Bibliography: p. 209
1. Deacons—History of doctrines.
2. Deacons. I. Title.
BV680.B37 1981 262'.14 81-9041
ISBN 0-8164-0497-6 AACR2

To my wife, Marian,
and my four sons,
Mark, John, Thomas, and Paul

Contents

PART TWO
The Renewal of the Diaconate in the Church Today 133

Foreword

From time to time I am invited to preach a sermon at the ordination of a deacon. The old Episcopal Prayer Book of 1928 prescribed the subjects of the sermon which I always tried to follow conscientiously. The preacher was required to declare *inter alia* "how necessary that Order is in the Church of Christ" (BCP 1928, p. 530). I always longed to say, Yes, so necessary that in many dioceses there are no deacons around to speak of between Christmas and Trinity! No wonder that excellent rubric has (however regrettably) been removed from the new Prayer Book! It was sheer hypocrisy to claim that we regarded the diaconate as "necessary" to the Church. Another thing I wanted to say was that the Presbyterians and Baptists were in this instance more Catholic than we were: if they had lost episcopacy they had at least restored something more like diaconate as it was in the Primitive Church. The German Lutherans also have a genuinely caritative diaconate, doing social service in parishes and running charitable institutions like Bethel, Bielefeld, for epileptics and other handicapped people.

The removal of that embarrassing rubric and of the post-communion prayer which referred to the diaconate as "this inferior office" (BCP 1928, p. 555) has not improved matters all that much. Now the overall impression is that a person being ordained to the diaconate is being ordained primarily to a ministry of the word. See the New Testament reading from 2 Corinthians 4:1–6, which is *all* about the apostolic ministry of preaching the Word. And then, as the Bishop hands the newly ordained person the Bible, he says, "Receive this Bible as a sign of your authority (*sic!*) to proclaim God's word . . ." Worse than that, every preacher, Roman Catholic or Episcopalian, who exalts the importance of the *diakonia* in the Church of him who came among us as One who serves knows full well that this person in front of him, now being ordained with such solemnity, will to all intents and purposes have to go through it all again in six months or a year's time to be ordained as a priest. Of course, we say, "Once a deacon, always a deacon," but that is pious fiction. The ordination of a deacon, as at present practised, is usually little more than a farce. In the Roman Catholic Church, as with us, the diaconate—despite some attempts since Vatican II—is still seen primarily as a stepping stone to the priesthood.

Dr. Barnett's scholarly study, drawing from Scripture and Antiquity, points the way to the abolition of the apprentice diaconate and the recovery of the Office in its primitive authenticity. I commend his work to all who on the one hand are concerned for the Catholicity of the Church, and to all who on the other hand accept the Reformation principle, *ecclesia semper reformanda.*

REGINALD H. FULLER
Virginia Theological Seminary
Alexandria, Virginia

Preface

This study was originally begun as a thesis for the Master of Sacred Theology degree at the suggestion and under the direction of Dr. Massey H. Shepherd, Jr., who at that time was director of The Graduate School of Theology of the University of the South, a school designed to allow parish priests to do graduate study under some of the Church's most outstanding scholars. Dr. Shepherd is not only one of the great patristic and liturgical scholars of today but is also a gracious Christian gentleman to whom I shall always feel grateful for his inspiration and guidance, not only in this work but in my pursuit of greater and deeper knowledge in the theological disciplines.

This work grew beyond what I had at first envisioned. As my interest in it grew, the program at the University of the South, Sewanee, Tennessee, was enlarged to offer a Joint Doctor of Ministry Program with Vanderbilt University. My study of the diaconate became a dissertation for the program requirement.

However, it has not been done primarily to meet the requirements for a degree. The more I studied the diaconate the more fascinated I became with the order and the more I came to believe in its importance to the renewal of the whole life and ministry of the Church. I found, in addition, that previous studies did not do justice to an order which has a history, in some respects at least, as the most glorious and Christ-like of all ministries. Most of these works are relatively brief, and none seems to have attempted to deal with the diaconate in the context of the nature of the Church and its total ministry. To consider it in isolation is like seeing an uncut diamond as only a pebble or trying to understand and appreciate a boat sitting on dry land.

For me the diaconate has become the most exciting order within a splendid ministry when it is viewed in the context of the whole and seen as it can and should be—the order which informs all orders of the primary work we are all sent to do, though in different ways with varying functions.

This study is, I believe, the most thorough, accurate, and complete work which has been done. Returning to the original sources has in some instances led to conclusions at variance with those which have usually been set forth. A most notable example is that related to the idea that preaching is a function inherent in the diaconate of the early Church, an error of importance far beyond what might appear at first and involving among other things a confusion of orders, a confusion which tends to negate a truly organic conception of the Church.

Another important instance in which the original sources fail to support rather widely held ideas is that relating to *cursus honorum*, the concept of the orders of ministry as a graded structure like rungs in an ecclesiastical ladder to be climbed from the least to the greatest. *Cursus honorum* as a rule and requirement actually came about many centuries later and for far different reasons than is frequently thought.

However, as important as the correction of such errors is, the primary significance of this work lies rather in that it provides the background necessary for an understanding of the diaconate which will enable it to become the exciting order which it can and should be in the Church of the late twentieth and early twenty-first centuries. The proposal for renewal emerges from and can only be understood and appreciated in the light of its historical roots. We should not indeed try to reproduce the order as it existed in the pre–Nicene Church, but the principles which informed it then and made it what it was in terms of that age and culture can do the same for our time.

Someone who read the manuscript in its original form commented that the work is like a giant jet airplane which seems to taxi slowly down the runway until suddenly it takes off in a surge of power. I have not changed this because to do so would mean the loss of much of its value. For most, like myself, I believe an understanding of and appreciation for the diaconate can come only by wrestling with the problem of the nature of the Church and carefully weighing the biblical and historical evidence relating both to the diaconate and to the development and transformation of the Church's total ministry.

I have gradually come to believe that the restoration of the diaconate as a full and equal order can and will do more than any other single act of renewal to bring about the sweeping restoration of the organic character given by Christ to his Church. This statement almost certainly will seem extreme to many, and perhaps it is. However, time may nevertheless prove it to be true.

I am indebted to many for their various contributions in connection with this work. First of all, my parish has been very patient in allowing me the time, especially in the summers, to study and write. In addition to what I have already said in reference to Dr. Shepherd, I am further indebted to him for reading the manuscript and making invaluable notes and comments. Dr. Donald S. Armentrout, my advisor and the director of the Sewanee–Vanderbilt Joint Doctor of Ministry Program, who is a most gifted teacher and an extraordinary preacher, has been most thoughtful and helpful in my research and in reading the manuscript, giving many valuable suggestions. Dr. Marion J. Hatchett has always been available for counsel and advice and has generously given the benefit of his own profound scholarship as well as his warm friendship and support. Thomas Edward Camp, Associate Librarian of the University of the South and Librarian of the School of Theology, provided much kind, efficient, and valuable assistance in finding and obtaining needed works.

Dr. Reginald Fuller graciously helped in translating some references as well as giving other advice and allowing me to audit his course in "Early Catholicism in the New Testament." Fr. Ron Del Bene read an early draft of the manuscript, offered helpful comments and encouraged its publication. Dr. O. C. Edwards, Dr. J. Robert Wright, Fr. Patrick McCaslin, Msgr. Ernest J. Fiedler, Fr. Joe Morris Doss, and Mel Hunke, one of the original deacons in the Archdiocese of Omaha's diaconate program, read all or part of the manuscript and made valuable suggestions from diverse viewpoints.

Fr. McCaslin in addition shared at length some of his experience as Director of the Permanent Diaconate Program for the Archdiocese of Omaha and as national President of the Association of Diaconal Directors. Msgr. Fiedler, Executive Director of the Bishops' Committee on the Permanent Diaconate of the National Conference of Catholic Bishops, also graciously supplied information and encouraged the publication of the work.

Dr. Laura Franklin, retired professor of English at Wayne State College, Wayne, Nebraska, spent many hours checking and proofreading these pages. Her work and suggestions, far beyond the call of duty, are truly appreciated.

Brother Thomas McDermott, a Dominican and friend, spent many hours obtaining books and facilitating my research when a good theological library was not readily available to me. I am also indebted to others for their help: Mrs. Barbara Houser Stuart, for many years coordinator for the Sewanee summer D. Min. program and a good friend; Dr. Urban T. Holmes, Dean of the School of Theology at the University of the South; Fr. Conrad L. Harkins, O.F.M., Director of the Franciscan Institute at Saint Bonaventure University; Fr. Edward H. Konerman, S. J.,

Secretary of the Catholic Theological Society of America; and Dr. Stanley T. Vandersall, Professor of the Department of Classics, the University of Nebraska—Lincoln. The Diocese of Nebraska and its Bishop, James D. Warner, have provided encouragement and financial assistance, for which I am grateful. In the earlier years of my study, when other financial assistance was not available, my mother, Egeria Brooks Barnett, and my aunt, Marion Overton Brooks, made it possible. My editor, Howard Galley, at The Seabury Press, has been most understanding and supportive as well as giving me the benefit of his expert editorial counsel.

Above all, however, I am grateful to my wife, Marian, for her constant and unfailing encouragement, understanding, support, and love during all the time I have spent on this project. She has also had her part in it as my typist, a most efficient one at that, and patient too, especially when deadlines have been short indeed.

I would include here only a few brief notes about the pages which follow. I have used the Revised Standard Version of the Scriptures (RSV), I believe, in every instance unless noted otherwise. Though works of this type usually do not include the particular translations of the ancient documents and writings, I have made a special effort to include them for the convenience of those who may not be thoroughly conversant with them. For the same reason the bibliography includes some cross-references and full references which might otherwise have been omitted. A brief history of diaconal vestments from the works of various scholars has been included in the Appendix, first as a convenience to the reader but also because an accurate, clear, concise history is not available.

May 20, 1981
Feast of St. Alcuin,
Deacon and Abbot of Tours

James Barnett

The Diaconate

PART ONE

THE ORIGIN, DEVELOPMENT, AND DECLINE OF THE DIACONATE

CHAPTER 1

The Nature of the Church—Truly Organic

The principle of the diaconate as an office and function in the Church is rooted in the nature of the Church itself as it was originally founded and lived in the pre-Nicene world. The first principle of that Church as it came into being was that it was *laos*, the people of God. The Church was called into being by God and made "a chosen race, a royal priesthood, a holy nation, God's own people."[1] All were *laos*. There was no word to distinguish, in the sense of today, between clergy and laity. The clergy were laity along with others who belonged to the people of God.[2]

It is here that we must begin if we are to clarify our understanding of the Church's ministry, because we must first rethink our theology of the Church itself. As G. W. H. Lampe observes, the basic problem in many attempts to deal with the ministry is the failure to have dealt adequately first of all with the nature of the Church.[3] While references in the New Testament and the post-apostolic generation to the origin and development of the ministry, and especially to what today we term the clerical ministry, are inadequate, the greater factor resulting in different interpretations of the Church's ministry has been the differing theological assumptions regarding the nature of the Church.[4]

Although it is far beyond the scope of this study to discuss in detail the nature of the Church, some consideration of several fundamental aspects of its nature is necessary here. We need first of all to recall the Church's corporate, organic constitution, which for centuries has been lost from sight and obscured in large measure by a "clericalism" that has dominated the churches, whether Protestant, Anglican, Orthodox, or Roman Catholic. The first Christians did not think in terms of having particular persons set aside, by whatever means, as "ministers" to do the Church's ministering. Even less did they think "primarily of a hierarchy and secondarily of a Church whose catholicity was guaranteed thereby"[5] as many Christians do today.

In fact in the early Church we find no sacred persons or sacred places.[6] In Jesus there is the union of infinite God with the flesh of humanity in which the goodness and holiness of creation is forever affirmed. Therefore, the Church from the outset avoided taking over the false distinction from Judaism between the sacred and the secular. It saw all as sacred. This is not, of course, to say that those Christians did not hold and treat some things more reverently than others. But it is to say that they had new insight into the nature of the Church and its relationship to the world. They had the Eucharist *wherever* they happened to come together as the Church.[7] They avoided designating those who performed the various functions of the Church by titles that would have set them apart from or given them rank above the rest of the *laos*. As Hans Küng observes, the New Testament clearly avoids using the "current and obvious terms" which denote "primacy," "rank," or "the honour and dignity of office" in reference to Christian ministries.[8] New words were needed because the Greek words then in use "all express a relationship of rulers and ruled."[9]

In emphasizing that the charisma given all Christians in baptism excluded the possibility of sacred space, sacred time, and sacred persons in the primitive Church, Käsemann asks rhetorically,

> "Does not all this lead to the profanation of what is holy?" The answer is, that the opposite is true. The fenced-off boundaries of "religion" are broken through when grace invades the world and its everyday life. It is not mistrust of the cultic element as such which leads Paul to avoid as a general rule the terminology of Old Testament or heathen sacrifices. On the contrary, in Rom. 12:1f he deliberately resorts to cultic language of this kind in order to describe the sanctification of everyday life as the true sacrifice of Christendom. Thus sacramental worship stands at the very heart of the life of the Christian assembly.[10]

Sacramental worship brings together and makes sacred the whole of life.

As Jesus brought a new unity to the physical and the spiritual, so he also brings a new unifying principle to Israel in his own person. He used the analogy of the vine, saying, "I am the vine, you are the branches."[11] He likened the Church to a flock of sheep and himself to its shepherd.[12] Christ himself becomes the unifying principle of the Church, which is not simply commissioned and empowered, as has often been suggested in recent years, but is reconstituted into a truly organic society.

This understanding of the Church permeates the whole of the New Testament. The Church is said to be God's flock.[13] Paul writes, "There is one body and one Spirit, just as you were called to the one hope that belongs to your call, one Lord, one faith, one baptism, one God and Father of us all, who is above all and through all and in all."[14] But perhaps the greatest of the New Testament analogies for the Church is that used by Paul when he terms it the "body of Christ," likening its members to the various parts of the human body.[15] Though a number of other figures are used for the Church in the New Testament, none serves to weaken those setting forth its organic nature.

Further, from the outset Christian initiation has been through the new birth of baptism,[16] in which one is grafted into this body. And in a reference to the Eucharist Paul writes, "Because there is one bread, we who are many are one body, for we all partake of the one bread."[17] The Eucharist continually renews the paschal mystery and is indeed seen from the beginning to be both a creator and symbol of the Church's organic oneness with and in Christ. Here Paul goes beyond analogy and says the Church's members "*are* one body." We see the primary importance of the Eucharist in this connection when Ignatius expresses the universal practice of the early Church:

> Be careful, then to observe a single Eucharist. For there is one flesh of our Lord, Jesus Christ, and one cup of his blood that makes us one, and one altar, just as there is one bishop along with the presbytery and deacons, my fellow slaves. In that way whatever you do is in line with God's will.[18]

One Eucharist in one place in one day remained the ideal of the Church until it was finally forgotten in the later middle ages. For centuries after the Church at Rome began to have Sunday Eucharists in the parish churches, fragments of the Bread consecrated at the pope's Eucharist were sent by acolytes to be placed in the chalice of every church, thereby symbolically making all Eucharists one as the Church is one and uniting all with Christ and one another.[19] Though obviously there must be more than one Eucharist in a city or town of any size, the multiplication of Eucharists in one church on one day contradicts, as the early Church clearly saw, the fundamental theology of its organic nature. The single Eucharist symbolized and created the oneness of the Christian community. Multiple Eucharists divided it symbolically and actually. Though the consequences of this contradiction are impossible to assess, they have undoubtedly been much more far-reaching than it would seem on the surface.

In the practical realm the multiplication of Eucharists has made possible the growth of many parishes until they are so large that the Christian community is more community in theory than in practice. But even smaller parishes have multiplied Eucharists for no other reason than convenience. Most Christians today seem to have little sense of being an integral and important part of a community—a caring, loving family—which needs each one in all of his or her uniqueness to be whole. This means among much else that far fewer people are actively participating in the Church's work. Much of the Church's ministry goes undone. This lack of community also is probably the principal cause for the high rate of dropouts among adult converts experienced by the major churches in America in recent times.

It is worthy of note that the Church's organic nature and unity are but the reflection of God. God is within himself a community of persons who are united with one another in perfect harmony and oneness, yet each person of the Trinity possesses individually personality and function. God has called and constituted the Church to be such a community of persons in the world, realizing the oneness of humanity and expressing the unity in perfect harmony of life together as each member grows into his or her own fullness.

Something of the Church's nature is to be seen in the word "church" itself. Though the derivation of the English word "church" is from the Greek *kuriakon,* meaning "the Lord's house" or a building designated for Christian worship, it is not so in the New Testament. Reginald Fuller observes that in the New Testament "church" is the Greek "ecclesia," which "always means an assembly of people and cannot mean a building."[20] It is apparently for this reason that the Greek-speaking Christians chose *ecclesia* and not "synagogue" to designate the messianic community.[21] The name *ecclesia* was used to designate those whom God had called and who had responded to his call with faith and obedience to live in a divinely constituted community. The idea of community is fundamental to the nature of this *ecclesia,* but it is a community which points in two directions. It is the assembly on the one hand of those called by God to live together as his people and, more important, on the other hand of those who meet with and live together with God.[22]

Interestingly, Walter Lowrie also declares in his illuminating discussion of the meaning of *ecclesia* that "holy" was used to describe the actual character of those belonging to the *ecclesia* by the New Testament writers and others afterwards.[23] Holiness in the Church was redefined to refer to the Church as an institution only after large numbers of half-converted people entered. He writes,

> Even in the early Catholic period the Church was still defined with sole reference to its true members; and so long as the character of the great majority of the disciples corresponded substantially with the ideal, it was possible to ignore the exceptions. It was only when widespread corruption forced men to *dwell* upon this incongruity, that they

> felt obliged to choose between a radical purification of the Church, or a new definition of it such as the trend of Catholic development demanded, that is, as an *institute*, which enjoyed the character of holiness apart from any consideration of the character of its members.[24]

This does not mean, of course, that these Christians in the very early period did not sin. It does mean that their lives were substantially different from those of others outside the *ecclesia,* so different the New Testament could unhesitatingly call them "saints," "holy ones." No small part of this difference was to be seen in the servant-ministry of all the people of God as came to be exemplified in the diaconate.

Hans Küng notes that as Christianity spread, though *ecclesia* was used in the New Testament to mean a local church or a group of congregations, it was so used in the sense that "each single *ekklesia* was a copy of the original community, each represented the universal *ekklesia.*"[25] Walter Lowrie writes on this theme:

> Where the Lord is, the head of the body, there is Christendom; where two or three are gathered in Christ's name, there is the *people of Christ,* the New Testament Israel; there is *the whole of Christendom* with all of its promised privileges; for Christ is in the midst, and that is all in all. Where Christ is, there is the Ecclesia—the people of God. . . . Hence it is that *every assembly of Christians,* whether it be great or small, which is gathered in the name of the Lord is called Ecclesia . . . The *whole* Church is not composed of individual Churches, neither is the individual Church regarded as a part of the whole. . . . There is but *one* Ecclesia, the assembly of *the whole of Christendom* but this one Ecclesia has innumerable manifestations.[26]

This view is in some ways radically different from that commonly held regarding the nature of the Church and has the broadest of implications, far beyond the scope of our subject. But only in this context can we see the full extent of the Church's organic character. To think of the Church throughout the world as it exists today as the universal Church is great, but there is a sense in which it is even greater to think of the Church in any parish as being the universal Church, as being *the* Body of Christ with all of its power and gifts and life!

Further, the Christian *ecclesia* of the New Testament age saw itself as Israel. It was the remnant that had been called by God to be Israel and to live then, already, in the age to come.[27] As Jesus himself had worked within the system,[28] the primitive Church continued to do so. It regarded the whole system as essentially valid, continuing to worship in the Temple, attend the synagogues, and keep the Law. It formed no revolutionary party but saw its mission as being sent to call the whole of Israel into the

Church, the true Israel of God.[29] Gradually it did come to see that the Church of God was a "reconstituted" Israel in which the sacrificial system[30] and the Law,[31] symbolized by circumcision, had been fulfilled by Christ and were no longer needed. Then, rejected finally by the Jews of the old Israel as had been their Lord and cast out of the synagogues, c. 65, they were not only free to develop their own institutions apart from the Jews, but the necessity for doing so was far more apparent.

It was only natural at the outset that the primitive Church was not greatly concerned with questions of organization and structure. It already had the organization and structure of the old Israel, which it was.[32] It also had the Twelve and the apostles, which seemed quite adequate for its needs. And when they were not, it had the authority and the flexibility to provide what was needed, as is seen by the appointment of the Seven in Acts 6. Further, it was "too near the heart of a vast explosion of spiritual power" to be concerned with such questions.[33] It had experienced not only the resurrection but the outpouring of the Holy Spirit.[34] It had found the Holy Spirit to be the energizing principle of its life and knew itself to be "the Spirit-possessed body of the redeemed who had passed from death into life, who had received the earnest of the Spirit, and were now awaiting the imminent Parousia. . . ."[35] Therefore, since these Christians were not concerned with questions of constitutional order, the answers to most questions about the nature of the ministry are not answered directly by the New Testament.

However, not only may certain inferences be made with confidence but the Scriptures do provide us with fundamental principles, some of which seem often to be overlooked, perhaps in some cases because of their very simplicity. We have already set forth the social nature, first of all, of God. Then we saw that the Church by its fundamental nature is a social, organic society. Due to the highly individualistic philosophy of human nature that permeates the thinking of the West in modern times but now seems to be waning, it might be well to note with Arnold Toynbee and others that humanity is primarily social by its nature and only secondarily are we individuals apart from other human beings.[36] It follows from human nature then that for society to exist as such there must be order.

The fact that God is a God of order is to be seen throughout the universe: the stars stay in their courses; sugar is always sweet; acorns always produce oak trees and never puppies. So true is this basic principle that the disorder we do observe can be seen as evil, a perversion or privation of good, as Augustine taught.[37] The structure of ancient Israel reflects this order with its high priest and priesthood, sacrificial system, synagogues and their rulers, Law, Sanhedrin, and theocratic monarchy. When we come to the Christian community called into being by God in

Christ, we expect to find order, an order which in fact is evident from the beginning of the New Testament period, even with its eschatological outlook and charismatic ministries.[38] We see it in the replacement of Judas,[39] in the appointment of the Seven,[40] in the authority of the Twelve,[41] in the "administrators" of Paul,[42] in the appointment of elders,[43] in the authority of "the apostles and the elders" of Acts 15, and elsewhere.

This is not to say that Jesus dictated every aspect of the structure of the Church anymore than did God when he instituted the Old Covenant with Abraham or renewed it later with Moses. Evidence from the Gospels indicates that Jesus gave few instructions for the Church's organizational structure.[44] John records that Jesus said "I have yet many things to say to you, but you cannot bear them now. When the Spirit of truth comes, he will guide you into all the truth; for he will not speak on his own authority, but whatever he hears he will speak, and he will declare to you the things that are to come."[45] There would not be the same imperative for Jesus to dictate during his incarnate life the details of organization as there would be for another, because he was to return in the person of the Spirit to be the energizing principle of the New Covenant Church. What Jesus did, it would seem probable, though we cannot expect the New Testament by its nature to provide adequate information, is to provide all the initial authority needed in his commissioning of the Twelve, of Paul, and perhaps of other apostles for those first years when the Church was to continue as part of the old Israel and to provide under the guidance of the Holy Spirit for its continuance thereafter. His emphasis was on the nature of the authority his disciples were to exercise, an authority of service.[46]

Käsemann strongly affirms the guidance of the Spirit in the primitive Church's transition from the charismatically called and authorized ministries of Paul's genuine letters, to the ordained and apostolically validated ministries found in the Lucan writings, the Pastorals, 1 Clement, and the Ignatian letters.[47] He sees this "revolution" as a historical necessity because the Pauline understanding of "office, worship, Christian freedom and responsibility" encouraged an uncontrolled and apparently uncontrollable enthusiasm which threatened the Gentile churches.[48] In the face of this danger Pauline Christianity turned to forms of Church government already proven in Jewish Christianity. Käsemann continues:

> It is precisely in this respect, in my opinion, that the revolution can be called legitimate. For I think that the Holy Spirit manifests itself in the Church most clearly when, in the midst of the pressing need and perplexity of men, it awakes the courage and spiritual gifts for new ways which are appropriate to the situation. Apostles do not justify retain-

> ing old orders, when they can no longer serve contemporary life. That Church which does not stand ready at all times to break out of its traditional walls and is not willing to bear the risks inevitably associated therewith cannot seriously appeal to her Master for her stance.[49]

The Church must indeed adapt itself to the age in which it lives, and it has been given not only the latitude and freedom it needs but also the power of the Holy Spirit to guide it according to the times and circumstances.

The principle of the Spirit's guidance contains within itself the necessity for testing every direction and adaptation against the scriptural norms of God's revelation in Christ. For example, making "sacred persons" of the clergy is not commensurate with the revelation in Christ wherein the distinctions between the sacred and the secular of the old Israel are abolished and the unity of all creation is affirmed. In like manner the shift from a Church whose ministry encompassed all its people, each with a special function, like the organs of a body, for the good of the whole, to a Church whose ministry was one of ascending grades characterized by rank, status, and power is to be found wanting when tested by the revelation in Christ.

It is somewhat ironic that those pentecostal groups who put great emphasis today on the place of the Spirit in the Church often deny his guidance in those early years in this most vital area.

The commission given to the Twelve, as Massey Shepherd notes, "implies, at the least, the formation and governance of a specific historical community of Christian disciples."[50] They are to extend Jesus' work of preaching and healing,[51] take the gospel to the world,[52] baptize all nations,[53] and forgive sins.[54] They are pictured in the first chapters of Acts directing the Church in its varied activities. This is true though, as many have observed, the Church's outlook was predominately eschatological. The argument that since Jesus expected the eschaton immediately he could not have intended to found a Church is quickly and effectively countered by Reginald Fuller's assertion that the Church is eschatological: "*ecclesia* in NT usage is itself an eschatological term—the community which is promised the Kingdom of God."[55] Though the *parousia* did not come within the lifetime of the apostles as they apparently at first expected, the *Kingdom* had been ushered in and they lived at the end of history.

NOTES

1. 1 Pet. 2:9. (Unless otherwise noted, quotations are from the RSV.)

2. Reginald Fuller, *Early Catholicism in the New Testament,* lectures at the Graduate School of Theology, Sewanee, Tn., 1970. Cf., Ernst Käsemann, *Essays on New Testament Themes* (London: SCM Press Ltd., 1964), pp. 63–87 (hereafter cited as *N. T. Themes*).

3. G. W. H. Lampe, *Some Aspects of the New Testament Ministry* (London: S.P.C.K., 1949), p. 3 (hereafter cited as *N. T. Ministry*). Lampe rightly states that such is the case with Charles Gore's *The Church and the Ministry* and Kenneth Kirk's *The Apostolic Ministry.*

4. Massey H. Shepherd, Jr., "Ministry, Christian," in *The Interpreter's Dictionary of the Bible,* ed. George A. Buttrick, 5 vol. (New York: Abingdon Press, 1962), 3:386.

5. Lampe, *N. T. Ministry,* p. 2.

6. Massey H. Shepherd, Jr. *The Christian Year,* lectures at the Graduate School of Theology, Sewanee, Tn., Summer, 1970. Cf., Käsemann, *N. T. Themes,* p. 78.

7. Ibid.

8. Hans Küng, *The Church,* trans. Ray and Rosaleen Ockenden (New York: Sheed and Ward, 1976), p. 389.

9. Ibid.

10. Käsemann, *N. T. Themes,* p. 78.

11. John 15:5.

12. John 10:1–16; 21:15–17.

13. Luke 12:32; Acts 20:28; 1 Pet. 5:2.

14. Eph. 4:4–6.

15. 1 Cor. 12:12–27; Rom. 12:4–5f: Col. 1:18, 24; 3:15.

16. John 3:3–8. Cf. Lampe, *N. T. Ministry,* p. 2.

17. 1 Cor. 10:17.

18. Ignatius, *To the Philadelphians* 4.1, in *Early Christian Fathers,* ed. Cyril C. Richardson (Philadelphia: Westminster Press, 1953), 1:105.

19. Dom Gregory Dix, *The Shape of the Liturgy* (Westminster: Dacre Press, 1945), p. 21.

20. Reginald H. Fuller, "Church," in *A Theological Word Book of the Bible,* ed. Alan Richardson (New York: Macmillan, 1951), pp. 46–47. Cf. Walter Lowrie, *The Church and Its Organization in Primitive and Catholic Times* (New York: Longmans, Green, and Co., 1904), pp. 102–40. Lowrie discusses here at length and with profound insight the significance of the name *ecclesia,* Jesus' use of the term which he regards as genuine in Matt. 16:18ff and 18:17ff, and that of the New Testament writers.

21. Fuller, "Church," pp. 46–47.

22. Lowrie, p. 106.

23. Ibid., pp. 106–107.

24. Ibid., p. 108 (italics original).

25. Hans Küng, *Structures of the Church,* trans. Salvator Attanasio (New York: Thomas Nelson & Sons, 1964), pp. 11–12. Cf. Fuller, "Church," p. 47.

26. Lowrie, pp. 136–37 (italics original).

27. Lampe, *N. T. Ministry,* p. 2.

28. Eduard Schweizer, *Church Order in the New Testament*, trans. Frank Clarke (London: SCM Press Ltd., 1961), pp. 34–38.
29. Pierson Parker, *Violence in the Gospels*, lectures at the Graduate School of Theology, Sewanee, Tn., 1972.
30. Heb. 10:1–25.
31. Acts 15:1–29.
32. Schweizer, p. 47.
33. Lampe, *N. T. Ministry*, pp. 2–3.
34. Acts 2.
35. Lampe, *N. T. Ministry*, p. 2.
36. Arnold Toynbee, *A Study of History*, 2 vol. abridgment by D. C. Somervell (New York: Oxford University Press, 1957), 2:79.
37. Augustine, *Concerning the Nature of the Good Against the Manichaeans* (De Natura Boni) 3, 4, in vol. 4: *St. Augustin: The Writings Against the Manichaeans and Against the Donatists*, in *Nicene and Post-Nicene Fathers of the Christian Church, A Select Library of the*, First Series, 14 vol., ed. Philip Schaff, (Grand Rapids, Mi.: William B. Eerdmans Publishing Co., 1956), 4:352; *On the Morals of the Manichaeans* (De Moribus Manichaeorum) 5.7, in *Nicene and Post-Nicene Fathers*, First Series, 4:70; *City of God* 11.9, in vol. 2: *St. Augustin's City of God and Christian Doctrine*, in *Nicene and Post-Nicene Fathers*, First Series, 2:210. Cf. Gerald Bonner, *St. Augustine of Hippo, Life and Controversies* (Philadelphia: Westminster Press, 1963), pp. 199–201, 204–06.
38. Lampe, *N. T. Ministry*, p. 7. Cf. Schweizer, pp. 14, 178–79.
39. Acts 1:15–26.
40. Acts 6:1–6.
41. Mark 3:13–19; Acts 1–6.
42. 1 Cor. 12:28.
43. Acts 14:23. Cf. Acts 20:17.
44. "A Report on the Restoration of the Office of Deacon as a Lifetime State," a Committee of eleven theologians of the Catholic Theological Society of America, chair. Edward Echlin, made at the request of the Bishops' Committee on the Permanent Diaconate (Roman Catholic), published in *The American Ecclesiastical Review* (March 1971) 164:3, par. 9, p. 193.
45. John 16:12–13.
46. "Restoration of the Office of Deacon," p. 11, par. 9.
47. Ernst Käsemann, *New Testament Questions of Today* (London: SCM Press Ltd., 1969), pp. 245–47 (hereafter cited as *N. T. Questions*).
48. Ibid., p. 247.
49. Ibid.
50. Shepherd, "Ministry, Christian," 3:387.
51. Mark 3:14–15 and parallels.
52. Luke 24:46–48; Acts 1:8.
53. Matt. 28:19.
54. John 20:23.
55. Fuller, "Church," p. 47.

CHAPTER 2

Ministry in the New Testament: Sent to Serve

The Varied Ministries Constituting The Ministry

In the New Testament period and throughout the pre-Nicene age the Church's ministry was that of the whole people of God. Each member exercised his or her function in and for the whole body. It is in this context that every ministry and office in the Church must be understood. Thus, the apostolic ministery of the Church is rightly conceived in terms that comprehend and envision the totality of the widely varied forms of ministry found in the New Testament and is not limited to the narrow confines of the threefold ministry of bishops, priests, and deacons.

One of the greatest sources of misunderstanding of the ministry of the early Church stems from our looking back, preconditioned as we are, to that period and seeing the leadership of the Church then as "the ministry." This is to forget that all were "laity" (*laos*), even the leaders. More subtle perhaps, but closely connected, is the tendency to think in terms of a clerical ministry which guarantees the catholicity of the Church[1] or even constitutes it. The New Testament view is that the action of the clergy is the action of the Church. The clergy act for the Church just as other members act for the Church in doing other ministries. A. T. Hanson rightly states that the New Testament does imply a distinction between clergy and laity in the modern sense of these terms and that the distinction is between

> those who lead in certain actions and those who are led. But the actions are not the actions of the clergy, but of the Church. Ordination does not confer authority to be the Church; it confers authority to act on behalf of the Church, and whatever the ordained man does (be it celebrating the Eucharist or granting absolution) the laity on behalf of whom he acts do it in some sense also through him. . . .[2]

However, Hanson's statement that the idea of the clergy being a special group "marked out by the fact that they are empowered or permitted to perform certain actions which the laity are not permitted to perform" is "to introduce a distinction between clergy and laity which is quite alien to the New Testament" is perhaps pressing the evidence too far.[3] The very idea of an organic society implies that its various members have different functions. Paul affirms this:

> For as in one body we have many members, and all members do not have the same function, so we, though many, are one body in Christ, and individually members one of another. Having gifts that differ according to the grace given to us, let us use them. . . .[4]

Paul then lists gifts such as prophesying, teaching, and serving. There would seem to be little evidence in the New Testament to support such a confusion of ministries as is suggested by Hanson.

The basic argument here would seem to be essentially that of Schweizer, though he makes an exception of the office of "apostle":

> The New Testament agrees that God does not bestow all the gifts of grace on every Church member . . . The apostle is marked out from the rest by his special call from the risen Lord; but he is the one who regards his ministry as teamwork with fully authorized fellow workers. . . . Except for the apostolic ministry, therefore, which is unique through a special call, no ministry in the New Testament is forbidden to any member of the Church. It is only in the Pastorals that women are excluded from preaching and that an age limit is fixed for widows. Otherwise, God decides by his gift what ministry is to be performed by one, what by another. The Church can confirm this by its order, but it must remain open to God's correction, and must not, through its order, completely exclude others from that ministry. . . . It is God's spirit who marks out in freedom the pattern that Church order afterwards recognizes; it is therefore functional, regulative, serving, but not constitutive, and that is what is decisive.[5]

There would seem to be a subtle but fundamental contradiction in the position taken by Hanson and Schweizer. On the one hand, they do recognize and assert that God has called the varying members of the Church to different ministries and given them varying gifts for these ministries ("God does not bestow all the gifts of grace on every Church member") but on the other hand, they seem to maintain that all can perform the same function ("Except for the apostolic ministry . . . no ministry in the New Testament is forbidden to any member of the Church.")

Yet an organic society is not like that. In the human body the eye cannot perform the function of the nose, nor the heart of the lungs. The same is true of the Church. Käsemann shows how often the watchword "To each his own" occurs in connection with charisma in the ministry of the primitive Church.[6] The Spirit gives to each Christian what is needed for his or her particular ministry for the benefit of the whole: "There is differentiation in the divine generosity. . . . No one goes away empty, but no one has too much."[7] Each is responsible to use the gifts given by the Spirit responsibly in accord with the particular grace given.[8]

More than anything else it is probably because the Church largely came to act as though the clerical ministry could perform all the functions of the Church's ministry—and much theology maintained in effect that the clerical ministry was the essence of the ministry, if not the whole ministry—that some have come to deny any special power or position to any ministry or function. Though we may tend to think of Catholic Christianity as being the offender here with its all-encompassing clerical ministry, certainly Protestant Christianity has not escaped from such clericalism. But as we shall see later, this type and degree of confusion of function was foreign to the pre-Nicene Church. It is this confusion actually, and not so much a distinction between "clergy" and "laity," to use modern terminology, which is alien to the New Testament.

Further, it is to be noted that the Church has always sought to confirm by its order those whom God has chosen, though at times individuals within the Church have shown little regard for this concern. But to maintain, as Schweizer does, that Church order is "functional, regulative, serving, but not constitutive, and that is what is decisive" would seem to lead to a kind of subjectivism that is not in accord with the record of Scripture and that serves to weaken the unity of the Church. The place of Judas was filled by Matthias through casting lots. He thereby became (though we are not told whether there was any other manner of appointment) one of the Twelve.[9] This would appear constitutive. Acts 6 tells us that the people chose the Seven, who were to be appointed by the Twelve, to provide for the distribution to the Hellenist widows. Through prayer and the laying on of hands by the Twelve, Luke writes, they were constituted to their office with apparent effectiveness. We read immediately that Stephen, "full of grace and power, did great wonders and signs among the people."[10] The apostles go from Jerusalem to Samaria to give apostolic approval to the converts of Philip in Samaria and bestow the Holy Spirit through the laying on of hands according to Acts 8:14–17. The elders of 1 Timothy 4:14 convey the Spirit through the laying on of hands and in v. 22 Timothy is warned about being hasty in laying on hands. Paul is said to have given Timothy the "gift of God" through the laying on of hands in 2 Timothy 1:6.

Even if the gift of the Spirit through the hands of the apostles in Acts

8 is the insertion of material from other sources by the Lukan author, as Käsemann convincingly argues,[11] and though the Pastorals are not genuinely Pauline, the instances are still part of the tradition of the Church and do illustrate that Church order is constitutive even in the New Testament.

A major concern of Schweizer and others is to maintain the freedom of the Holy Spirit to work in the Church. However, it is surely limiting the freedom of the Spirit to argue that he does not act here in a constitutive way. Further, this is not to say that this type of Church order even concerned the whole of the Church's ministry. It did not. To say that God does act through his Church in answer to its prayers in granting the grace of particular functions is not to limit God to that only. Nor does it insure that the one who receives the grace will use it. But it does make order in the Church possible by providing a degree of objectivity.

Sent With Authority

Two words sum up the basic characteristics of the ministry both of Jesus and of those exercising the various ministries of the New Testament Church. They are "sent" (*apostellein*) and "serve" (*diakonein*).[12] So central is the first of these characteristics that Bishop Frank Wilson wrote at the outset of his book on Church history, "Our Lord did not write a book; neither did He erect an organization. The one thing He did was to issue a Divine Commission to certain selected persons which Commission they were to perpetuate."[13] While this statement standing alone might be interpreted as neglecting particularly Jesus' empowering of the Church, it does serve to point out the essential "sentness" of the Church.

But Jesus first of all knew himself to have been sent. Luke records the incident in the synagogue at the outset of Jesus' ministry when he stood up and read from Isaiah, " 'The Spirit of the Lord is upon me, because he has anointed me to preach good news to the poor. He has sent me to proclaim release to the captives and recovering of sight to the blind'. . . ." Afterwards, he said, "Today this scripture has been fulfilled in your hearing."[14] He was "sent for this purpose," to "preach the good news of the kingdom of God to the other cities also."[15] In another context he says, "Whoever receives me, receives not me but him who sent me."[16] It is the Father who has sent him: "For the works which the Father has granted me to accomplish, these very works which I am doing, bear me witness that the Father has sent me."[17]

Jesus then sent the Twelve. In what appears to be a training mission, Matthew tells us that they are sent at this point only to "the lost sheep of the house of Israel,"[18] but their commission is later made universal.[19] They are to extend Jesus' work of healing and casting out demons.[20] Mark reports that they are also to preach.[21] Luke records the appointment and sending first of the Twelve and then of the Seventy, which indicates that Jesus extended the number of those sent to do his work in the world beyond the Twelve, whatever the meaning of the number seventy (or seventy-two).[22] The Spirit sends Barnabas and Saul after selecting them.[23] Paul speaks of himself as one who is sent: "For Christ did not send me to baptize but to preach the gospel. . . ."[24] Indeed, the idea that Jesus has sent his Church into the world is implied in the fact that the principal forms of ministry are gifts to the Church: apostles, prophets, evangelists, pastors, and teachers.[25] The idea underlies the whole of New Testament thought.[26]

However, the divine commission which Jesus had and then transmitted to his disciples went beyond simply being "sent." He possessed both power and authority from God, so much so that people were amazed.[27] He corrected the Mosaic Law, which was to the Jews of ancient Israel divinely instituted.[28] He exorcised demons, which was either a divine or demonic activity,[29] and healed all manner of disease.[30] He forgave sins, a prerogative belonging only to God.[31] He claimed authority over life and death, as given to him by his Father.[32] The power to give eternal life to humanity had been committed to him by his Father.[33] Indeed, he had been given "all authority in heaven and on earth.[34]

The idea of "sending" is closely related to that of "authority" in the sending of the disciples, and especially of the Twelve, as it is with Jesus' own commission. The Twelve are given authority specifically to heal the sick and cast out demons,[35] to preach,[36] and to baptize.[37] The Seventy are sent with power to heal and have "authority . . . over all the power of the enemy."[38] Peter is given the authority of "binding" and "loosing,"[39] an authority which is later extended to "the disciples."[40] On Easter Day Jesus gives authority to "the disciples" to forgive sins, which is probably a reference to baptism,[41] and tells them, "As the Father has sent me, even so I send you."[42] We might note also that Paul as well was given authority,[43] having been called to be an apostle.[44]

To Serve

The thing that seems to stand out above all else in the sending forth of the Church then is that it is sent with power and authority to extend the work of Jesus in the world. This work is service, *diakonia,* the second great characteristic of the ministry of Jesus and of the Church.

The word *diakonos* (deacon) literally means a servant and in particular a waiter.[45] Most of the New Testament uses of *diakonos, diakonia,* and *diakoneō* clearly bear the general meaning of service and were applied to Christ and to all sorts of others.[46] In its noun form *diakonos* occurs thirty times in the New Testament and ranges in meaning from the most menial service, as in Mark 9:35, to the highest service of God, as in Colossians 1:23.[47] Jesus uses the word of himself: "I am among you as one who serves (*diakoneō*),"[48] the context emphasizing the kind of service denoted by "serving at tables." Again when James and John asked for the chief places of honor, Jesus contrasted the way of the world with his way, saying that "whoever would be great among you must be your servant, and whoever would be first among you must be slave of all. For the Son of Man also came not to be served but to serve (*diakoneō*). . . ."[49] He also by implication again applies the term to himself by saying that when the master of the house returns from the wedding feast and finds his servants waiting, "he will gird himself and have them sit at table, and he will come and serve (*diakoneō*) them."[50]

Paul says that Jesus became a "servant" (*diakonos*) to the Jews to show God's truthfulness in order that the promises given to the patriarchs might be confirmed and the Gentiles might glorify God.[51] He applies the word *diakonos* again to Jesus in asking if his critics would be right under the circumstances in claiming Christ is the "agent" (*diakonos*) of sin.[52] Paul also uses this term to describe himself and his own ministry: He was made "a minister" (*diakonos*) of the gospel[53] and also of the Church.[54] He describes Epaphrus as a "minister" (*diakonos*) of Christ and Timothy as God's "servant" (*diakonos*)[55] and uses the term in the plural of himself and others.[56] He also describes the civil ruler as "God's servant" (*diakonos*)[57] and uses the term elsewhere for the servants of Satan.[58]

The "ministry" of the Twelve is referred to as *diakonia* in reference to filling the place of Judas.[59] The "varieties of service" (*diakonia*)[60] mentioned by Paul include "the ministry" (*diakonia*) "of the word,"[61] "of reconciliation,"[62] and "of the Spirit."[63] In Romans Paul refers to his "service" for Jerusalem as *diakonia*[64] and in 2 Corinthians calls the "offering" of the Church at Corinth for that at Jerusalem *diakonia.*[65]

In the Gospels certain women of Galilee are said to have "ministered" (*diakoneō*) to Jesus.[66] The "service of tables" is implied by Luke in connection with Martha's work[67] and made explicit in this regard by John.[68] There is a definite financial connotation when Luke records that a number of women "provided for" (*diakoneō*) Jesus and the Twelve "out of their means"[69] and again when Paul goes to minister (*diakoneō*) to "the saints."[70] Timothy and Erastus are those who help (*diakoneō*) Paul.[71]

From these references it becomes clear that the word "service" (*diakonia*), with broad application, is the key New Testament word for the ministry of the Church and the word "servant" (*diakonos*) is key for those who exercise the function of ministry.[72] It is also readily apparent that this ministry points in two directions at the same time.[73] It has first of all been sent by God in Christ and therefore has God as its reference point. Secondly, it has been sent to serve others, all others, but especially those in the Church.[74]

A point often missed today in the Church in reference to Jesus' command to love is that the New Testament emphasis regarding the love Christians are to have towards others is on their love for fellow members of the Christian community. When Christians are genuinely concerned to love one another, this love overflows into the world and the world is drawn to seek the source of such love.

There can be little doubt that Jesus intended to create a radically new consciousness in his disciples regarding their "ministry."[75] Under the Old Covenant all were well aware of the "service" they were to render to God in worship and obedience to his Law. However, they had little consciousness of being sent by God to serve the needs of their fellow human beings. Like the "Gentiles," they thought of greatness in terms of rank, power, and authority. Jesus clearly reversed this system of values:

> You know that the rulers of the Gentiles lord it over them, and their great men exercise authority over them. It shall not be so among you; but whoever would be great among you must be your servant, and whoever would be first among you must be your slave; even as the Son of man came not to be served but to serve, and to give his life as a ransom for many.[76]

Again, in the great picture of the judgment Jesus makes humble service to others the crux of entrance into heaven. Those who fed the hungry, gave drink to the thirsty, welcomed the stranger, clothed the naked, and visited the sick and those in prison did it to Jesus: "As you did it to one of the least of these, my brethren, you did it to me."[77]

But above all the whole character of Jesus' ministry and that of any who would follow him is epitomized in a most vivid and dramatic way at the Last Supper when he girded himself with a towel as the lowest household servant and washed the feet of his disciples, commanding his followers to do likewise.[78] The character of the apostolic ministry is there indelibly marked as *diakonia.* This passage from the thirteenth chapter of John's gospel could appropriately be read at the ordination of every deacon.

It is just here that we find a source of misunderstanding regarding Jesus' intention towards the organization and structure of his Church. He intended to change the character of the ministry of the Church under the New Covenant, that is of the whole body of the Church, from that of "exclusive privilege and ritual performance" to one of "lowly and devoted service" to others in the name of Christ.[79] But in speaking of this ministry and the word *diakonia* to describe it, Eduard Schweizer goes beyond affirming this point:

> The very choice of the word, which still clearly involves the idea of humble activity, proves that the Church wishes to denote the attitude of one who is at the service of God and his fellow-men, not a position carrying with it rights and powers.[80]

The two ideas, an office created for humble service but possessing rights and powers, are not mutually exclusive. In fact, such things as the rights and powers given to the Twelve and exercised by them in Acts 1–6, the authority exercised by Paul over the churches he founded, the authority of the apostles and elders at Jerusalem in Acts 15, and the authority of other apostles, prophets, and teachers, among other factors, would seem to bear this out. Jesus did not condemn or reject the order of the Old Covenant. He rather "fulfilled" it and established a new order in which service to God is service to others. The *radically different thing is the attitude towards office* and not the failure of an office to possess rights and authority. These, as we have seen, are necessary for order in any social organization.

It is not that Schweizer and others necessarily deny there were those in the Church who had rights and authority. Obviously, this was not the case even in the New Testament age. They instead hold that rights and authority were not attached to an office as such but rather simply belonged to those who exercised them. Schweizer avers,

> It is certainly quite true that the prophet has authority only as far and as long as his prophecy goes on. But exactly the same is true of the apostles and of the overseers, superintendents, elders, and whatever else they are called; for only where the apostle's words can really inwardly prevail in the Church do they become its real authority. It is certainly true that the Church acknowledges, or even chooses, as its leaders those people from whom it has repeatedly experienced such authoritative guidance and who have proved themselves.[81]

The view here is not that of an organic society, where there is an inherent difference between members as to function. He maintains that every member of the Church can baptize, celebrate the Eucharist, and preach, arguing on this basis, "The assertion that the gift of grace is bestowed on *every* church member, and that therefore *every* member is called to service, is constant in the New Testament. . . ."[82]

It is true that in the New Testament every member of the Church has received the gift of grace and has been called to service; but what follows here is Paul's assertion, which runs throughout his writings, that all ministries are charismatic gifts of the Spirit. The gift of the Spirit's grace brings rather "varieties of service"[83] such as we see in organic societies. In the natural family the father by virtue of his office can never fulfill the function either of the mother or of the child in that family, nor in the body can the hands do that of the vocal chords.[84] In the New Testament we find diversity of function and office, so that, even in such a task as providing for the Gentile widows, those chosen are appointed with prayer and the laying on of hands by the Twelve.[85] Surely in the Church at Jerusalem grace is bestowed by the Spirit for the office through the Church's prayer and the laying on of hands, even though the Spirit is not limited to the Church's selection and appointment to bestow gifts for various ministries within the Church.

The principle involved here is seen also in the Lukan tradition when Luke says the apostles at Jerusalem sent Peter and John to Samaria to investigate the preaching of the gospel there. According to the tradition they prayed and laid hands on those who had been baptized for the receiving of the Holy Spirit, and they thereby did receive the Spirit,[86] thus giving apostolic validation to the work of Philip.[87] Again in Acts Luke says that Paul baptized about twelve at Ephesus; and then, when he laid his hands on them, they received the Spirit.[88] When the Spirit directed the prophets and teachers of the Church at Antioch to set apart Barnabas and Saul for the work he was calling them to do, they did so with fasting, prayer, and the laying on of hands. In this way apparently they were "sent out by the Holy Spirit."[89] The author of 1 Timothy speaks of not neglecting "the gift you have, which was given you by prophetic utterance when the elders laid their hands upon you."[90]

The point in this connection is not so much about the laying on of hands (which is only the means)[91] as the tradition recorded here which clearly indicates that the Church was confident that God would give the Spirit to those upon whom its leaders laid their hands with prayer for specific purposes.

The New Testament does teach that ministerial function is given by the *charisma* of the Holy Spirit.[92] But it does not teach that the ministry of the Church is constituted as the wind, which "blows where it wills, and you hear the sound of it, but you do not know whence it comes or whither it goes." Jesus is speaking of the individual ("So it is with every one who is born of the Spirit"[93]) and the fact that the *source* of the inward power of the individual Christian is not apparent for the world to see. Rather than constituting the Church's ministry haphazardly, the Holy Spirit fills all the various ministries with his presence and power. It is this primary fact that we find expressed in Paul's writings. Though he does speak of the duty of his congregations to love, respect, and be subject to their leaders,[94] he has little to say about the "official ministries" of the Church other than that of apostle. He thought of ministry primarily as a function given by the grace of the Spirit and not in terms of office. And he saw it in the broadest terms: "It was an exercise by each and every member of the Church of his own charism of the Spirit to the edification of all. . . . Even apostleship was to Paul a 'spiritual gift'. . . ."[95]

Urban Holmes sees the most relevant text relating to Paul's conception of the ministry to be 1 Corinthians 12:28–31:

> And God has appointed in the church first apostles, second prophets, third teachers, then workers of miracles, then healers, helpers, administrators, speakers in various kinds of tongues. Are all apostles? Are all prophets? Are all teachers? Do all work miracles? Do all possess gifts of healing? Do all speak with tongues? Do all interpret? But earnestly desire the higher gifts.

He previously stated that, except for the "apostolate," the ministry for Paul is "essentially functional charismatic." He then states, "Here we do not have an authorized, ordained (i.e., a 'laying on of hands' by men in a certain office) ministry; but one whose validity was tested by its right teaching (1 Timothy 4:1, for example, is perhaps a reflection upon the dangers of a divisive charismatic ministry)."[96]

Holmes fails to make any distinction here between the first three "offices" and the others. Both C. K. Barrett and Reginald Fuller have noted that a twofold break in the sentence calls attention to an important distinction between the two groups.[97] The first three in the list refer to persons, the others to functions or gifts, though the difference is somewhat blurred in the RSV and in many other modern translations. The King James Version follows more closely the Greek and reads "first apostles, secondarily prophets, thirdly teachers, after that helps, governments, diversities of tongues." Further, the numerical sequence ends after "teachers," indicating that those which follow are of lesser consequence. Barrett notes that the first three have to do with the ministry of the word and observes, "This threefold ministry of the word is, according to Paul, the primary Christian ministry. By it the Church is founded, and built up."[98]

This certainly is not the picture which emerges in the second century with the monepiscopate, the term denoting the use of *episkopos* (bishop) to designate a single officer as president of the local Christian community, or even that in Acts and the Pastoral Epistles. However, Paul's concept of ministry in I Corinthians would seem to be more than that of a ministry "whose validity was tested by its right teaching." Right teaching is undoubtedly important to Paul. But the picture here starts with the apostle, who has been a witness to the resurrection and possessed authority, having been commissioned directly by the risen Christ.[99] The apostle may not have been ordained through the laying on of hands, but he was certainly authorized and commissioned.

The basis of the authority of prophets and teachers is not so apparent, but they do seem to possess it in the Church. It is at least possible that, in light of the evidence we shall allude to in connection with the appointment of the bishops and deacons of Philippians 1:1 in the next chapter, the prophets and teachers at least were often appointed with the laying on of hands. If this is true, it might be interpreted more in the sense of connecting them with Paul and his authority and of Paul's recognition of their possessing the Spirit's charisma than of an ordination in which Paul conveyed the charisma. Those who worked miracles, healed, and spoke in tongues would need no special authority by the nature of their service. However, those who acted in administering the Church's affairs, if not also those who gave help to others, such as the needy, would need some form of authorization by the Church. These latter ministries are not concerned with teaching and so *could not* have been validated by "right teaching."

The important thing here is to see that the whole of the Church of the New Testament age was sent into the world with power and authority to serve. At least certain of its primary leaders were authorized and commissioned for special functions and held what may rightly be called "offices." However, the word chosen by that Church to describe the ministry of all is one which was unbiblical and nonreligious and excludes all pretentions to rank and status. All are sent for *diakonia,* for ministry which is exercised foremost in service to others.

NOTES

1. G. W. H. Lampe, *Some Aspects of the New Testament Ministry* (London: S.P.C.K., 1949), p. 2 (hereafter cited as *N. T. Ministry*).
2. A. T. Hanson, "Shepherd, Teacher and Celebrant in the New Testament Conception of the Ministry," in *New Forms of Ministry,* ed. David M. Paton, Research Pamphlets, No. 12, World Council of Churches Commission on World Mission and Evangelism (London: Edinburgh House Press, 1965), p. 17.
3. Ibid.
4. Rom. 12:4–6.
5. Eduard Schweizer, *Church Order in the New Testament,* trans. Frank Clarke (London: SCM Press Ltd., 1961), pp. 203–04.
6. Ernst Käsemann, *Essays on New Testament Themes* (London: SCM Press Ltd., 1964), p. 76 (hereafter cited as *N. T. Themes*).
7. Ibid.
8. Ibid., p. 77.
9. Acts 1:21–26.

10. Acts 6:8.
11. Käsemann, *N. T. Themes*, pp. 85–89.
12. Lampe, *N. T. Ministry*, p. 3. Cf. Massey H. Shepherd, Jr., "Ministry, Christian," in *The Interpreter's Dictionary of the Bible*, ed. George A. Buttrick, 5 vol. (New York: Abingdon Press, 1962), 3:386.
13. Frank E. Wilson, *The Divine Commission—A Sketch of Church History* (New York: Morehouse-Gorham, 1946), p. 3 (original in italics).
14. Luke 4:16–21.
15. Luke 4:43. Cf. Matt. 15:24.
16. Mark 9:37.
17. John 5:36ff. Cf. Acts 3:26; 1 John 4:9, 10, 14; John 3:16–17; 6:29, 57; 7:29 et al.
18. Matt. 10:5–6. Cf. Mark 6:7–13.
19. Matt. 28:16–20. Cf. Acts 1:8.
20. Matt. 10:1, 8.
21. Mark 3:14.
22. Luke 9:1–6; 10:1–12.
23. Acts 13:2–4.
24. 1 Cor. 1:17. Cf. Acts 26:16–17.
25. Eph. 4:11.
26. Lampe, *N. T. Ministry*, p. 5.
27. Mark 1:22, 27.
28. Matt. 5:22, 28, 32, 34, 39, 44.
29. Luke 11:14–20.
30. Matt. 4:23–24; Mark 1:23–45; Luke 4:23, 33ff; John 4:46ff.
31. Mark 2:3–12. Cf. Matt. 9:1–8; Luke 5:17–26.
32. John 10:18.
33. John 17:2.
34. Matt 28:18. Cf. Eph. 1:21–23.
35. Mark 3:14–15; 6:7; Matt. 10:8; Luke 9:1–2.
36. Mark 3:14; Matt. 10:7; Luke 9:2.
37. Matt. 28:19, though here it is the Eleven.
38. Luke 10:9, 19.
39. Matt. 16:19.
40. Matt. 18:18.
41. Reginald Fuller states that in this passage John "associates the gift of the Spirit with the apostolic mission, here defined not as the proclamation of the kerygma, but as the forgiving and retaining of sins. The primary reference here is probably to baptism rather than to the sacrament of penance." *Preaching the New Lectionary: The Word of God for the Church Today* (Collegeville, Mn.: The Liturgical Press, 1974), p. 39 (hereafter cited as *Preaching*).
42. John 20:21–23.
43. 2 Cor. 10:8.
44. Rom. 1:1; Gal. 1:1.
45. Hans Lietzmann, *A History of the Early Church*, vol. 1: *The Beginnings of the Christian Church;* vol. 2: *The Founding of the Church Universal* (bound together), trans. Bertram Lee Woolf (New York: The World Publishing Co., Meridian Books, 1961), p. 155. Cf. Lampe, *N. T. Ministry*, pp. 5–6.
46. C. F. D. Moule, "Deacons in the New Testament," *Theology* 58 (London: 1955), 405–06.

47. Burton Scott Easton, *The Pastoral Epistles* (New York: Charles Scribner's Sons, 1947), p. 181.
48. Luke 22:27.
49. Mark 10:43–45. Cf. Matt. 20:26–28; Luke 22:24–27; Mark 9:35.
50. Luke 12:37.
51. Rom. 15:8.
52. Gal. 2:17.
53. Eph. 3:7. Cf. Gal. 1:23.
54. Col. 1:23, 25.
55. Col. 1:7; 1 Thess. 3:2.
56. 1 Cor. 3:5; 2 Cor. 3:6; 6:4; 11:23.
57. Rom. 13:4.
58. 2 Cor. 11:15.
59. Acts 1:17, 25.
60. 1 Cor. 12:5.
61. Acts 6:4.
62. 2 Cor. 5:18.
63. 2 Cor. 3:8.
64. Rom. 15:31.
65. 2 Cor. 9:1.
66. Mark 15:41. Cf. Matt. 27:55.
67. Luke 10:40.
68. John 12:2.
69. Luke 8:3.
70. Rom. 15:25.
71. Acts 19:22.
72. Cf. Moule: 405; Lampe, *N. T. Ministry*, p. 6; Urban T. Holmes III, *The Future Shape of Ministry: A Theological Projection* (New York: Seabury Press, 1971), p. 17 (hereafter cited as *Future Shape*); J. C. Lambert and George Johnston, "Minister," in *Dictionary of the Bible*, ed. James Hastings, rev. ed. Frederick C. Grant and H. H. Rowley (New York: Charles Scribner's Sons, 1963), p. 662.
73. Lampe, *N. T. Ministry*, p. 6.
74. Gal. 6:10; John 13:34.
75. Moule: 405.
76. Matt. 20:25–28.
77. Matt. 25:31–46.
78. John 13:1–15.
79. Lambert and Johnston, p. 662.
80. Schweizer, p. 177.
81. Ibid., p. 187.
82. Ibid., pp. 187–88 (italics in original).
83. 1 Cor. 12:5.
84. 1 Cor. 12:12–26.
85. Acts 6:1–6.
86. Acts 8:14–17.
87. Käsemann, *N. T. Themes*, p. 166.
88. Acts 19:1–7.
89. Acts 13:1–4.
90. 1 Tim. 4:14.

91. It is worth noting, however, that this is the means used by Jesus to bless the children (Mark 10:16) and to heal the sick at times (Mark 6:5; Luke 13:13).
92. Lampe, *N. T. Ministry*, p. 6.
93. John 3:8.
94. 1 Cor. 16:15–16; 1 Thess. 5:12–13.
95. Shepherd, "Ministry, Christian," 3:389.
96. Holmes, *Future Shape*, pp. 14–15.
97. C. K. Barrett, *A Commentary on the First Epistle to the Corinthians* (New York: Harper & Row, 1968), p. 295 (hereafter cited as *1 Corinthians*); Reginald Fuller, *Early Catholicism in the New Testament*, lectures at the Graduate School of Theology, Sewanee, Tn., 1970. Note the discussion on 1 Cor. 12 in chap. 3.
98. Barrett, *1 Corinthians*, p. 295.
99. 1 Cor. 9; Rom. 1:1–6; 2 Cor. 10:8; 12:1–5.

CHAPTER 3

The Diaconate in the New Testament

Acts 6:1–6

It was natural that the specialized ministry of the deacon would develop to express in representative form the basic principle of the apostolic ministry which the whole Church was called upon to render.[1] The need for such an office developed very early in the life of the Church that had been "sent" into the world to "serve." The picture of the communal life of the Church in Jerusalem given in Acts shows that almost from the outset the Church found it necessary to appoint those who would assist in looking after its poor. The implication of Acts 6:1–6 is that the Christian community at Jerusalem had such "distributors" even before the appointment of the Seven.

The problem of the neglect of the "Hellenist" widows referred to in Acts 6:1 came about as "the disciples were increasing in number," Luke says, because those whom he calls "Hellenists" "murmured against the Hebrews because their widows were neglected in the daily distribution." The population of Jerusalem included many Greek-speaking Jews who had been born abroad in the diaspora. Among these there were many devout Jews who had settled in Jerusalem towards the end of their lives in order to be buried near the holy city.[2] The Christian community had gained adherents from among these Jews, and there may have been a relatively large number of the Christian widows who were widows from among this group and, therefore, were dependent upon charity, because they had no relatives in Jerusalem to take care of them.[3] Following Jewish custom, the Jerusalem Church apparently already had relief officers to distribute aid.[4]

The Twelve proposed the election of the Seven to the whole assembly of disciples. The reason they gave, that "it is not right that we should give up preaching the word of God to serve tables," does not imply that the Twelve had been handling the "daily distribution" but rather that they proposed the selection of others so that this would not become necessary for them in the future.[5] For the Twelve prayer and the proclamation of the word are of first importance and must take precedence over social work.[6]

Critical study of this passage has led increasingly to the conclusion that a deeper problem existed in the Jerusalem Church than appears on the surface.[7] Vischer sees the activity of the Seven as "scarcely different from that of the apostles" and suspects that the Seven are appointed to "preserve unity" in a situation of tension much deeper than that noted in Acts between the Greek-speaking Christians ("Hellenists") and the Aramaic-speaking Christians ("Hebrews") in Jerusalem.[8] Haenchen argues convincingly that this tension is basically due to the "Hellenists," led by Stephen, going far beyond the "Hebrews" in "the exercise of great freedom in relation to the law," so that in the Church's distributions to the poor the "Hellenist" widows were deliberately neglected by the "Hebrews" in charge.[9] Acts 6:12–14 gives evidence of such freedom of interpretation by recording that, when Stephen was arrested and brought before the council (the Sanhedrin), he was accused of never ceasing

> to speak words against this holy place [the Temple, which was adjoined by the senate-house][10] and the law; for we have heard him say that this Jesus of Nazareth will destroy this place and will change the customs which Moses delivered to us.

It is important to note that those who objected to Stephen's teaching and instigated his arrest were Jews who were "Hellenists," not "Hebrews,"[11] further indicating the distinctiveness of the "Hellenists." The destruction of the Temple and change of the customs given by Moses, which Stephen is accused of teaching, threatened "the whole Jewish system of civil and religious life."[12]

The freedom referred to is that taught by Jesus himself, as when his disciples broke the Mosaic Law by picking ears of grain on the sabbath. Jesus justified this breach by saying, "The sabbath was made for man, not man for the sabbath."[13] The Church generally would adopt this freedom, but in the "Jewish period" of the Church, prior to the controversy over circumcision reported in Acts 15, there is ample evidence to indicate a much stricter view regarding the Law on the part of the Twelve and many other Jewish–Christians at Jerusalem, most of whom were probably Aramaic-speaking "Hebrews" in the sense of Acts 6.

Two such groups would explain why, immediately following the stoning of Stephen, in the "great persecution" of the Jerusalem Church reported in Acts 8, "the apostles at Jerusalem" were *not* arrested.[14] Stephen was killed, and then another of the Seven "Hellenist" leaders, Philip, is named as representing those who were "scattered" in this persecution and "went about preaching the word."[15] But Acts 8:14 clearly says that the apostles, including two of the Twelve, Peter and John, were still in Jerusalem, apparently living in peace. The inference, as drawn by Haenchen, that there were then two recognizably distinct groups within the primitive Christian community at Jerusalem, the "Hellenists" interpreting the Law with the freedom taught by Jesus and the "Hebrews" traditionally keeping the whole of the Mosaic Law, would explain first of all why the apostles were not touched by the persecution. At the same time it would also perhaps best account for the appointment of the Seven and their subsequent work as Acts describes it.[16] As Fuller suggests, the Seven were already leaders of the "Hellenists" at the time of their election, and their appointment stemmed from the concern of the Twelve to avoid a split between the two groups.[17]

The position of the Seven emerges then as one considerably beyond that of those who wait on tables. The responsibility of the "daily distribution" for the Christian "Hellenist" widows was no doubt given them, but given them as the leaders of the "Hellenists" of the Christian community. The evidence in Acts of the nature of the ministries of Stephen and Philip does lead to the conclusion of Schweizer that the Seven "stand out as men who have the gift of missionary preaching and a special insight into the new nature of the Church."[18]

The Seven then were chosen by the Church, and commissioned for their work by the Twelve with prayer and the laying on of hands.[19] The number "seven" could have suggested itself to the Twelve not only because it was a sacred number among the Jews[20] but also because in Jewish towns the local council known as "the 'Seven of the Town' or 'Seven Best of the Town' " usually was composed of seven men.[21]

Vischer maintains that the appointment of the Seven gave them a special position, so that they worked "beside" and "not simply subordinate to" the apostles.[22] In the sense that they formed the leadership of the "Hellenists," a group sufficiently distinct so as to have been subject to severe persecution and scattered while the rest of the Christian community remained untouched, their position does seem to have been "beside" the apostles. However, they were appointed by the Twelve with the laying on of hands, a practice taken from Judaism, which "formally associated the seven with the twelve, as their deputies to discharge a special duty"[23] and was seen as directly transmitting to them blessing and power.[24] The Seven and the "Hellenists" were part of the primitive community and, as such, subordinate to the Twelve.

But the primitive Church did not think in terms of "subordination" as we do today. The subordination of the Seven is not that which was to develop later. We do not find rank and dignity of office there. Rather the subordination is one simply of authoritative leadership exercised for the welfare of the community.

Further, the Seven are not called "deacons" here or elsewhere in the New Testament, and it is almost certain that they did not hold that office.[25] Their office was unique and was not continued in the Church.[26] The word "deacon" is, in fact, never used in Acts.[27] André Lemaire in reviewing recent research on ministries in the New Testament reports that the majority of scholars support this conclusion: the Seven were not deacons.[28] However, even though they were not deacons, they are significant in the development of the office because at an early time they were looked to as a model for the diaconate.[29] Irenaeus (c. 185) was the first of the early Church fathers to call the Seven deacons. In writing of Stephen's speech to the Sanhedrin in his work *Against Heresies,* Irenaeus speaks of "Stephen, who was chosen the first deacon by the Apostles. . . ."[30]

Though many of the early fathers, following Irenaeus, did regard the Seven as deacons, the view was not universal. John Chrysostom wrote in one of his homilies and was later quoted with approval by the Council of Trullo (692) in reference to the question of their office:

> Was it that of deacons? But this office did not yet exist in the churches. But was it the dispensation of a presbyter? But there was not as yet any bishop, but only apostles, whence I think it is clear and manifest that neither of deacons nor of presbyters was there then the name.[31]

Canon 16 of Trullo concludes that "the Seven deacons are not to be understood as deacons who served at the mysteries . . ." but were those who were entrusted with philanthropic works.

Since the Seven did serve as a model, facts about them recorded in Acts are worthy of our attention. First, we note that their qualifications are threefold: They are to be men of good reputation, full of the Spirit, and filled with wisdom.[32] The only duty mentioned for them at their appointment is the responsibility to see to the "daily distribution" for the "Hellenist" widows. This would have included "serving tables" at the common meal of the community as well as other distributions.[33] However, it seems likely the Seven fulfilled this responsibility through the assistance of subordinates, just as the Twelve did,[34] rather than making the actual distribution themselves. They might be termed "charity commissioners," as Kirsopp Lake calls them.[35]

The picture of the ministries of Stephen and Philip may well be illustrative of the Seven. Though Norbert Brockman says that what both Stephen and Philip are reported doing in Acts is essentially "catechetical instruction" and would be an appropriate type of witness for any good Christian,[36] they appear to function much like the apostles, particularly in the proclamation of the word and in working miracles.[37] Not only does Stephen address the council (Sanhedrin) with what may be called a sermon,[38] but the "false witnesses" set up against him accused him of being one who "never ceases to speak words against this holy place and the law."[39] Philip goes down to Samaria to proclaim Christ, his mission being so effective that multitudes heeded what he said, witnessed the miracles he did, and were baptized.[40] He converted and baptized the Ethiopian eunuch.[41] Philip is also called an evangelist.[42]

It is significant that, in spite of the important place preaching had in the ministries of Stephen and Philip, and even though the Seven were thought to have been deacons and were used as models for the diaconate from the time of Irenaeus, preaching was not part of the deacon's function as the office developed in the Church of the sub-apostolic age, so far as is known, and it did not become so in the early Church.

Philippians 1:1

In the opening verse of Paul's letter to the Philippians he addresses "all the saints in Christ Jesus who are at Philippi, with the bishops and deacons." Some authorities understand "bishops and deacons" to refer simply to the function of exercising oversight and of serving the Christian community.[43] Others, like F. W. Beare, see them as officers but not in the technical sense.[44] It is true that Paul's inclusion of these terms in his address is unique here. But we must remember that in this period in which "status" has little meaning or place and the Church is characterized by a truly organic nature, it would have been natural simply to address the Church as a whole in a given place without mention of any particular officers, as we find in Paul's other letters. In this instance the occasion for singling out "bishops and deacons" probably arises from their special responsibility in collecting and sending the gift to Paul for which he thanks the Church there.[45] But that they were singled out is in itself a strong indication that they were recognized officials of the Church at Philippi.

Fuller asserts that the ministries of the Pauline churches are essentially charismatic, being "set" in the Church by God.[46] He interprets the "bishops and deacons" of Philippians 1:1 in the light of the list in 1 Corinthians 12, which he sees to be the most important of the charismatic lists because it is systematic. As we noted earlier, the first three of the list, apostles, prophets, and teachers, are people. The rest are gifts or powers, which are exercised temporarily and so do not attach themselves to persons. Among these are "governments" corresponding to the "bishops" of Philippians 1:1 and "helps" corresponding to the "deacons" of that passage.[47] Though Fuller sees these bishops and deacons to be charismatics, he rightly assigns a difference to them. First, though they correspond to the "governments" and "helps" of 1 Corinthians 12, they also correspond to the "apostle, prophets, and teachers" in that they are people. Therefore, the charismatic gifts tend to attach themselves to the persons, and the "bishops and deacons" exercise their functions on a more or less permanent basis. This difference, he asserts, is a step towards "Early Catholicism," the term denoting a time in which the traditional offices are already present.

It would also appear that officials always existed who exercised pastoral and administrative responsibilities side by side with the apostles, prophets, and teachers, to whom Paul assigns special precedence. They may have been volunteers at first, but gradually they must have acquired official recognition.[48]

The question of their appointment or commissioning through prayer and the laying on of hands must remain speculative. Fuller believes that there is no ordination, as we know it, recorded in Paul's writings.[49] However, these Jewish Christians almost from the beginning seem to have used the long-revered Judaic sign of laying on of hands to authorize and empower those appointed to serve as leaders in the Church. The Seven of Acts 6 are so appointed by the Twelve with fasting and prayer after election by the Jerusalem community. When the Holy Spirit directs prophets at Antioch to "set apart" Barnabas and Saul for their missionary work, it is done by the laying on of hands after fasting and prayer.[50] Though there is no question of ordination conveying power and authority for ministry here, but rather the sign of blessing for their work as they were sent forth, it does indicate its use and associate it with Paul. Luke's statement in Acts 14:23 that Barnabas and Paul appointed elders in every church with fasting and prayer represents a tradition of such long standing that Luke assumes it to have been true, though apparently he is reading this back into the founding of the Pauline churches.[51]

In light of such evidence it is not unreasonable to believe it even likely that Paul used this sign of appointment to recognize, authorize, and confirm charismatic ministries, especially the chief ones of prophet and teacher, as he founded his churches. It is certainly possible that the "bishops and deacons" of Philippians 1:1 could have been commissioned through the laying on of hands with prayer, though if this is true it is probable that it did not possess the full meaning of later ordination. As G. W. H. Lampe has stated,

> There is no sufficient evidence to suggest that the exercise of the ancient sign of delegation of authority (and of spiritual blessing), the im-

position of hands, was confined to those possessing any particular status in the Church; until Christian unity began to be threatened, and until the ministry came to be associated with the Old Testament priesthood, the importance of the rite was probably not so overwhelmingly great as we should naturally expect it to be.[52]

Käsemann sees ordination with the same meaning it had in Judaism only in the Pastorals, 1 Timothy 4:14, 5:22 and 2 Timothy 1:6. Along with most Pauline scholars he regards these as not genuinely Pauline but rather as representing Christian communities with Pauline characteristics in the province of Asia.[53] Here ordination originating in the Jewish–Christian communities is brought into the Pauline communities.[54] As in Judaism it bestows the Spirit and gives special authorization and power to administer the *depositum fide*, the faith as contained in the Pauline tradition.[55]

In addition, in view of Paul's failure to mention bishops and deacons anywhere else in this connection at least and of his use of different terms in his other letters for those who perform various tasks in the Church, it is reasonable to think that there was no uniform structure of offices in the Pauline churches of the early New Testament period.[56] However, when we add the clear emergence of these offices in their technical sense by the late New Testament period and their probable origin in the Pauline churches to what has already been said, we must conclude that these "bishops and deacons" are officers of the Church at Philippi and not simply men exercising leadership.[57]

This is, however, not to say that either the diaconate or the episcopate of the Church at Philippi was the more fully developed office of the second century.[58] No mention is made here of the functions of the "bishops and deacons," so we cannot know the exact nature of their offices at this date, c. 60.[59] It is apparent that the deacons are associated with the bishops in the leadership of the Church. They represent the first stage of the office as it emerges in more developed form in the Pastoral Epistles. This would, then, be the first reference in the New Testament to the specific office of deacon.[60]

1 Timothy 3:8–13

Most scholars would agree that by the time of the later strata of the New Testament the term "deacon" is used unquestionably to denote the office in the technical sense.[61] Most of the New Testament information regarding the office is to be found in 1 Timothy 3:8–13. Though there is considerable divergence regarding the date of this epistle, it probably should be put early in the second century.[62]

We should note here that the offices of bishop and of deacon probably originated in the Pauline or Hellenistic churches, which had no presbyters during Paul's lifetime,[63] and that the office of presbyter probably originated in the Jewish–Christian churches, particularly at Jerusalem.[64] Lemaire reports in his survey of recent research in New Testament ministries that all studies relating to the presbyterate in the New Testament find its origin to be in the Jewish–Christian communities, where it is first attested.[65] These communities borrowed the office directly from the traditional organizational structure of the Jewish synagogue. Like their Jewish counterparts, Christian presbyters (elders) were ordained by the laying on of hands to govern the community as part of the presbyteral council.[66] And like their synagogue prototypes they were given places of honor at the liturgy.[67]

Reginald Fuller conjectures that presbyters came into being around the decade of the 50s at Jerusalem. They are mentioned there in Acts 21. A synthesis afterwards occurs. Presbyters are adopted by the Pauline churches and, as Vischer points out, are linked with the bishops, so that in Acts 20 the terms are interchangeable.[68] The bishops and deacons of the Pauline churches are joined with the presbyters of the Judaistic churches. The synthesis, Fuller maintains, had taken place by 110. There are then the three orders of bishops, presbyters, and deacons. He further sees the emergence of one bishop as head of the presbyteral council, or the monepiscopate, in the Ignatian bishops. The link in the "tunnel" period is seen in Timothy and Titus, who are "apostolic men" or "apostolic delegates" forming the link between the apostles and the Ignatian bishops.[69]

This theory seems quite plausible and will provide a general framework at least into which the office of deacon fits as we find it in the later New Testament period.

As we turn to 1 Timothy 3, we note first of all that again the offices of bishop and deacon are mentioned together, indicating their close connection as they developed in the Church. Though the duties are not given for either office, the qualifications are listed and are nearly identical. Clearly, both offices are filled from respected men in the community. The requirements for deacons, no less than those for bishop, are "strict because of the dignity of the office."[70]

In examining these qualifications we also must take into account that considerable evidence indicates the lists of virtues required for these offices are not of Christian origin but were in general use in the Hellenistic world and have here simply been applied to Church offices.[71] Martin Dibelius and Hans Conzelmann argue convincingly for this view and state emphatically,

> Such a schema underlies the teaching of duties in 1 Timothy 3. This explains why so little is mentioned which would especially characterize a bishop or deacon. For this reason the specifically Christian element is missing.[72]

Bearing this in mind, it would seem that the use of these lists to shed light on the nature and duties of these offices must be quite limited.

Further, the similarity of the two lists of qualifications is such that it seems unwise to attempt to draw too much from the differences.[73] However, a brief comparison is in order and helpful. First, let us examine the requirements for deacons, which are directly paralleled by those for bishops. Deacons are to be "serious," which has to do with both inward temper and outward attitude and roughly corresponds to the requirements that the bishop be "sensible" and "dignified."[74] They are to be "not addicted to much wine," the requirement condemning not drinking but drunkenness.[75] They are to be "not greedy for gain," both because undue concern for money is inconsistent with Christian character and because the duties of the office relating to alms and other financial matters would create a temptation. In addition, deacons are "also to be tested first." This testing is best understood in the sense of an examination of character and conduct and not a probationary period, as some have thought.[76]

The meaning of the requirement for both offices that they be filled with men who are the "husband of one wife" is disputed. Some have interpreted it to mean "married to one wife," as against polygamy. E. K. Simpson finds this to be the obvious meaning, arguing that it was "practiced not uncommonly among the Jews of later days, and of course, excessively rife in pagan circles.[77] However, this was not a likely danger for Christians of any kind and would, therefore, be an improbable interpretation.[78]

Easton and Kelly are among those who see the meaning to be "married only once," the prohibition being against second marriage either after divorce or the death of a wife.[79] It is argued that there is abundant evidence from both literature and funerary inscriptions of antiquity to show that to remain unmarried under these circumstances was considered meritorious while to marry again was self-indulgent.[80] However, Dibelius and Conzelmann observe that this was "especially in contrast to a multiplicity of marriages as the result of separation."[81]

In the Roman Catholic and Eastern Orthodox Churches, according to Norbert Brockman, it is this interpretation of the passage which has led to the prohibition of a second marriage for deacons.[82] Though Brockman notes that a never-married deacon may not marry in either Church, he does not explain how the text can be interpreted to encompass this meaning which prohibits even a first marriage. The interpretation, "married only once" does prohibit a widower remarrying. However, Brockman, while observing that this interpretation is not likely to be abandoned in the Roman Catholic Church today, due particularly to the desire for rapprochement with the Orthodox, argues that the original meaning of the passage may better be understood to be that a deacon "be a man noted for fidelity to his wife, the example of an authentically Christian married life."[83]

The kind of requirement here, it is to be emphasized, in light of New Testament thought would not be limited to the Church's leaders but would be for all.[84] Simpson puts this aptly: "To postulate grades of official sanctity among members of the same spiritual body may be orthodox clericalism, but it is heterodox Christianity."[85] In this connection the Pauline teaching that marriage is dissolved by the death of the spouse leaving the other free to remarry as is set forth in Romans 7:1–3 would seem virtually to rule out a prohibition against such an interpretation. Though a double standard does develop with clerical celibacy later, Tertullian writes early in the third century, "Vain shall we be if we think that what is not lawful for priests is lawful for laics."[86]

In light of what has been said, the best understanding here is that this requirement is one of fidelity to one's wife and might best be interpreted as "faithful to his one wife"[87] or "a husband 'undividedly attached to his wife.' "[88] The bishop or deacon is to have a stable and harmonious marriage, which will give assurance that he will perform the pastoral service of his office with dignity and efficiency.[89] If this list is in fact a list of virtues describing public office and not specifically Christian in origin, this interpretation is strengthened. The Christian author would in this connection have been saying that Christian bishops and deacons are required to have standards at least as high as public officials. The general meaning here would have been that of fidelity in marriage.

Several requirements are listed for the deacon and not for the bishop. Deacons are to be "not double-tongued." The special responsibility of deacons in connection with the poor and other pastoral concerns of the Church would make it especially important that they be truthful and consistent in their dealings with others. The deacon also must "hold the mystery of the faith with a clear conscience." Easton argues that this requirement is made for deacons alone because the bishops acted only as members of a council, where one man's mistakes can easily be corrected by the group, but a deacon acted individually with the poor, "whom he could influence profoundly."[90] While interesting, this is perhaps pressing the differences unduly. Kelly puts the emphasis on "clear conscience," noting that sound faith without such a clear conscience is sterile. He asserts, and rightly, that this qualification of Christian conviction is the most important listed.[91]

The "women" mentioned here are probably wives of the deacons.[92] Though some scholars argue that these women are "women deacons," the Greek has only "women similarly" and the reasons for selecting the other reading seem insufficient.[93] Their special mention would be due to their close association with their husbands in the pastoral and charitable work of the deacon. It may well be supposed that they often accompanied their husbands on visits to the homes of members of the Christian community. Therefore, they also would need to be "serious" and "no slanders, but temperate, faithful in all things."

The qualifications for the bishop not given in the deacon's list are that the bishop is to be "hospitable," "an apt teacher," and "not a recent convert," qualities which would not seem to need additional comment for our purposes.

Up to this point nothing has been said regarding the relationship of the bishops and deacons. It seemed best to look first at the pertinent New Testament texts. These, as we have now seen, simply mention the two offices together, leaving us with little more than the order of first bishops and then deacons to note in this connection. And in light of subsequent development we correctly see here an order of precedence. However, it has all too often been true that the later subordination based on rank and status of the deacon to the bishop has been read back into this early period.

Easton rightly observes that, though the Greek word "deacon" means "servant" or "assistant," it would be misleading to translate it as such. The deacons were not the assistants of the bishops at this time but rather "dispensers of the Church's charities; they 'served' the poor and the sick," not the Church's primary leaders.[94] To think in terms of subordination to the bishops at this time is largely to forget the character of the Church of the late New Testament period.

Prototype for Deacons

The effort to find a prototype in Judaism or pagan religions for this office has met with scant success. The term "deacon" is used in Greek inscriptions to denote officials of pagan cults and other groups in all parts of the Mediterranean world. Here "deacon" frequently denotes a waiter, an inference drawn from the fact that it frequently refers to boys and cooks, but the evidence is insufficient to conclude that any such office provided a Christian prototype.[95] The ruler of the Jewish synagogue did have an assistant called a *hazzan* whose liturgical function is somewhat analogous but who had no similar pastoral or sacramental duties. Also, the title is entirely unlike that of "deacon." In classical Greek writings the word has the meaning of ordinary servants, messengers, and civil officials. Josephus and Epictetus at times use the term to refer to a "servant" of God.[96]

Though Edward Echlin states, "The similarity between Jewish levites and Christian deacons is striking,"[97] the evidence does not support the implication that they were prototypes. Henry Gwatkin sees "no likeness to the Levite, who was rather a porter of the temple, who looked after the beasts, and sang in the Choir." In his view the nearest Jewish parallel is the "collector of alms," though he does not find this office analogous.[98] Dix sees a parallel

> between the deacon who placed the bread and mingled cup before the president (at the Eucharist), ministered the *lavabo* [a ceremony which he points out in a footnote is not attested to before the fourth century at the Eucharist] and ministered the elements to the communicants, and the Jewish "attendant" who ministered the ceremonial hand-washing, set the bread for breaking, and the mingled cup for blessing before the president of the *chaburah* and served the food and drink of the religious meal.[99]

Again, though there may be some similarity of function, there seems no connection between this "attendant" and the Christian deacon. It is most probable that the office of deacon was without direct antecedents either in Judaism or paganism, growing out of the distinctive character of the *diakonia* Jesus gave to the nature of the Church and its ministry.

NOTES

1. Lukas Vischer, "The Problem of the Diaconate," in *The Ministry of Deacons*, ed. Department of Faith and Order (Geneva: World Council of Churches, 1965), p. 19. Cf. C. F. D. Moule, "Deacons in the New Testament," *Theology* 58 (London: 1955), 405.
2. Ernst Haenchen, *The Acts of the Apostles, a Commentary* (Philadelphia: Westminster Press, 1971), pp. 260–61.
3. Ibid.
4. Joachim Jeremias, *Jerusalem in the Time of Jesus* (Philadelphia: Fortress, 1969), pp. 130–32. Cf. Haenchen, pp. 261–62. Kirsopp Lake, Note 12, "The Communism of Acts 2 and 4–6 and the Appointment of the Seven," in Part 1: *The Acts of the Apostles*, ed. F. G. Foakes and Kirsopp Lake, in *The Beginnings of Christianity* (Grand Rapids, Mi.: Baker Book House, 1979 [paperback ed.]), 5:148–49 (hereafter cited as Note 12).
5. Haenchen, p. 262. Cf. Richard B. Rackham, *The Acts of the Apostles* (London: Methuen [13th ed.], 1947), p. 83.

6. Edward Echlin, *The Deacon in the Church Past and Future* (Staten Island, N. Y.: Alba House, 1971), p. 8.

7. Haenchen gives a good detailed analysis of Acts 6:1–7 and a helpful summary of the history of criticism relative to the election of the Seven, pp. 259–69.

8. Vischer, pp. 15–16.

9. Haenchen, pp. 268–69. Cf. G. W. H. Lampe, "Acts," in *Peake's Commentary of the Bible,* ed. Matthew Black and H. H. Rowley (London: Nelson, 1962), pp. 893–94 (hereafter cited as "Acts"). Cf. Vischer, p. 16. It might be observed, human nature being what it is, that in such a situation of tension the neglect could have been more imagined than real.

10. Rackham, p. 91.

11. Haenchen, p. 271. Cf. Rackham, pp. 89–90.

12. Rackham, p. 91.

13. Mark 2:27.

14. Kirsopp Lake (Note 12, p. 141) maintains that a major cause of the failure of the communal experiment of the Jerusalem Church was that the Seven "administrators" were killed or driven out of Jerusalem.

15. Acts 8:4–5.

16. Haenchen, pp. 266–68.

17. Reginald Fuller, *Preaching the New Lectionary: The Word of God for the Church Today* (Collegeville, Mn.: The Liturgical Press, 1974), p. 185 (hereafter cited as *Preaching*).

18. Eduard Schweizer, *Church Order in the New Testament,* trans. Frank Clarke (London: SCM Press Ltd., 1961), p. 30.

19. Acts 6:5–6.

20. Rackham, p. 83.

21. Haenchen, p. 263.

22. Vischer, p. 16.

23. F. F. Bruce, *Commentary on the Book of the Acts,* The New International Commentary on the New Testament (Grand Rapids, Mi.: William B. Eerdmans Publishing Co., 1956), pp. 130–31.

24. Haenchen, p. 264. Cf. Rackham, p. 85.

25. Moule: 406–07. Cf. Haenchen, pp. 265–66; Rackham, p. 86; Fuller, *Preaching,* p. 185; G. H. C. Macgregor, "*Exegesis,*" of "The Acts of the Apostles," in *The Interpreter's Bible,* 12 vol. (New York: Abingdon Press, 1954), 9:90; Echlin, pp. 7–8.

26. Vischer, p. 16. Cf. Macgregor, 9:90. But for an opposing view, see Easton, pp. 182–83.

27. Massey H. Shepherd, Jr., "Deacon," in *The Interpreter's Dictionary of the Bible,* 5 vol. (New York: Abingdon Press, 1961), 4:785 (hereafter cited as "Deacon"). Cf. Rackham, p. 86.

28. André Lemaire, "The Ministries in the New Testament: Recent Research," *Biblical Theology Bulletin* III:2, June 1973: 147.

29. Vischer, p. 17.

30. Irenaeus, *Against Heresies* 3.12.10, in vol 1: *The Apostolic Fathers with Justin Martyr and Irenaeus* (1956), in *The Ante-Nicene Fathers: Translations of the Writings of the Fathers down to A.D. 325,* ed. Alexander Roberts and James Donaldson, Amer. reprint ed. A. Cleveland Coxe (Grand Rapids, Mi.: William B. Eerdmans Publishing Co., 1956), 1:434. Cf. Ibid., 4.15.1, *Ante-Nicene Fathers* 1:480 for an almost identical statement.

31. John Chrysostom, *Homily* 14, *On Acts 5:34*, in vol. 11, *St. Chrysostom: Homilies on the Acts of the Apostles and the Epistle to the Romans*, in *Nicene and Post-Nicene Fathers of the Christian Church, A Select Library of the*, First Series, 14 vol., ed Philip Schaff (Grand Rapids, Mi.: William B. Eerdmans Publishing Co., 1956), 11:90–91. However, the translation used here is a better rendering of the passage and is given in Canon 16 of Trullo, in vol. 14, *The Seven Ecumenical Councils*, ed. Henry R. Percival, in *Nicene and Post-Nicene Fathers of the Christian Church, A Select Library of the*, Second Series, 14 vol., ed. Philip Schaff and Henry Wace (Grand Rapids, Mi.: William B. Eerdmans Publishing Co., 1956), 14:373.

32. Acts 6:3.

33. Acts 2:46 speaks of the daily meal; Acts 4:35 mentions other distributions.

34. Rackham, p. 83.

35. Lake, Note 12, p. 149.

36. Norbert Brockman, *Ordained to Service: A Theology of the Permanent Diaconate* (Hicksville, N.Y.: Exposition Press, 1976), p. 8.

37. Acts 6:8.

38. Acts 7:1–53.

39. Acts 6:13.

40. Acts 8:4–13.

41. Acts 8:26–40.

42. Acts 21:8.

43. For example, Bo Reicke, "Deacons in the New Testament and in the Early Church," in *The Ministry of Deacons*, ed. Department of Faith and Order (Geneva: World Council of Churches, 1965), p. 10. Cf. Lietzmann, 1:146.

44. F. W. Beare, *A Commentary of the Epistle to the Philippians* (New York: Harper & Brothers, 1959), p. 49; Ernest F. Scott, "The Epistle to the Philippians," in *The Interpreter's Bible*, 12 vol. (New York: Abingdon Press, 1955), 11:16.

45. J. Hugh Michael, *The Epistle of Paul to the Philippians*, The Moffatt New Testament Commentary (New York: Harper & Brothers, n.d. [Preface dated 1927]), pp. 6–7. Cf. Massey H. Shepherd, Jr., "Ministry, Christian," in *The Interpreter's Dictionary of the Bible*, 5 vol., ed. George A Buttrick (New York: Abingdon Press, 1962), 3:390; Reicke, p. 10.

46. Reginald Fuller, *Early Catholicism in the New Testament*, lectures at the Graduate School of Theology, Sewanee, Tn., 1970. Cf. Vischer, p. 18; Käsemann, *Essays on New Testament Themes* (London: SCM Press Ltd., 1964), pp. 63–94, especially p. 81 (hereafter cited *N. T. Themes*).

47. Cf. J. N. D. Kelly, *A Commentary on the Pastoral Epistles: 1 Timothy, 2 Timothy, Titus* (New York: Harper & Brothers, 1963), p. 81 (hereafter cited *Pastoral Epistles*).

48. Ibid., pp. 71–72.

49. Fuller, *Early Catholicism.*

50. Acts 13:1–3.

51. Haenchen, p. 436.

52. G. W. H. Lampe, *Some Aspects of the New Testament Ministry* (London: S.P.C.K., 1949), pp. 14–15 (hereafter cited as *N. T. Ministry*).

53. Käsemann, *N. T. Themes*, pp. 86–87.

54. Ibid., p. 87.

55. Ibid.

56. Vischer, p. 17.

57. Among those supporting this view: J. B. Lightfoot, *St. Paul's Epistle to the Philippians* (Grand Rapids, Mi.: Zondervan Publishing House, 1963 [reprint of 1913 ed.]), pp. 95–99; J. Hugh Michael, *The Epistle to the Philippians* (New York: Harper & Brothers, n.d.), pp. 4–6; J. Müller, *The Epistles of Paul to the Philippians and to Philemon,* The International Commentary on the New Testament (Grand Rapids, Mi.: William B. Eerdmans Publishing Co., 1955), p. 35; Echlin, p. 9; J. C. Lambert and Geroge Johnston, "Minister," in *Dictionary of the Bible,* ed. James Hastings, rev. ed. Frederick C. Grant and H. H. Rowley (New York: Charles Scribner's Sons, 1963), p. 662; Moule: 406; Vischer, p. 17.

58. Joseph A. Fitzmyer, "The Letter to the Philippians," in *The Jerome Bible Commentary,* 2 vol., ed. Raymond E. Brown, Joseph A. Fitzmyer, Roland E. Murphy (Englewood Cliffs, N.J.: Prentice-Hall, 1968), 2:249. Cf. Echlin, p. 5.

59. Philippians is dated c. 55 (Michael, p. xxi) to c. 64 (Beare, p. 24), though the weight of evidence seems to favor the latter years.

60. J. J. O'Rourke, "Deacons: In the Bible," *New Catholic Encyclopedia,* prepared by an editorial staff at the Catholic University of America (New York: McGraw-Hill, 1967), 4:667.

61. Vischer, p. 19. Cf. Reicke, p. 10.

62. Kelly, who makes a strong case for Pauline authorship, dates it c. 62–65, pp. 34–36; Burton Scott Easton (*The Pastoral Epistles* [New York: Charles Scribner's Sons, 1947]), sets it c. 105, p. 21; Barrett put it between 90 and 125 (C. K. Barrett, *The Pastoral Epistles in the New English Bible* [London: Oxford University Press, 1963], hereafter cited as *Pastoral Epistles*), p. 18; Titus sets the date between 100–150, suggesting c. 130 as likely (Eric Lane Titus, "The First Letter to Timothy," in *The Interpreter's One-Volume Commentary on the Bible,* ed. Charles M. Laymon [Nashville: Abingdon Press, 1971], p. 883).

63. Käsemann, *N. T. Themes,* p. 86.

64. This concept is briefly outlined by Vischer (p. 17) but was set forth in detail by Fuller (*Early Catholicism*). Cf. Cyril Richardson, "Introduction," to "The Letters of Ignatius," in vol. 1: *Early Christian Fathers,* in Library of Christian Classics (Philadelphia: Westminster Press, 1953), 1:177 (hereafter cited as "Ignatius").

65. Lemaire, p. 146.

66. Ibid., p. 147.

67. Ibid.

68. Vischer, p. 17.

69. Käsemann, *N. T. Themes,* p. 87; Fuller, *Early Catholicism.*

70. Easton, pp. 132–33. Cf. Echlin, p. 11.

71. Barrett, *Pastoral Epistles,* p. 57. Cf. George A. Denzer, "The Pastoral Letters," in *The Jerome Biblical Commentary,* 2 vol., (Englewood Cliffs, N.J.: Prentice-Hall, 1968), 2:354.

72. Martin Dibelius and Hans Conzelmann, *The Pastoral Epistles,* trans. Philip Buttolph and Adela Yarbro, ed. Helmut Koester (Philadelphia: Fortress Press, 1972), p. 51.

73. W. J. Lawstuter, "The Pastoral Epistles: First and Second Timothy and Titus," in *The Abingdon Bible Commentary,* ed. Frederick Carl Eiselen, Edwin Lewis, and David G. Downey (New York: Abingdon Press, 1929), p. 1278.

74. Kelly, *Pastoral Epistles,* p. 81.

75. Ibid., p. 77.

76. Easton, p. 10. Cf. Kelly, *Pastoral Epistles,* p. 84.

77. E. K. Simpson, *The Pastoral Epistles: The Greek Text with Introduction and Commentary* (Grand Rapids, Mi.: William B. Eerdmans Publishing Co., 1954), p. 50.
78. Barrett, *Pastoral Epistles,* p. 58.
79. Easton, p. 10; Kelly, *Pastoral Epistles,* p. 84.
80. Kelly, *Pastoral Epistles,* p. 75.
81. Dibelius and Conzelmann, p. 52.
82. Brockman, p. 17.
83. Ibid., pp. 17–18.
84. Barrett, *Pastoral Epistles,* p. 58; Dibelius and Conzelmann, p. 52.
85. Simpson, p. 50.
86. Tertullian, *On Exhortation to Chastity* 7, vol. 4: *Tertullian, Part Fourth; Minucius Felix; Commodian; Origen, Parts First and Second,* in *The Ante-Nicene Fathers,* 4:54. Quasten dates this at between 204–212 (Johannes Quasten, *Patrology* [Westminster, Md.: Newman Press, 1950], 2:305).
87. Barrett, *Pastoral Epistles,* pp. 58–59.
88. Jean-Paul Audet, *Structures in Christian Priesthood: A study of home, marriage and celibacy in the pastoral service of the church,* trans. Rosemary Sheed (New York: Macmillan and Co., 1967), p. 60. See also André Lemaire, "Pastoral Epistles: Redaction and Theology," Biblical Theology Review, II:1 (February 1972):32, who affirms this view.
89. Ibid., pp. 57–61.
90. Easton, p. 9.
91. Kelly, *Pastoral Epistles,* p. 82.
92. Moule: 406. Cf. Easton, pp. 132–33.
93. Kelly, *Pastoral Epistles,* pp. 83–84.
94. Easton, p. 132.
95. Shepherd, "Ministry, Christian," 3:389–90. Cf. Schweizer, p. 174.
96. Shepherd, "Deacon," "Deaconess: KJV Servant," 4:786; "Ministry, Christian," 3:389.
97. Echlin, p. 4. (He gives Dix, "The Ministry in the Early Church c. A.D. 90–410," in *The Apostolic Ministry: Essays on the History and the Doctrine of Episcopacy,* ed. Kenneth E. Kirk [London: Hodden & Stoughton, 1946], as his reference here, but without a page number. I am unable to find the support.)
98. Henry M. A. Gwatkin, "Deacon," in *A Dictionary of the Bible Dealing with its Language, Literature, and Contents,* ed. James Hastings (New York: Charles Scribner's Sons, 1911), 1:574.
99. Dix, "The Ministry in the Early Church," p. 246.

CHAPTER 4

Age of the Apostolic Fathers

The Golden Age: A.D. 100–600

The five centuries from 100 to 600, or from Ignatius of Antioch to Gregory the Great, have been called the Golden Age of the diaconate.[1] In this period deacons flourished in numbers and in importance. They oversaw the pastoral care of the Church. They were administrators of the Church's charities. They were assistants of its bishops, often succeeding them in office. They had a major role in the Church's liturgies. They were the great symbol of the servant ministry to which the Church has been called by Christ.

Councils in the early fourth century, such as Arles and Nicaea, demonstrate the importance of the diaconate by admonishing deacons to "keep within their proper bounds"[2] as presbyters were growing in importance by assuming the functions of the pre-Nicene bishop. At Rome in the time of Pope Damasus, 366–384, Ambrosiaster could write his treatise "On the Boastfulness of Roman Deacons."[3] Jerome, writing in the late fourth or early fifth century, reports that presbyters at Rome are ordained only on recommendation of a deacon and are "less thought of."[4] Even the seventh century Council of Toledo, 633, finds it necessary to direct that in choir deacons "are not to raise themselves above the presbyters."[5] There is no doubt, as we shall see, that their very importance, coupled with the lack of any clear definition of their relationship to the presbyter, was a major factor in their decline.

Guided by the Holy Spirit

It is when we move outside of the New Testament, in the sub-apostolic age, that we see more clearly the character and function of the various offices within the Church as they underwent a transformation from the apostolic age. This change, however, is not to be considered simply a natural development in a human society. The charisma of the Holy Spirit was fully at work in the Church, guiding its development. Lampe reminds us, "Though in one aspect, the change was due to the natural pressure of altered circumstances, it did not happen without the guidance and authority of the Holy Spirit."[6]

The Letter of the Church at Rome to the Church at Corinth (*1 Clement*)

References to the diaconate outside the New Testament in the subapostolic age are relatively plentiful. The first of these, the letter of Clement to the Church at Corinth (c. 96), provides the only other reference generally assigned to the New Testament period mentioning bishops and deacons.[7] This writing is of great importance, having been held in such esteem in antiquity that it was counted among the Scriptures by the Syrian Church and appended to the biblical *Codex Alexandrinus.*[8] Clement, the author, was listed by Irenaeus as the third Bishop of Rome[9] but he can better be described as one of the leading presbyters or, possibly, presbyter-bishops of Rome.

Cyril Richardson rightly points out that to call Clement the third Bishop of Rome implies that the monepiscopate was already established at Rome, which is highly unlikely, since Clement himself refers to the Church rulers both as bishops and as presbyters, using the terms interchangeably. Richardson believes that a hint in the *Shepherd of Hermas* may indicate that Clement acted as a "kind of foreign secretary for the church." He adds, "It must suffice to call him a leading—perhaps *the* leading—presbyter-bishop of the Roman Church."[10] Echlin calls Clement "a leading Roman presbyter."[11] Shepherd says that the Roman Church at this time was governed by a council of presbyters, which probably had a chairman appointed by seniority.[12] There is much to be said for the interpretation of Walter Lowrie that in 1 Clement not all presbyters were bishops but only those *appointed* to liturgize.[13]

Clement wrote anonymously but on behalf of the Church at Rome to help settle a controversy in which a group in the Corinthian Church had thrust their leaders out of office.[14] He tells us that the apostles

> after receiving their orders and being fully convinced by the resurrection of our Lord Jesus Christ and assured by God's word, went out in the confidence of the Holy Spirit to preach the good news that God's Kingdom was about to come. They preached in country and city, and appointed their first converts, after testing them by the Spirit, to be bishops and deacons of future believers.[15]

Clement further writes in reference to the office of bishop that the apostles "appointed the officers we have mentioned. Furthermore, they later added a codicil to the effect that should these die, other approved men should succeed to their ministry." He also speaks of appointment being by the apostles "or later on and with the whole church's consent, by others of proper standing."[16] Clement calls the leaders of the Church at Corinth "bishops and deacons," as we have seen, but he uses "presbyters" for these leaders elsewhere.[17] While it does seem apparent that the terms "bishops" and "presbyters" are used here interchangeably, a careful reading of the text does not enable us to say that the "deacons" are in that category. In light of what we know subsequently, it seems likely that Clement means to include them here as important leaders of the Corinthian Church but not the same as the presbyter-bishops.

Dom Gregory Dix sees in this letter the first Christian description of the way in which the Eucharist was performed. He renders his own translation of the pertinent lines:

> Unto the high-priest (= the celebrant-bishop) his special "liturgies" have been appointed, and to the priests (= presbyters) their special place is assigned, and on the levites (= deacons) their special "deaconings" are imposed; the layman is bound by the ordinances for the laity. Let each of you, brethren, make eucharist to God according to his own order, keeping a good conscience and not transgressing the appointed rule of his "liturgy."[18]

However, this would seem to be reading back into Clement later thought. As we have seen, the Corinthian Church apparently had presbyter-bishops and deacons, but not yet the later threefold structure. The term "priest" was not yet applied to any Church official. The reference of Clement here would rather seem to be, when taken in context, to the order found in the religion of the Old Testament. He moves from that to speak of the order in the Church established by God through Jesus Christ.[19]

As valuable as 1 Clement is, it does not shed any light upon the function of the deacon at that time.[20] It does assert that apostolic authority and succession is to be transmitted in an orderly fashion by the direction of the apostles through the proper appointment of the presbyter-bishops and deacons with the assent of the whole Church. We may see in this an apostolic succession for both the bishops and deacons.[21]

The Shepherd of Hermas

The *Shepherd of Hermas,* once widely read and considered Scripture by Clement of Alexandria, Origen, and Irenaeus,[22] contains in its original section (c. 96)[23] a reference showing the importance of the deacons in the life of the Church. In his vision Hermas sees a tower under construction as a symbol of the building of the triumphant Church. Some stones fit perfectly, others are rejected, as will be those in the Church who do not repent. Hermas writes,

> Now hear about the stones that go into the building. The stones that are square and white and fit their joints are the apostles and bishops and teachers and deacons who have lived in the holiness of God, and have been bishops and teachers and deacons for God's chosen in purity and reverence.[24]

Hermas again mentions deacons in one of the parables towards the end of his work.[25] These are men who have betrayed the trust of their office. In his concern for repentance he writes,

> The ones that are spotted are deacons who served badly and plundered the living of widows and orphans, and made profit for themselves from the ministry they had accepted to perform. So if they persist in the same desire, they are dead and have no hope of life. But if they turn and perform their service purely, they will be able to live.[26]

The care of the poor and especially of widows and orphans was a special and major concern of the Church in the ancient world, and here as elsewhere the evidence shows that the deacons had direct responsibility in this work.

The Didache

Though the date of the *Didache* is uncertain, its section on Church order, Chapters 6 to 15, seems to reflect the rural churches of Syria in the sub-apostolic age. It probably was originally a separate document dating from the late first century, which was placed with the first section and the last chapter and edited by a scribe in Alexandria c. 150.[27]

Therefore, consideration of the *Didache* belongs in the sub-apostolic age, when the primary leadership of the Church was undergoing a transformation from that of apostles, apostolic delegates, prophets, and teachers to that of bishops, presbyters, and deacons. The author of the *Didache* first discusses teachers, apostles, and prophets in that order.[28] He then writes,

> You must, then, elect for yourselves bishops and deacons who are a credit to the Lord, men who are gentle, generous, faithful, and well tried. For their ministry to you is identical with that of the prophets and teachers. You must not, therefore, despise them, for along with the prophets and teachers they enjoy a place of honor among you.[29]

The clear implication here is that bishops and deacons are being added to the leadership of the Church for the same functions as had heretofore been rendered by the prophets and teachers alone.[30] The admonition to give them honor along with the older form of prophets and teachers suggests that they are not yet considered on a par and entirely accepted by all. Further, whereas the prophets and teachers had been primarily charismatic, the bishops and deacons are apparently elected by the Church and commissioned through the laying on of hands. They too then are given the charisma of the Spirit but in a more orderly fashion.[31] This commissioning through the laying on of hands is to be seen as the confirmation of the charisma given by the Spirit.[32]

It is noteworthy that in the *Didache* the term "bishops" is used in the plural not the singular. Further, the bishops and deacons are lumped together and are said to fulfill the same function as the prophets and teachers did. Clearly, the office of bishop was not the same office as that of deacon, just as that of prophet was not the same as that of teacher. Rather, the mention of the two together may well have been due to their together constituting a ruling council for the local Church, though we cannot be certain.

Echlin argues from the text cited of the *Didache* that both bishops and deacons preached and taught as well as performing certain other functions.[33] Brockman maintains, on the other hand, that deacons were chosen by the community for only a "catechetical role . . . to undertake the instruction of the faithful with edification."[34] He consistently avoids ascribing to deacons the role of preaching liturgically. In light of the evidence here and elsewhere it would seem likely that the bishops and not the deacons took over the prophets' functions of presiding at the Eucharist, preaching, and teaching. It seems highly unlikely in view of the lack of other evidence that deacons preached. The deacons would, as other sources indicate, have liturgical functions at the Eucharist in addition to their other functions. But it is important to remember that functions in the Church were not then so rigidly defined and "the official *charismata* of the early church were not severally exclusive. Any individual could perform as many functions as his spiritual endowments allowed."[35]

Ignatius

In the letters which Ignatius, the martyr-bishop of Antioch, wrote as he journeyed from Syria to suffer his martyrdom in Rome in the reign of Trajan, 98–117,[36] there emerge for the first time the clearly distinguishable orders of bishops, presbyters (or elders), and deacons. This picture represents a stage of development beyond that found in the Pastoral Epistles and 1 Clement.[37] In the latter the local churches are governed by councils of officials, probably presbyters and/or presbyter-bishops, with deacons possibly being included in some places. These councils were subject to apostolic delegates such as Timothy and Titus.

But in the Ignatian letters the single bishop emerges as the leading figure in the Church. The Ignatian bishop represents the monepiscopate, a term denoting rule of the local church by a council of presbyters (possibly including deacons)[38] over which one bishop presides.[39] Though the Ignatian letters have often been thought to picture the monarchical episcopate in the churches of Asia Minor in the early years of the second century,[40] the Asian bishops did not possess the autocratic authority implied by that term.[41] Lemaire thinks the language of the Ignatian letters probably indicates that "the ministerial vocabulary first became fixed at Antioch and that the word *episkopos* has designated the president of the local Christian community."[42] He quotes K. A. Strand in seeing the struggle of the Church with heresy as a major reason for the development of the monepiscopate as it did at that time in the East.[43] The monepiscopal Ignatian bishop was not a monarch ruling over the Church but rather was president of the community and of the presbyteral council, which possessed the authority to rule in the local church.

Ignatius uses the symbolism of the bishop as the type of God the Father, the presbyters as that of the college of the apostles, and the deacons as Jesus Christ:

> Correspondingly, everyone must show the deacons respect. They represent Jesus Christ, just as the bishop has the role of the Father, and the presbyters are like God's council and an apostolic band. You cannot have a Church without these.[44]

Dix sees here the same ordering of the Church in its Eucharistic assembly that he finds reflected in the Revelation. The "Church," which at this time was never thought of in terms of a building,[45] was arranged so that the bishop sat at the front in a chair covered by a white linen cloth facing the people across the altar. The presbyters were seated in a semicircle on either side of the bishop. Two of the deacons stood beside the bishop with the others either at the front of the congregation or scattered through it.[46]

The subdeacons and acolytes assisted the deacons and guarded the doors. Other members, men on one side and women on the other, faced the bishop with the catechumens and visitors at the back. Dix believes this arrangement was adopted by the end of the first century, because it is reflected in the vision of the heavenly assembly in the Revelation, which he dates c. 93.[47] Whether or not Dix is correct in this early date, and some details such as the presence of subdeacons and acolytes by Dix's own testimony do not come until later, the general arrangement pictured is that of the universal practice as it shortly came to be and reflects both the nature of the Church and the character of its offices which continued throughout the pre-Nicene period.

In Ignatius's letter to the Trallians we find specific references to the liturgical function of the deacons at the Eucharist:[48] "Those too who are deacons of Jesus Christ's 'mysteries' must give complete satisfaction to everyone. For they do not serve mere food and drink, but minister to God's Church."[49] In 1 Corinthians Paul speaks of being "stewards of the mysteries of God."[50] Though the Greek word "mystery," used here, generally refers to sacred rites, and Christians later applied it to the sacraments, Paul uses it rather to mean secret knowledge of God's plan revealed in the gospel.[51] Thus, Ignatius's use of "mysteries" in connection with the deacons would not in itself be sufficient to infer liturgical function. However, his statement that the deacons "minister to God's Church" when set beside his contrast to their not merely serving food and drink, a probable reference to the Christian "agape" or "fellowship meal," does indicate their participation in the Eucharist liturgically. Ignatius uses the terms "eucharist" and "agape" to denote the same type of assembly, both describing the entire service of worship. Conclusive evidence for the separation of the Eucharist and the agape into independent gatherings comes, at least in the East, only at the end of the second century.[52]

It is also probable that Ignatius's exhortation to a single Eucharist implies a liturgical function for the deacons:[53]

> Be careful then, to observe a single Eucharist. For there is one flesh of our Lord, Jesus Christ, and one cup of his blood that makes *us* one, and one altar, just as there is one bishop along with the presbytery and deacons, my fellow slaves.[54]

The admonition to "a single Eucharist" here is probably due to separate Eucharists held by a group of Judaizers.[55] But his mention of "one flesh," "one cup," "one altar," and "one bishop," all being an integral part of the Eucharist, would clearly indicate that along with the "one bishop," "the presbytery and deacons," who are his "fellow slaves," also have a prominent place in the Eucharist.

It has been asserted that deacons are said to preach in Ignatius's letters.[56] In one of the texts cited Ignatius writes,

> Consequently, it would be a nice thing for you, as a church of God, to elect a deacon to go there [Antioch] on a mission, as God's represent-

> ative, and at a formal service to congratulate them and glorify the Name.[57]

The function of this deacon would, however, seem to be that of a special representative or ambassador to the Church at Antioch. In the light of no other evidence it seems unlikely that the phrase "glorify the Name" is a reference to preaching. Echlin refers to another passage in *Philadelphians* to support diaconal preaching in the Ignatian letters, though a fair translation of the passage will not bear this interpretation. Richardson renders the text, "Now about Philo, the deacon from Cilicia. He is well spoken of and right now he is helping me in God's cause. . . ."[58] Echlin bases his argument on a translation which runs, "Philo . . . is at present giving me his help in preaching God's word."[59] Other authorities do not support this reading.[60] It must be concluded that there is insufficient evidence in these letters to maintain that preaching was a function of the diaconate in these writings.

It is sometimes assumed that the deacon's position as seen in the writings of Ignatius was that of assistant to the bishop, as the latter emerged a single figure in the monepiscopate.[61] It is true that at times they did act in this capacity. Philo, the Cilician deacon, was helping Ignatius at the time he wrote to the Philadelphians; but in the same sentence we are told that so was Rheus Agathopus, who is described as "a choice person" and is apparently not a deacon.[62] Ignatius asks the Church at Ephesus to let their deacon, Burrhus, whom he describes as "my fellow slave," remain with him.[63] But Burrhus is said to be a deacon of the Church at Ephesus, not of the Bishop, and his position seems incidental to the request. The position of the deacon in these letters appears to be that of a servant of the Church, who naturally at times acts to assist its leading officer.

However, the most striking aspect of Ignatius's letters regarding the place of the deacon in the Church is his reference to their symbolizing Jesus Christ. Ignatius at this point refers to the bishop as a figure of God the Father and the presbyters as symbolizing the apostolic council. He then says, "Let the deacons (my special favorites) be entrusted with the ministry of Jesus Christ who was with the Father from eternity and appeared at the end (of the world)."[64] In a similar context, as we have noted before, he writes that they are to be respected because "they represent Jesus Christ."[65] Ignatius can think in these terms and use this order with the deacons in the third place yet representing Jesus Christ because ministerial order was not conceived by him or others in terms of status or rank but rather of function. So long as we think in categories of rank and status we cannot understand the development of these orders in the ancient Church.[66] The office of the deacon, though mentioned third, is not inferior but is in fact that of Christ himself.

It is because of the high esteem in which the deacon was held that he may have been included in the governing council and was mentioned at one point along with the bishop and presbyters as among those to whom obedience is to be given. The basic concern of Ignatius is for the unity of the Church as he writes,

> Flee from schism as the source of mischief. You should all follow the bishop as Jesus Christ did the Father. Follow, too, the presbytery as you would the apostles; and respect the deacons as you would God's law. Nobody must do anything that has to do with the Church without the bishop's approval. You should regard the Eucharist as valid which is celebrated either by the bishop or by someone he authorizes.[67]

It is also to be noted that in view of the functional nature of the offices, the respected place of the deacon, and the liturgical function already possessed by the deacon, it is entirely conceivable that the bishop could have authorized a deacon to preside at the Eucharist when he was unable to be present at this early time.[68]

Polycarp

In the letter of Polycarp to the Philippians, which comes after the martyrdom of Ignatius and is probably to be dated c. 115–120,[69] the qualifications set forth for deacons are reminiscent of those in 1 Timothy:

> Likewise the deacons should be blameless before his [God's] righteousness, as servants of God and Christ and not of men; not slanderers, or double-tongued, not lovers of money, temperate in all matters, compassionate, careful, living according to the truth of the Lord, who became "a servant of all."[70]

Here it is worth noting that the deacons are to be "servants of God and of Christ and not of men," which in effect indicates that the deacons have not yet become assistants of the bishop. Polycarp also speaks of the necessity of the people within the Church "being obedient to the presbyters and deacons,"[71] who together may have comprised the ruling council at Philippi.

The End of the Post–Apostolic Age

By the end of the age of the apostolic fathers the leadership of the Church is clearly passing from the charismatically appointed apostles, prophets, and teachers of the primitive Church to the threefold orders of bishops, presbyters (or elders), and deacons. While at first the bishops and deacons may have had responsibilities only for the business affairs of the Church,[72] they seem almost immediately to have begun to assume liturgical and pastoral functions. Though various factors were involved in this change, such as the decreasing number of prophets possessed with charismatic gifts, and the threat of Gnosticism, it is to be remembered, also, that the change did not occur "without the guidance and authority of the Holy Spirit,"[73] and in this sense "can be understood as of divine institution."[74]

The three orders, however, do not constitute the ministry of the Church. The ministry of the Church continues to be, as it had been from the first, the service rendered by all of the Church's people to God, to one another, and to others. The three orders were delegated certain functions within this ministry. At this time the monepiscopate has developed in some churches with a single bishop presiding both over a council of presbyters (and deacons?) and over the Eucharistic assembly. Presbyters acted as a council for the governance of the local Church, and deacons served those in need and participated liturgically at the Eucharist.

The deacons had liturgical and administrative functions of their own. They were a full order with *leiturgia* and *diakonia* which were distinctive. These functions were firmly bound together and were increasingly not to be interchanged with those of other orders.[75] But we must wait to learn from succeeding writers more about these functions.

Though the deacons were subject to the ruling council of the local Church, they were "servants of the Church" and "of God," not of another order or official. It is undoubtedly true that the deacon from the outset had a close relationship with the bishops. However, it is all too easy to read back into the first and second centuries what is to be found later in this connection. It would seem probable that it was more as the monarchial episcopate developed, following the monepiscopate, and assimilated the rule of the corporate presbyterate that the deacons came more and more to be thought of as the liturgical and administrative assistants of the bishop rather than of the Church. From the time the primary leadership of the Church passed from the apostles or apostolic delegates, prophets, and teachers to the bishops (or presbyter-bishops), presbyters, and deacons, the bishop did possess a sacramental and liturgical dominance.[76] But it is to be remembered that this was only in the context of the Church. The bishop was the "high priest" and not the "priest," because the priesthood was in this early period seen to belong to the whole body of the Church.[77] The presbyter had no liturgical function, though he may have been designated by the bishop to assume liturgical functions at the Eucharist when the bishop could not be present, as reported by Ignatius.[78] It is, however, entirely possible, as we have observed, that a deacon could have been the one so authorized. But, in any event, the deacon appears from the earliest time to have had liturgical function which was not derived from the bishop.

NOTES

1. Edward R. Hardy, "The Deacon in History and Practice," in *The Diaconate Now*, ed. Richard T. Nolan (Washington: Campus Books, 1968), p. 15. Echlin (Edward Echlin, *The Deacon in the Church Past and Future* [Staten Island, N.Y.: Alba House, 1971], pp. 25, 57) refers to the golden age of the diaconate as being from Ignatius to Nicaea. Though the decline begins in the fourth century, the diaconate continues to flourish long after.
2. Canon 18, Nicaea, in *A New Eusebius: Documents Illustrative of the Church to* A.D. *337*, ed. J. Stevenson (New York: Macmillan, 1957), p. 363.
3. S. L. Greenslade, "Introduction," to *Letter* 146 of Jerome, in *Early Latin Theology*, trans. S. L. Greenslade, in Library of Christian Classics (Philadelphia: Westminster Press, 1956), 5:383.
4. Jerome, Epistle 146.2, in *Early Latin Theology*, 5:388. The translator dates this letter after 388 (5:383–84). The evidence might suggest c. 400. Jerome died in 419 or 420 (5:286).
5. Charles Joseph Hefele, vol. 4: *A History of the Councils of the Church, from the Original Documents.* A.D. *451 to* A.D. *680*, trans. William R. Clark in *A History of the Councils of the Church* (Edinburgh: T. & T. Clark, 1895), 4:454.
6. G. W. H. Lampe, *Some Aspects of the New Testament Ministry* (London: S.P.C.K., 1949), p. 20 (hereafter cited as *N. T. Ministry*).
7. C. D. F. Moule, "Deacons in the New Testament," *Theology* 58 (London: 1955):407.
8. Berthold Altaner, *Patrology*, trans. Hilda C. Graef (New York: Herder and Herder, 1960), p. 99.
9. Irenaeus, *Against Heresies* 3.3.3., in vol. 1: *Early Christian Fathers*, in Library of Christian Classics (Philadelphia: Westminster Press, 1953), 1:372. Irenaeus also says that Clement, along with many others still alive, had known the apostles and had "their traditions before his eyes," 1:373.
10. Cyril C. Richardson, "The Letter of the Church of Rome to the Church of Corinth, Commonly called Clement's First Letter—Introduction," in *Early Christian Fathers*, 1:36–37.
11. Echlin, p. 14.
12. Massey H. Shepherd, Jr., "Smyrna in the Ignatian Letters: A Study in Church Order," *Journal of Religion* 20(1940):156 (hereafter cited "Ignatian Letters"). Cf. Richardson, "Clement," p. 39.
13. Walter Lowrie, *The Church and Its Organization in Primitive and Catholic Times* (New York: Longmans, Green, and Co., 1904), pp. 341–50. Lowrie, however, is probably not correct in arguing that the term "presbyter" ("elder") in 1 *Clement* does not denote an office (pp. 348–52) except when they are called "appointed presbyters."
14. I *Clement* 44; in *Early Christian Fathers*, 1:63–64.
15. Ibid., 42, p. 62.
16. Ibid., 44, pp. 63–64.

17. Ibid., 44, 47, 57, pp. 63–65, 69.

18. Dom Gregory Dix, *The Shape of the Liturgy*, (Westminster: Dacre Press, 1945), p. 1. (Reference is to 1 *Clement* 40 and 41.)

19. 1 *Clement* 42, in *Early Christian Fathers*, 1:62–63.

20. Echlin argues that since deacons were associated with the bishops "both in their ministry and in their expulsion, we may conclude that the diaconal function involved ministry of liturgy and charity." His reference is to 1 *Clement* 44, but this has nothing to say at all about liturgical function.

21. Bo Reicke, "Deacons in the New Testament and in the Early Church," in *The Ministry of Deacons*, ed. Department of Faith and Order (Geneva: World Council of Churches, 1965), p. 11.

22. Edgar J. Goodspeed, *A History of Early Christian Literature*, rev. & enlarged, Robert M. Grant (Chicago: University of Chicago Press, 1966), p. 32 (hereafter cited *Early Christian Literature*).

23. The first section of the *Shepherd*, Visions 1–4 (in Edgar J. Goodspeed, *The Apostolic Fathers—An American Translation* [New York: Harper & Brothers, 1950]), probably was written during the last years of the leadership of Clement of Rome, which ended in 97 (see Goodspeed, *Early Christian Literature*, pp. 30–34). Cf. Johannes Quasten, vol. 1: *Beginnings of Patristic Literature* in *Patrology* (Westminster, Md.: Newman Press, 1950), 1:92–93.

24. Hermas, *Shepherd*, Vision 3.5.1, in Goodspeed, *Apostolic Fathers*, p. 112.

25. The second section of Hermas, *Shepherd*, Vision 5 through the end, is to be dated in the second century a few years after the first, though Parables 9 and 10 may be still later additions. Goodspeed and Grant's (*Early Christian Literature*, pp. 30–34) argument for this dating and against the time of Pius I (140–155) is to be preferred.

26. Hermas, *Shepherd*, Parable 9.26.2, in Goodspeed, *Apostolic Fathers*, p. 193.

27. Cyril C. Richardson, "The Teaching of the Twelve Apostles, Commonly Called the Didache," in *Early Christian Fathers*, 1:162–65.

28. *Didache* 11–13, in *Early Christian Fathers*, 1:176–78.

29. *Didache* 15, in *Early Christian Fathers*, 1:178.

30. Reginald Fuller, *Early Catholicism in the New Testament*, lectures at the Graduate School of Theology, Sewanee, Tn., 1970. Cf. Lowrie, pp. 331–42.

31. Fuller, *Early Catholicism*.

32. Lowrie, p. 342.

33. Echlin, p. 17.

34. Norbert Brockman, *Ordained to Service: A Theology of the Permanent Diaconate* (Hicksville, N.Y.: Exposition Press, 1976), p. 21.

35. Shepherd, "Ignatian Letters": 154.

36. Eusebius dates the martyrdom of Ignatius at 107 in his *Chronicles*, fn. *Church History* 3:36, in vol. 1: *Eusebius: Church History, Life of Constantine the Great, and Oration in Praise of Constantine*, trans. and ed. Arthur Cushman McGiffert, in *Nicene and Post-Nicene Fathers of the Christian Church*, Second Series, ed. Philip Schaff and Henry Wace, 14 vol. (Grand Rapids, Mi.: William B. Eerdmans Publishing Co., 1952), 1:169. However, modern scholars generally agree only that he was martyred in Rome in the reign of Trajan (98–117): Kirsopp Lake, "Introduction" to "The Epistles of Ignatius," in *The Apostolic Fathers*, vol. 1 (Cambridge, Ma.: Harvard University Press, 1912 [reprint 1970]), 1:166; Cyril Richardson, "Introduction," to "The Letters of Ignatius," in *Early Christian Fathers*, 1:75.

37. Massey H. Shepherd, Jr., "Ministry, Christian," in *The Interpreter's Dictionary of the Bible*, ed. George A. Buttrick (New York: Abingdon Press, 1962), 3:391. Cf. Richardson, in *Early Christian Fathers*, 1:76.

38. Shepherd, "Ignatian Letters:" 142.

39. Richardson, *Early Christian Fathers*, 1:76. Reginald Fuller (*Early Catholicism*) sees the same development and the emergence of the monepiscopate in Ignatius.

40. E.g., Eduard Schweizer, *Church Order in the New Testament*, trans. Frank Clarke (London: SCM Press Ltd., 1961), p. 154; Hans Lietzmann, *A History of the Early Church*, vol. 1: *The Beginnings of the Christian Church;* vol. 2: *The Founding of the Church Universal* (bound together), trans. Bertram Lee Woolf (New York: The World Publishing Co., Meridian Books, 1961), 2:58; and John Knox, *The Early Church and the Coming Great Church* (New York and Nashville: Abingdon Press, 1955), p. 121.

41. Shepherd, "Ignatian Letters:" 141.

42. André Lemaire, "The Ministries in the New Testament: Recent Research," *Biblical Theology Bulletin* III:2, June 1973: 145.

43. Ibid.: 145–46.

44. Ignatius, *Trallians* 3, in *Early Christian Fathers*, 1:99. Cf. Ignatius, *Magnesians* 6, in *Early Christian Fathers*, 1:95.

45. Dix points out that the word "church" means "invariably . . . the solemn assembly for the liturgy, and by extension those who have a right to take part in this" until the third century. (Dix, *Shape of the Liturgy*, p. 20). Cf. Reginald H. Fuller, "Church," in *A Theological Word Book of the Bible*, ed. Alan Richardson (New York: Macmillan, 1951) p. 46.

46. Dix, *Shape of the Liturgy*, p. 28.

47. Dix may have intended rather that the *general arrangement* was adopted by the end of the first century, since he states later (*Shape of the Liturgy*, p. 35) that the "minor orders" came into existence by the end of the second century.

48. Richardson, in *Early Christian Fathers*, 1:99 fn.

49. Ignatius, *Trallians* 2, in *Early Christian Fathers*, 1:99.

50. 1 Cor. 4:1. Cf. 1 Cor. 2:7; 13:2; 14:2.

51. C. K. Barrett, *A Commentary on the First Epistle to the Corinthians* (New York: Harper & Row, 1968) pp. 99–100 (hereafter cited *1 Corinthians*).

52. Shepherd, "Ignatian Letters:" 149.

53. Echlin, p. 21.

54. Ignatius, *Philadelphians* 4, in *Early Christian Fathers*, 1:108.

55. Richardson, in *Early Christian Fathers*, 1:108 fn.

56. Urban T. Holmes III, *The Future Shape of Ministry: A Theological Projection* (New York: Seabury Press, 1971), p. 25 (hereafter cited *Future Shape*). Echlin, p. 21.

57. Ignatius, *Philadelphians* 10, in *Early Christian Fathers*, 1:111.

58. Ignatius, *Philadelphians* 11, in *Early Christian Fathers*, 1:111.

59. Echlin, p. 21.

60. See Gerald G. Walsh, "The Letters of St. Ignatius of Antioch," in vol. 1: *The Apostolic Fathers*, in *The Fathers of the Church*, trans. Francis X. Glimm, Joseph M. F. Marique, and Gerald G. Walsh (New York: Cima Publishing Co., 1947), 1:117, which reads "ministering in the word of God." A similar reading is found in vol. 1: *The Apostolic Fathers with Justyn Martyr and Irenaeus*, in *The Ante-Nicene Fathers: Translations of the Writings of the Fathers down to* A.D. *325*, ed. Alexander Roberts and James Donaldson, Amer. reprint ed. A. Cleve-

land Coxe (Grand Rapids, Mi.: William B. Eerdmans Publishing Co., 1956), 1:85: ". . . who still minister to me in the word of God." Lake's translation reads, ". . . who is at present serving me in the word of God," *Apostolic Fathers,* 1:251. J. B. Lightfoot renders the phrase, ". . . who now ministereth to me in the word of God. . . ." (*The Apostolic Fathers,* ed. J. R. Harmer [Grand Rapids, Mi.: Baker Book House, 1956 (reprint of 1891 ed.)]), p. 82.

61. Richardson, in *Early Christian Fathers,* 1:76.

62. Ignatius, *Philadelphians* 11, in *Early Christian Fathers,* 1:111.

63. Ignatius, *Ephesus* 2, in *Early Christian Fathers,* 1:88.

64. Ignatius, *Magnesians* 6, in *Early Christian Fathers,* 1:95.

65. Ignatius, *Trallians* 3, in *Early Christian Fathers,* 1:99.

66. Shepherd, "Ignatian Letters:" 158.

67. Ignatius, *Smyrneans* 8, in *Early Christian Fathers,* 1:115. Cf. Ignatius, *Polycarp* 6, in *Early Christian Fathers,* 1:119.

68. Echlin, p. 22.

69. Massey Shepherd argues convincingly for the unity of Polycarp's letter and, therefore, for the traditional dating of it ("Introduction" to "The Letter of Polycarp, Bishop of Smyrna, to the Philippians," in *Early Christian Fathers,* 1:122–23). However, some follow the theory of P. N. Harrison, in which chap. 13 and possibly 14 are considered one letter and dated at this time and chap. 1–12 are thought to be another letter from c. 135 (in Altaner, p. 111).

70. Polycarp, *Philippians* 5, in *Early Christian Fathers,* 1:133.

71. Ibid.

72. Shepherd, "Ignatian Letters:" 152–53. Cf. Lietzmann, 1:193, 2:58.

73. Lampe, *N. T. Ministry,* p. 20. I do not mean to imply here that the Holy Spirit is always the guiding force behind all that happens in the Church. Though he is always present, obviously he is not always heeded. However, in this early period, especially the pre–Nicene age, of more costly Christianity and of undeniably great zeal for and commitment to Christ within the Church generally, the guidance of the Holy Spirit is clearer and more apparent and assuredly present in the emerging order of the offices within the Church's ministry.

74. Karl Rahner, *Bishops: Their Status and Function,* trans. Edward Quinn (Baltimore: Helicon Press, 1964), p. 17.

75. Dix, *Shape of the Liturgy,* p. 112.

76. Ibid., p. 33.

77. Ibid., pp. 29–34. Cf. Dom Gregory Dix, "The Ministry in the Early Church c. A.D. 90–410," in *The Apostolic Ministry: Essays on the History and the Doctrine of Episcopacy,* ed. Kenneth E. Kirk (London: Hodden & Stoughton, 1946), p. 282 fn.

78. Ignatius, *Smyrneans* 8, in *Early Christian Fathers,* 1:115. Cf. Dix, *Shape of the Liturgy,* p. 34.

CHAPTER 5

From the Post-Apostolic Age to the Constantinian Era

Justin Martyr

Justin Martyr, one of the most learned and the most voluminous Christian writers up to his time, describes the worship of the Church at Rome c. 150[1] in his *Apology.*[2] In this valuable account of the Eucharist Justin records that after "the prayers" had been concluded and the kiss of peace exchanged, bread and wine mixed with water are brought to "the president of the brethren," who gives praise and glory to God and offers thanks at length over them. Then Justin continues:

> When the president has given thanks and the whole congregation has assented, those whom we call deacons give to each of those present a portion of the consecrated bread and wine and water, and they take it to the absent.[3]

For the first time we have specific mention of this liturgical function of the deacons. It is to be noted here that this earliest record makes it the function of the deacons alone to administer both the Bread and the Wine at the Eucharist. We see too the depth of their understanding of the organic nature of the Church by the deacons' taking the eucharisticized Bread and Wine to those who were absent. The importance of this is emphasized by Justin's repeating in reference to the weekly Eucharist each Sunday that "they [the consecrated elements] are sent to the absent by the deacons."[4]

Dix thinks that the administration of both the Bread and the Wine by the deacons is the authentic practice of the Church and that it continued after Justin's time.[5] Later evidence would seem to support this view, and John Bligh is probably correct in maintaining that for centuries after Justin deacons continued to administer the chalice even to priests and bishops, though probably not to a bishop celebrant. He reports that Durandus says it is still legally correct but is no longer done in the Roman Catholic Church.[6]

It is also of interest that only the office of deacon is mentioned here by Justin in his portrayal of Christian worship at Rome in the mid-second century. Justin's designation of the presiding officer at the Eucharist as "the president of the brethren" or "one of the brethren who was presiding,"[7] either of which are legitimate translations of the Greek,[8] should not be taken to imply that a single bishop had not yet emerged at Rome in what we have termed the monepiscopate. Justin, as an apologist, was writing for non-Christians[9] and therefore uses "president," a term they will understand, just as he uses "Sunday" instead of "the Lord's Day."[10] Irenaeus's account of the visit of the aged Bishop Polycarp to Rome a year or two before his martyrdom in 155 or 156[11] calls Anicetus, whom Polycarp came to visit, its bishop.[12] Clearly the monepiscopate is present at Rome in Justin's time.

Irenaeus

Irenaeus, who saw and heard Polycarp in Smyrna in his youth and later became Bishop of Lyons in Gaul, is the first to call Stephen of Acts 6 a deacon, as was previously noted. He writes (c. 185),[13]

> And still further, Stephen, who was chosen the first deacon by the apostles, and who of all men, was the first to follow the footsteps of the Lord, being the first that was slain for confessing Christ, speaking boldly among the people, and teaching them, says: "The God of glory appeared to our father Abraham. . . ."[14]

He also mentions Nicolas (or Nicolaus), whom he says "was one of the seven first ordained to the diaconate by the apostles," and credits him with founding the sect of the Nicolaitans[15] referred to in Revelation 2:6, though his connection with this heretical group is mere conjecture.[16] Irenaeus thus begins the tradition that the Seven of Acts 6 were the first deacons, at least so far as the written evidence is concerned. In this connection it is to be noted again that in spite of the mention of Stephen preaching in Acts and of Irenaeus's reference to Stephen in order that he might quote him both here and in Book 4, deacons do not apparently possess the function of preaching.

The Pseudo-Clementines

The "Epistle of Clement to James" introducing the *Homilies* in the *Pseudo-Clementines* speaks of the deacons being as eyes to the bishop:

> Moreover let the deacons of the church, going about with intelligence, be as eyes to the bishops, carefully inquiring into the doings of each member of the church, ascertaining who is about to sin, in order that, being arrested with admonition by the president, he may haply not accomplish the sin. Let them check the disorderly, that they may not desist from assembling to hear the discourses, so that they may be able to counteract by the word of truth those anxieties that fall upon the heart from every side, by means of worldly casualties and evil communications; for if they long remain fallow, they become fuel for the fire. And let them learn who are suffering under bodily disease, and let them bring them to the notice of the multitude who do not know of them, that they may visit them, and supply their wants according to the judgment of the president. Yea, though they do this without his knowledge, they do nothing amiss. These things, then, and things like to these, let the deacons attend to.[17]

The duties enumerated for the deacons here are these:

1. They are to be the "eyes of the bishop" for the purpose of seeing those about to sin, so that the "president" may exhort the person to refrain.
2. They are to "check the disorderly" in Christian meetings, so that the people may hear the "discourses" and have the "word of truth" to counteract temptation.
3. They are to learn of the sick and "bring them to the notice of the multitude," not the bishop, so that the people of the Church may visit them and supply their needs as the bishop deems necessary.

Yet, they are still primarily servants of the Church and not of the bishop. Speaking out of this tradition, the author here observes that even if they do these things without knowledge of the bishop, whom he prefers to call "the president," they do nothing amiss.

The pseudo-Clementine literature contains another mention of deacons, though it adds little to our knowledge. The author writes, "Let the deacons, going about, look after the bodies and the souls of the brethren, and report to the bishop."[18]

Tertullian

Tertullian, born in Carthage and destined to become the first great figure in Latin Christianity, was converted to Christianity at Rome, but returned to his native Carthage. He was an able and prolific writer. In his work *On Baptism,* c. 200,[19] he stated that deacons can baptize with the bishop's authority:

> Of giving it [baptism], the chief priest (who is the bishop) has the right: in the next place, the presbyters and deacons, yet not without the bishop's authority, on account of the honour of the Church, which being preserved, peace is preserved. Beside these, even laymen have the right. . . . But how much more is the rule of reverence and modesty incumbent on laymen—seeing that these powers belong to their superior—lest they assume to themselves the specific function of the bishop![20]

His interest in asserting the authority of the bishop seems to stem largely, like that of Ignatius, from his concern for the Church's unity, for he explains that schism can easily follow when others assume the bishop's functions. Laymen, therefore, should baptize only in case of necessity. But by laymen he does not mean women. In this chapter he denies the right of women to assume the functions either of baptizing or teaching.

Though function still seems to be uppermost, Tertullian's use of "superiors" to designate the place of the bishop in reference to the laity connotes a growing conception of rank and status attaching themselves to the offices of the Church. Of more importance, however, is his use of *summus sacerdos,* which above is translated "chief priest" but which may also be rendered "high priest."[21] The expression is not used elsewhere by Tertullian and is not known to have been used earlier.[22] Bishop Wordsworth writes in this connection of the emergence of the office of the bishop in the first half of the third century:

> The Bishop then, as a central authority in a sacrificial worship offered by the whole priestly race, became inevitably the *archiereus* or "sacerdos," terms which came into use about the first quarter of the third century and were accepted generally from the middle of the same period.[23]

Cyprian, who derived many of his ideas from Tertullian,[24] took over *summus sacerdos* and "built on it—and on the use of *ara*—his doctrine of the ministry, separating the Episcopate from the Presbyterate, and the clergy from the laity."[25]

But Tertullian himself asserts strongly the organic and functional nature of the Church and its people. In *The Exhortation to Chastity,* c. 205,[26] one of his last works before his Montanist period, he argues that not only those chosen for the "sacerdotal order" must be men of one marriage but so also the laity. The tradition that priesthood belongs to the whole Church is here asserted, when Tertullian asks, "Are not even we laics priests?" He further asserts that in cases of necessity, when no priests are present, laymen have the rights of priests. In such an event he says,

> You offer [celebrate the Eucharist], and baptize, and are priest, alone for yourself. But where three are, a church is, albeit they be laics. . . . Therefore, if you have the right of a priest in your own person, in cases of necessity, it behoves you to have likewise the discipline of a priest whenever it may be necessary to have the right of a priest. . . . Hence we are bound to contend that the command to abstain from second marriage relates first to the laic; so long as no other can be a presbyter than a laic, provided he has been once for all a husband.[27]

Though the purpose of his discussion is to show that digamy[28] is not allowed, and though many would not agree that laymen might celebrate the Eucharist, his argument does reveal that his conception of the Church is soundly organic and apostolic. He can say, "Where three are, a church is, albeit they be laics." The laity are as much the Church as are the clergy. He here sets forth a profound truth about the nature of the Church which the clericalism of later centuries almost totally obscured.

Hippolytus

Hippolytus, who as a young man was a pupil of Irenaeus and succeeded him as the foremost figure of Greek Christianity in the West, wrote *The Apostolic Tradition*, c. 215,[29] in the last part of the episcopate of Zephyrinus, Bishop of Rome from 198–217, whom he strongly opposed, considering him "an ignorant and illiterate individual and one unskilled in ecclesiastical definitions," who was "accessible to bribes and covetous."[30] In this compact manual we have the earliest text of the ordinal[31] and the first detailed information about ordination to the diaconate.[32] The tradition given here undoubtedly in some important respects represents the practice of the Church at Rome long before the third century.[33]

The Apostolic Tradition directs that deacons are to be chosen like the bishops and presbyters, which is by election of all the people.[34] Hippolytus states clearly the place of the deacon in the Church in Rome at this time when he explains why only the bishop lays hands upon him in ordination:

> When the deacon is ordained, this is the reason why the bishop alone shall lay his hands upon him: he is not ordained to the priesthood but to serve the bishop and to carry out the bishop's commands. He does not take part in the council of the clergy; he is to attend to his own duties and to make known to the bishop such things as are needful. He does not receive that Spirit that is possessed by the presbytery, in which the presbyters share; he receives only what is confided in him under the bishop's authority.[35]

Here the deacon is not part of the ruling council of presbyters over which the bishop presides. But rather the deacon has become here the servant of the bishop, carrying out his orders, a position somewhat different from that in Ignatius where they are "servants of the Church" and "subject to the bishop and presbytery," or in Polycarp where they are "servants of God" and may share in the rule of the Church. This change, as we shall soon note, is even to be seen in the difference between the wording of the ordination prayer in the *Apostolic Tradition* and Hippolytus's explanation of it.

It is helpful for us to remember in understanding the place of the deacon in Hippolytus's writings that the leadership and rule of the Church at Rome seems originally to have been set in a council of presbyters or presbyter-bishops and probably to have remained so longer there than in most churches originally governed by such presbyteral councils. As Rome adopted the threefold offices, the deacon would not have had the prestige on this account he had in churches where the leadership had been vested in the bishops and deacons and would more easily have become subject to and assistant of the bishop. In addition, Easton rightly points to the importance of the development of the monarchial bishop in deacons becoming the assistants and delegates of the bishops. As the bishop assumed rule of the local Church and controlled Church activity, the deacons would in the normal course of events become his assistants. Easton is also probably right in maintaining that the emphasis placed by Hippolytus on explaining why the bishop alone lays his hands on a deacon in ordaining him shows that the custom, while of long standing in Rome, was still questioned.[36]

The prayer of ordination given at this point in the *Apostolic Tradition* refers to the part the deacon has in the Eucharistic offerings:

> O God, who hast created all things and hast ordered them by thy Word, the Father of our Lord Jesus Christ, whom thou didst send to minister thy will and to manifest to us thy desire; grant [the] Holy Spirit of grace and care and diligence to thy servant, whom thou hast chosen to serve the church and to offer in thy holy sanctuary the gifts that are offered to thee by thine appointed high priests, so that serving without blame and with a pure heart he may be counted worthy of this exalted office, by thy goodwill, praising thee continually. Through thy Servant Jesus Christ, through whom be to thee glory and honour, with [the] Holy Spirit, in the holy church, both now and always and world without end. Amen.[37]

In the prayer God is asked to give the Holy Spirit to the man being ordained deacon. The twofold nature of the office is seen in the mention of charitable and liturgical functions: "to serve the Church" and "to offer in the holy sanctuary the gifts." Here we find the concept of "high priest"[38] as the president of the Eucharist. We would note also that the office of the deacon is described as "exalted."

However, one of the most significant things to be seen here is that this prayer appears to represent an older stratum of tradition than Hippolytus's introduction to it. In the introduction, as we have seen, emphasis is laid on the bishop alone laying hands on the deacon with the explanation that the deacon is ordained to serve the bishop, but in the older ordination prayer embodying the original tradition, the deacon is clearly "to serve the Church," a subtle but significant departure.

Hippolytus makes one further point regarding the ordination of deacons. He tells us that a confessor, "if he has been in bonds for the name of the Lord," shall not have hands laid on him for either the diaconate or the presbyterate, "for he has the honour of the presbyterate by his confession." But to qualify, a confessor must have either been "punished with bonds" or "shut up in prison."[39] Bishops, however, must receive the laying on of hands, a requirement which may have been due to the necessity for unquestionable designation of this office since there was only one bishop in one place.[40]

The *Apostolic Tradition* tells us something of the liturgical function of the deacon. In describing the baptismal Eucharist at Easter, Hippolytus relates that the deacons bring the offerings of the people to the bishop, who eucharistizes or consecrates them.[41] The offerings of this period at the Eucharist were small loaves of bread and probably a little wine in a flask brought by each person.[42] The deacons probably arranged the oblations on the altar, standing on the people's side. Then, Hippolytus directs, the bishop with all the presbytery lays his hand upon the offering and says the Thanksgiving.[43]

However, in contrast to the practice of the deacon administering both the Bread and the Wine reported by Justin Martyr, Hippolytus says that the bishop shall distribute the Bread "with his own hand."[44] Though in the description of the paschal Eucharist the deacons are to assist with the chalice and the cups of water and milk only if enough presbyters are not available,[45] the text of the next statute clearly indicates that it was the deacons and not the presbyters who still at this time normally administered the chalice.[46] The discrepancy here may be due to a faulty reconstruction of the document in the description of the Easter Eucharist, in which later tradition is incorporated into the text.

Jalland states that Ambrose of Milan speaks of the deacons administering only the chalice at Milan in *Duties of the Clergy*.[47] In the passage cited Ambrose relates that Lawrence, martyred c. 258, a deacon of Bishop Xystus (Sixtus II) of Rome, asks his bishop if he is not "a fitting servant" to suffer martyrdom with him. Speaking of himself, he says, "To him to whom thou hast entrusted the consecration of the Saviour's blood, to whom thou hast granted fellowship in partaking of the Sacraments, to him doest thou refuse a part in thy death?"[48] As the translator points out, "consecration" is a strange expression for a deacon to use in reference to himself.[49] However, taken in the context of the practice of the Church, it is rightly understood to mean simply that Lawrence, as a deacon, administered the chalice. The fact that Lawrence is speaking of joining his bishop in martyrdom makes the reference to the deacon's liturgy in administering Christ's Blood especially appropriate. Though the Bread is not mentioned here, it is apparent, especially in light of the *Apostolic Tradition*, that this was administered by his bishop.

It may be, as Jalland also states, that deacons administer only the chalice in North Africa by the middle of the third century.[50] But at the point in Cyprian's *Treatise on the Lapsed* which he gives as his reference,[51] the deacon is simply said "to offer the cup to those present" and nothing is said about the Bread. It is more likely that the deacon lost his function of distributing the Bread at the Eucharist in the course of the fourth century with the transformation of the presbyterate, though the practice may have survived much later in Syria and perhaps elsewhere.[52]

It is further to be noted in Hippolytus's account that the deacons play a prominent part in the administration of baptism. The baptism is administered by a presbyter or, possibly, a bishop, assisted by deacons. Prior to the baptismal candidates entering the water, deacons stand on either side of the presbyter holding the oils the presbyter will use in anointing. The deacon on the left holds the oil of exorcism, so named for its purpose and because it is exorcised, not blessed. The deacon on the right holds the oil of thanksgiving (chrism), the name derived from its blessing still being in the form of a thanksgiving.[53] The presbyter anoints each candidate with the oil of exorcism after the renunciations, probably over the entire body,[54] the clothing having been removed at the beginning of the baptismal rite. No impropriety was involved because all non-Jews in the Graeco-Roman world were accustomed to nakedness in the public baths.[55] A deacon, likewise naked, goes into the water with the candidates for the baptism, the presbyter probably standing beside the water. After the baptism, the presbyter anoints each with the oil of thanksgiving, again presumably over the whole body.[56] They are then clothed and brought into the Church, where the bishop lays his hands upon them with prayer and then anoints them on their foreheads with the oil of thanksgiving, using a Trinitarian formula.[57]

The duty of the deacons to be alert to inform the bishop of any who are sick is repeated by Hippolytus, though now they are to do this along with the subdeacons.[58] The bishop at this point is referred to as the "high priest."

It would also appear that the deacons at Rome may have had the duty of teaching. The *Apostolic Tradition* directs,

> Let the deacons and the presbyters assemble daily at the place which the bishop may appoint; let the deacons (in particular) never fail to assemble unless prevented by sickness. When all have met they shall instruct those who are in the church, and then after prayer, each shall go to his appointed duties.[59]

These assemblies for instruction are apparently those discussed by Hippolytus in succeeding sections.[60] They seem to have been held on weekdays and were frequent, though probably not every day. Instruction was intended for the people of the Church generally, who "will hear God speaking through the instructor."[61] The only mention of a teacher in this later section is in the sense of one specially gifted,[62] which could mean one endowed with a special charisma who might or might not have been a clergyman. However, it would seem likely that the ordinary instruction at these meetings was given by the deacons, since they are not only mentioned here before the presbyters but are to be present without fail.

If the bishop is not present at an *agape* or special Christian fellowship meal, Hippolytus tells us that the faithful must take the "blessed bread," which is not the Eucharist, and the catechumens the "exorcised bread" only from the hand of a presbyter or deacon. The text makes it apparent that deacons can bless this non-eucharistic bread:

> And even if the bishop should be absent when the faithful meet at a supper, if a presbyter or a deacon is present they shall eat in a similar orderly fashion. . . . But if (only) laymen meet, let them not act presumptuously, for a layman cannot bless the blessed bread.[63]

The Apocalypse (Vision) of Paul

The Apocalypse (or Vision) of Paul, a document which probably originated in Egypt c. 245 and had much influence on the middle ages,[64] pictures presbyters, bishops, and deacons as among the ranks of the damned in that order. The author writes relative to his vision of a deacon:

> I saw another man in the fiery river up to his knees. Moreover his hands were stretched out and bloody, and worms proceeded from his mouth and nostrils and he was groaning and weeping, and crying. He said: Have pity on me! for I am hurt above the rest who are in this punishment. And I asked, Sir, who is this? And he said to me: This man whom thou seest, was a deacon who devoured the oblations and committed fornications and did not right in the sight of God, for this cause he unceasingly pays this penalty.[65]

It is interesting that the order here at this date lists the presbyter first and then the bishop and the deacon, perhaps reflecting the importance of the presbyteral council with the monepiscopate in this area at this date. It is further to be noted that it is the deacon who is said to suffer more than any other. This is apparently due to his having "devoured the oblations," since the presbyter is also guilty of fornication. The close association of the deacons with the oblations of the people is here affirmed, and the implication is that the deacons took for themselves offerings intended for the poor, especially widows and orphans.

The Latter Half of the Third Century (and Beyond)

The poor and needy had always been a major concern of the Church and were the special responsibility of the deacons. Though this ministry of service, by the middle of the third century, was probably not stressed so much as it had been previously,[66] it was and remained one of the Church's great concerns. At Rome in the time of Bishop Fabian, who died in the Decian persecution of 250, the deacons had been so burdened with this work that the bishop divided the city into seven regions corresponding to the number of deacons, which had been fixed at Rome and in some other places at seven due to the influence of Acts 6. A deacon was put over each and the office of subdeacon created to assist the deacons and then to succeed them.[67] The churches of the Roman deaconries became at a much later time the titles of the cardinal deacons.[68]

The legend of Lawrence, deacon of the Church at Rome martyred in 258, serves to illustrate the importance of the care of the poor in the work of the diaconate. The legend relates that, when arrested and ordered to hand over the treasures of the Church, Lawrence brought the poor of the Christian community.[69]

DEACONS MADE BISHOPS

At Rome, as Lietzmann affirms, "the college of deacons stood next to the bishop, and constituted his executive, and the papal throne was usually filled from one of its members."[70] Often in fact throughout the Church of the second and third centuries the senior deacon was elected to succeed the bishop, whose executive assistant he had been.[71] And the practice continues long after. Joseph Bingham observes in this connection that it was not necessary to be ordained presbyter to be made bishop and adds, "Deacons were as commonly made bishops as any other."[72] The selection of deacons rather than presbyters oftentimes to fill vacancies in the bishop's office was logical, since many of the bishop's duties were administrative, as were the deacon's, following the emergence of the monepiscopate and later the monarchial episcopate.

Various examples of deacons being made bishops may be cited.[73] Eusebius as a deacon represented Dionysius, Bishop of Alexandria, at the Council of Antioch called in 264 to deal with Paul of Samosota.[74] The Laodiceans came to know him there and elected him their bishop.[75] Caecilian was archdeacon when ordained Bishop of Carthage in 311 at the beginning of the Donatist schism.[76] Athanasius was the principal deacon of Alexandria when he succeeded Alexander as its bishop in 328.[77] Felix, a deacon of the Roman Church, was appointed to succeed Liberius, Bishop of Rome, when the latter was sentenced to exile by the Emperor Constantius, c. 355, for resisting Arianism,[78] though Liberius afterwards accepted the Arian formula and was allowed to reoccupy his see.[79] John Chrysostom, who became Bishop of Constantinople in 398,[80] made one of his own deacons, Hercalides, Bishop of Ephesus.[81]

Beyond the fourth century we continue to find examples of deacons being elected bishop. In the fifth century, c. 446, Leo the Great, Bishop of Rome, wrote that metropolitans are to be chosen from "the presbyters of that same church or from the deacons. . . ."[82] The most famous of these deacons was Gregory the Great, who as a deacon had been sent by Pelagius II of Rome as his *apocrisiarius* to the Imperial Court in Constantinople and after returning to his monastery in Rome was elected bishop of that city while still a deacon in 590 to succeed Pelagius.[83] Andronicus, a deacon of the Church of Angelium when chosen, succeeded Anastacius as Jacobite Patriarch of Alexandria in 614.[84] As late as the twelfth century we find that upon the death of Chail IV, Jacobite Patriarch of Alexandria, in 1102, one of the two candidates for his successor was John, a deacon, though his rival Macarius was elected by the synod.[85]

The election of deacons to the episcopate serves to illustrate the importance of the office and the esteem in which it was held. In the third century the deacons seem often to have overshadowed the presbyters in their importance and influence. Though this was soon to change, at least as a common occurrence, the office did retain much of its former respect and honor for many centuries before it declined into relative insignificance.

DIDASCALIA

In the Syrian *Didascalia,* dating probably from c. 220–250,[86] the number of deacons, which was fixed at seven in some places, is to be in proportion to the size of the local Church.[87] The author sees a close relationship between the bishop and the deacons. They are to "be of one mind,"[88] a point made even stronger later in the work when the bishop and the deacon are to be "of one counsel, and of one purpose, and one soul dwelling in two bodies."[89] As in the Ignatian letters the deacon is to "make all things known to the bishop, even as Christ to His Father."[90] But the deacon is now, a century after Ignatius, first to take care of all the work that he can, reflecting the increase in numbers in the churches. The office of the bishop has become more remote than before. The deacons are to be intermediaries, and the people are to have

> very free access to the deacons, and let them not be troubling the head at all times. For neither can any man approach the Lord God almighty except through Christ. All things therefore that they desire to do, let them make known to the bishop through the deacons.[91]

The *Didascalia* is also dependent upon Ignatius's writings in likening the bishop to God the Father, the deacons to Jesus Christ, and the presbyters to the apostles.[92] It is to be noted here that the deacons are mentioned just after the bishops, due undoubtedly both to their close association with the bishop and to their importance in the Church.

The *Didascalia*, unlike Ignatius, adds two other classes of offices. Between the deacons and the presbyters in the section just referred to, the document directs that "the deaconess shall be honoured by you in the place of the Holy Spirit," the expression originating as a result of "spirit" being feminine in Semitic languages such as Hebrew, Aramaic, and Syriac.[93] Then, following the presbyters, the Church order states that "the orphans and widows shall be reckoned by you in the likeness of the altar." Such symbolism is repeated elsewhere in the document, especially in connection with the widows. Their association with "the altar" would seem to derive from the fact that they offer prayers for the Church and receive gifts from the Church for their support.[94] They are not, of course, to be considered with the major orders, but both classes do represent a development in the century since Ignatius.

These deaconesses have many but not all of the functions of the male deacons. The *Didascalia* says that they are required for the ministry to women. They are needed to go to visit some women in places where sending a deacon might cause scandal, especially among the heathen, to visit women who are sick and others who are in need, and to bathe those recovering from sickness.[95] The liturgical function of the deaconess is that of anointing women in baptism, since this anointing apparently covered the whole body but was restricted to the head when no woman was present. The deaconess is also to instruct the women following their baptism in how to keep the seal of baptism unbroken by purity and holiness of life. The invocation of the divine names, however, is to be pronounced by a man.[96] The emphasis is on letting "a woman rather be devoted to the ministry of women, and a male deacon to the ministry of men."[97]

The author of the *Didascalia*, in contrast to the *Apostolic Tradition*, states that the presbyters and deacons are appointed by the bishop. In reference to the deacons he writes, "O bishop . . . those that please thee out of all the people thou shalt choose and appoint as deacons: a man for the performance of the most things that are required, but a woman for the ministry of women."[98] The same practice seems to be followed in North Africa at this time, though the North African bishops ordinarily acted with the advice of the clergy and people. Cyprian says that deacons are appointed by the bishop.[99] But he also teaches that bishops, presbyters, and deacons are to be appointed in the presence of all the people according to the example of the apostles given in Acts 4.[100] In a letter to the clergy and people of Carthage from his retreat he also explains that he has ordained Aurelius a reader without consulting them because the young man was "already approved by the Lord." But his custom was otherwise, for he states, "In ordinations of the clergy, beloved brethren, we usually consult you beforehand, and weigh the character and deserts of individuals, with the general advice."[101] Influences of the monepiscopate would seem to have persevered longer in North Africa than in Syria.

Throughout this Syrian Church order the presbyters seem secondary "though senior" to the deacons, who are the bishop's "close and constant" companions.[102] The presbyters are to be counselors of the bishop and councilors of the Church.[103] The presbyters and the deacons together are to form a council with the bishop for rendering judgments in disputes between members of the Church.[104]

The *Didascalia* also sees a close connection between the priests and the levites of the Old Testament and the clergy of the Church.[105] The comparison is to be found in many writings of the Church fathers, but it is clearest here.[106] It makes possible the application of the rules regarding the first-fruits, tithes, and other offerings to the Church and so providing for the clergy's support as well as for the orphans, widows, and others in need.[107] Instructions are given for the distribution of income among the clergy, though provision for the presbyters seems to be optional, indicating that the office of deacon developed into a full-time occupation before that of the presbyters.[108] In North Africa Cyprian mentions the "monthly divisions" in connection with ordaining men presbyters.[109]

In the *Didascalia* we find the first recorded liturgical formula for the deacon.[110] After the dismissal of the catechumens and before the beginning of the prayers, when the bishop stands in the church to pray, the author directs,

> Wherefore, O bishops, that your oblations and your prayers may be acceptable, when you stand in the Church to pray let the deacon say with a loud voice: Is there any man that keepeth aught against his fellow?[111]

Here we see also the organic nature of the Church as well as the liturgical formula. Peace and love among all members of the Christian community are needed if the oblations and prayers of the Church at the Eucharist are to be acceptable to God.

In another reference to the liturgical function of the deacon, two deacons with specific duties at the Eucharist are mentioned:

> But of the deacons let one stand always by the oblations of the Eucharist; and let another stand without by the door and observe them that come in; and afterwards, when you offer, let them minister together in the Church.[112]

The oblations are the offerings of the people, which may well have been put on a table near the entrance as the people arrived. It is almost certainly correct to assume that later in the third century, if not in fact at this time, deacons did bring the oblations of bread and wine to the bishop at the altar following the service of the word and just prior to the beginning of the Eucharist itself. However, there is no evidence to indicate, as has been asserted, that the deacons at this date spread a linen cloth over the altar before placing the oblations upon it. Though such a covering may well have been used, there is nothing to indicate that it was placed there in the course of the Eucharist or by the deacons.[113]

The author continues to discuss the arrangement of the assembly and instructs the deacon "who is within" to keep order and insure that "decency and decorum" prevail. It is an additional duty of the deacon to inquire of those coming from another congregation whether that person belongs to the Church.[114] And the *Didascalia* tells us the bishop may delegate either deacons or presbyters, mentioned in that order, to baptize.[115]

The third century was a period in which the dignity and importance of the deacon increased at the expense of the presbyter.[116] Perhaps the climax is recorded in the *Didascalia*, where the deacon usually takes precedence over the presbyter. The churches of the pre-Constantinian era were relatively small.[117] In most places a single bishop presided over the Church and could administer its needs with the assistance of the deacons. However, the situation was soon to change with the rapid growth of the Church in the next century, following the adoption of the Constantinian policy of toleration, with the resultant delegation of more and more duties to the presbyters.[118]

CYPRIAN

Cyprian is the "most clear and comprehensive" of all the fathers "in his conception of the body of Christ as an organic whole, in which every member has an honourable function."[119] Ignatius taught "Do nothing without the bishop," but Cyprian emphasizes the equally primitive concept, "Let bishops do nothing without the presbytery and people."[120] Cyprian, in writing to the presbyters and deacons from his retirement during the Decian persecution in 250, clearly expressed his concept of the interdependence of all orders within the Church. He declared it his principle that ". . . from the first commencement of my episcopacy, I made up my mind to do nothing on my own private opinion, without your advice and without the consent of the people."[121]

One cannot help but note the freedom and flexibility shown by the early Church. Much of this seems to have stemmed from the profound understanding of its organic nature. Cyprian could say that under extreme circumstances a deacon could convey sacramental absolution because it was the Church that possessed the ministry and the sacraments and administered the means of God's grace. He mentions this unusual function of the deacons when he directs that they may hear confessions of the lapsed who have certificates from the martyrs and are in imminent danger of death when a presbyter cannot be found. Then, "the imposition of hands upon them for repentance" will bring them forgiveness.[122] Some modern Roman Catholic theologians have maintained that this was sacramental confession.[123] There was order but not the sterile narrowness that has permeated so much of the Church's thinking in later centuries.

APOSTOLIC CONSTITUTIONS

Though the deacons would acquire the right to read the Gospel lesson in the Eucharist, it would not appear that they possessed this privilege in the third century as R. P. Symonds thinks probable.[124] Cyprian, in writing to the Church at Carthage during his temporary retirement from the city, regarding the ordination of Celerinus as a reader, speaks of this function as belonging to the readers.[125] It is in the *Apostolic Constitutions*, c. 380,[126] that a deacon or a presbyter *in that order* is directed to read the Gospel.[127] Jerome (d. c. 420) refers to deacons reading the Gospel, the context implying that it was a customary function at that time.[128] Sozomen says that at Alexandria the Gospel lesson was read by the archdeacon,

> whereas in many places it is read by the deacons, and in many churches only by the priests; while on noted days it is read by the bishops, as for instance at Constantinople, on the first day of the festival of the resurrection.[129]

Apparently, it was in the fourth century that the deacon acquired the prerogative of reading the Gospel at the Eucharist, though it was not exclusive. However, there seems to be no evidence that deacons were allowed to preach at this time. The sermon was given by the presiding officer, usually a bishop, seated in his chair.[130]

One of the liturgical functions sometimes ascribed to deacons of the third century is that of bidding the intercessory prayers of the faithful at the Eucharist.[131] While it is possible that the deacons began this practice in the third century, it is not mentioned in the Egyptian sacramentary of Serapion, which dates from c. 350.[132] Bishop Wordsworth says that in this sacramentary all prayers are said by the bishop, except one for the bishop and the Church, which may have been said by another bishop or a presbyter. He specifically remarks that there is nothing for the deacons to say.[133] The earliest reference to the deacons bidding the prayers of the people seems to be in the Syrian *Apostolic Constitutions*, c. 380.

There the deacons do have a most prominent part. In addition to reading the Gospel, as we noted above, they announce various stages of the service, such as dismissing the hearers: "Let none of the hearers, let none of the unbelievers stay."[134] They bid the various intercessory prayers of the Church.[135] They announce the kiss of peace, keep order, and with the subdeacons guard the doors.[136] They bring the oblations to the altar and two of them stand beside the altar with fans to insure that insects do not get into the chalices.[137] And at the conclusion a deacon says, "Depart in peace."[138] Dix rightly states that only the bishop spoke directly to God on behalf of the Church, while the deacon spoke *to* the Church.[139]

We have already seen that the *Didascalia* in the first half of the third century says that the deacons in Syria then called out, "Is there any man that keepeth aught against his fellow?" just after the catechumens had been dismissed and before the bishop began the prayers of the faithful. What we see a century and a half later in the *Apostolic Constitutions* regarding the deacon announcing phases of the service and bidding the prayers of the people would appear to be a logical development and is fully in accord with the pre-Nicene concept of the organic nature of the Church. Therefore, we may well assume that these functions of the deacon did grow, perhaps in the Syrian Church, spreading elsewhere between the time of the *Didascalia* and the *Apostolic Constitutions*.

Theodore Klauser observes that it is noteworthy that Hippolytus does not mention the deacon's call summoning the attention of the people with the words, "Listen, attend" or with his announcement, "The holy Things for the holy people!" However, he says, "It is possible, nevertheless, that both of these (or something similar) were in use at this time."[140]

Certainly, the position of the deacon shown in the *Didascalia* was of such prominence that it would be natural for him to assume added functions at the Eucharist in the third century in Syria. And in light of these factors we are probably justified in assigning to him the bidding of the prayers of the Church in this region by the end of the century. However, conditions following the Constantinian policy of toleration, particularly the marked increase in numbers in the Church and the acquisition of more permanent and suitable buildings for the Eucharist, were more conducive to the rather elaborate liturgical development in the deacon's office found in the *Apostolic Constitutions* and care should be exercised in ascribing them to the third century.

BAPTISM BY DEACONS

At the beginning of the third century we find evidence that the deacon was on a par with the presbyter in the administration of baptism. Tertullian's treatise *On Baptism* is extremely important not only as the earliest work on this subject but as the only pre-Nicene treatise on any of the sacraments.[141] He writes,

> The supreme right of giving (baptism) belongs to the high priest, which is the bishop: after him, to the presbyters and deacons, yet not without commission from the bishop, on account of the Church's dignity: for when this is safe, peace is safe. . . .[142]

Tertullian, writing c. 198–200,[143] in his early, orthodox period, adds that in emergencies even laymen baptize, but emphasizes that presbyters and deacons may ordinarily do so with consent of the bishop. We have already noted that the *Didascalia* not only affirms that the bishop may delegate to either deacons or presbyters the right to baptize but mentions them in that order.[144] Canon 77 of the Council of Elvira, c. 306, provides,

> If a deacon, that takes care of a people without either bishop or presbyter, baptizes any, the bishop shall consummate them by his benediction.[145]

Bingham sees this to mean that the canon "plainly supposes that deacons had the ordinary right of baptizing in such churches over which they presided"[146] and is certainly correct.

Jerome verifies this function of the deacon when he wrote *Against Luciferians*, c. 379:[147]

> I do not deny that it is the practice of the Churches in the case of those who living far from the greater towns have been baptized by presbyters and deacons, for the bishop to visit them, and by the laying on of hands to invoke the Holy Ghost upon them. . . . It is that without ordination and the bishop's license neither presbyter nor deacon has the power to baptize. . . .[148]

He also adds that of necessity laymen may and often do baptize. Cyril of Jerusalem, d. 386, strongly implies that deacons baptize sometimes at least in the smaller towns regularly as a matter of their office.[149]

It is to be remembered that, in the pre-Nicene Church when the organic principle prevailed and the functions of the various offices were not so sharply defined, the deacon was not an "inferior" order, and the Church was in the process of delegating liturgical functions to meet the needs of growing numbers. In this period even the Eucharist was at least at times presided over by a deacon. We recall Ignatius's instruction, "You should regard the Eucharist as valid which is celebrated either by the bishop or by *someone* he authorizes."[150] In the late third century, probably during the Diocletian persecution, some deacons offered (presided over) the Eucharist, a practice forbidden by the Council of Arles, 314,[151] but one which the Council did not declare invalid. The fact that deacons and congregations could easily accept the deacon offering the Eucharist, probably in the absence of both the bishop and presbyters, a practice which Landon says "in many places had been allowed,"[152] shows the importance of the deacon and his prominence in the practice of the Church's liturgies.[153] We may rightly include baptism as a function of the deacon by virtue of his office though with authorization by the bishop at this time.

DEACONS PUT OVER CHURCHES

Many of the same factors which led to the deacon being authorized to baptize along with the presbyter also apparently gave rise to his being given the charge of small congregations at least on occasion. Canon 77 of the Council of Elvira, c. 306, which we have noted, is unambiguous in this regard when it refers to a deacon who "takes care" of a congregation without either a bishop or presbyter (*Si quis diaconus regens plebem sine episcopo vel presbytero . . .*).[154] In his commentary on the Council of Elvira and fourth century Christianity, Alfred Dale states that new churches were not directed by bishops of their own but were under the charge of a presbyter or deacon.[155] Hefele probably rightly applies this to the expansion of the Church from larger towns into the countryside, a presbyter or deacon being sent from the larger place to the rural assembly, which remained under the bishop of the town.[156]

Bingham says that "country-presbyters and deacons" were put over churches, citing Canon 77 of Elvira, and with Hefele sees this in reference to country congregations. However, Bingham in the same chapter goes on to speak several times about "country-presbyters" being "fixed upon" country churches without including deacons,[157] indicating that though the practice existed presbyters were more frequently put in charge of rural congregations.

The *Testament* of the forty martyrs of Sebaste, who died c. 320, may be interpreted as indicating by implication that deacons in Armenia led rural congregations:

> We also salute the faithful in the district of Sarein, the priest with his people, the deacons with their people; Maximus with his people, Haesychius with his people, Cyriacus with his people.[158]

The writings of Jerome, *Against Luciferians*, and Cyril of Jerusalem, *Catechetical Lectures*, which have just been cited in connection with baptism, also lend some weight in the late fourth century to deacons having oversight of rural churches. The fact that they apparently baptize would lead to this conclusion. Also in connection with baptism the Council of Toledo, 400, directs that "before Easter deacons or sub-deacons shall fetch the chrism from (the bishop)," who alone may consecrate it.[159] Canon 3 of the First Council of Vaison, 442, is quite similar.[160] Gregory of Tours writes that Cautinus, who was later made bishop of Auvergne, was, "in his diaconate, in charge of the church of that village."[161] Schamoni sees in these references to Toledo, Vaison, and Gregory of Tours evidence that deacons as a normal practice were placed over parishes.[162] However, with the probable exception of Gregory's reference, it is certainly possible that there were both priests and deacons in these country churches, who together constituted the leadership.

A careful analysis of the evidence leads to the conclusion that deacons did exercise leadership in at least some rural congregations in the third and fourth centuries. However, this assertion must be a guarded one. As we have seen, the Church gradually delegated most of the liturgical functions of the bishop to the presbyter and not, at least generally speaking, to the deacon. Deacons did not preach nor "offer" (preside at) the Eucharist by virtue of their office, though exceptions have been noted particularly to the latter function. Therefore, they could not ordinarily have functioned as heads of congregations in the same way that bishops and later presbyters did. It is too much to claim, as Schamoni does, that "in the transitional period between antiquity and the early Middle Ages, when the Church expanded into the country areas, the deacon did great work as precursor and pioneer of the priest in the filial churches; by virtue of his ordination, he acted as leader of the community."[163]

The deacon's office did give him the prestige but not the requisite liturgical function to have the place as head of the Eucharistic assembly. And in light of the existence of the *chorepiscopi* there would seem to be no compelling reason that the Church at that time would have been hesitant to have ordained presbyters to preside at the Eucharist even in small rural churches. It would seem probable that in most places there were both presbyters and deacons in the country churches. Since deacons also had the right to baptize with the same authorization needed by the presbyter, they may well have baptized with a presbyter present, a possibility which would avoid the inference drawn from references that deacons headed congregations because they baptized, as cited in the passages from Jerome, *Against Luciferians*, and Cyril of Jerusalem, *Catechetical Lectures*.

Though contrary to the thinking of later centuries, the organic conception of the early Church along with the importance of the deacon and the permanency of his office would have made it possible for small places under a nearby bishop to have been put under the charge of a deacon even though there was also a presbyter there, but one who might have been much younger and less experienced. However, whatever the circumstances were when these small churches were put under the care of deacons, the practice would not appear to have been general.

The Blessing of the Paschal Candle

As we have seen, in Hippolytus deacons did have the authority to bless the non-Eucharistic "blessed bread" at an *agape*, at least in the absence of the bishop. Another blessing, one which belonged to the deacon then and is still the deacon's prerogative in the Roman and Anglican Churches today, is that of the paschal candle at the Easter Vigil. The lighting and blessing of the paschal candle, symbolizing the return of light to the spiritual world in the risen Christ, remains one of the Church's most impressive sacramentals. Its origin is, however, shrouded in antiquity.[164]

We do know from Eusebius that the deacons were closely associated with the lights used during the night of the Easter Vigil at Jerusalem, at least in the third century. In relating the report of a miracle by Narcissus, Bishop of Jerusalem c. 200, in which water was reputed to have been changed into oil through his prayer, Eusebius writes, "They say that the oil once failed while the deacons were watching through the night at the great paschal vigil."[165] Though the miracle is not to be thought genuine, the report does indicate the existence of the vigil as a long-established custom by the time of Eusebius in Jerusalem.

Elsewhere Eusebius also tells us that the Emperor Constantine "changed the holy night vigil into a brightness like that of day, by causing waxen tapers of great length to be lighted throughout the city: besides which, torches everywhere diffused their light, so as to impart to this mystic vigil a brilliant splendor beyond that of day."[166] The Great Vigil of Easter seems well established in the fourth century in the East.

The most important of the ceremonies relating to the lights of the Easter Vigil as they have come down to us is the lighting and blessing of the paschal candle by the deacon. Dix sees its origin to be in the ceremony at the beginning of the vigil service on Holy Saturday, which he believes was in use at Jerusalem in the fourth century, in which the deacon blessed the lamp put beside the lectern to provide light for the lector.[167] On the other hand, W. J. O'Shea argues that the paschal candle is not derived from the custom of symbolizing the resurrection of Christ with lights at the Easter Vigil, though this symbolism may subsequently have influenced it. Rather he thinks the probable origin is in the daily ceremony of the deacon lighting and blessing a lamp in the evening to provide needed illumination for the evening services, which in time became an elaborate ceremony accompanied by psalms, chants, and prayers called the *Lucernarium.*[168]

The truth probably encompasses both customs. The daily ceremony of lighting and blessing a lamp to provide light for the evening services would naturally take on greater significance at the Easter Vigil and be influenced by the use of the lighted lamps and candles symbolizing the risen Christ. It would seem almost inevitable that the lights of the Easter Vigil would have suggested the special paschal candle symbolizing the risen Lord at the daily ceremony of lighting and blessing a lamp when it was done at the Easter Vigil and is probably implied in Dix's discussion.

The lack of citations referring to the earliest mention of this rite is in part due to the fact that a letter to a deacon named Praesidius mentioning it, and attributed to Jerome, was thought to have been spurious from the sixteenth to the present century because of additions to it. However, critical studies increasingly attest to its authenticity, and we may consider it to be genuine.[169] Another citation from Augustine is doubtful, since the crucial phrase, which Augustine uses to introduce several lines of praise, is literally "verses in praise of a (the) candle,"[170] though Bettenson translates the sentence in the text, "This is how I put the same thought in some verses in praise of the paschal candle."[171] But Bettenson sees the reference as being to perhaps "a votive candle offered as a prayer or a thanksgiving," not a reference to the paschal candle blessed by a deacon on Holy Saturday.[172] Marcus Dods gives the first reading as, "It is this which some one has briefly said in these verses in praise of the Creator," with the alternate, "Which I briefly said in these verses in praise of the taper."[173] The three verses of praise which follow do end with a direct address to the Creator.

Jerome's letter to Praesidius, written no later than 384,[174] is the first clear reference to the blessing of the paschal candle.[175] The deacon, Praesidius, who served the Church at Piacenza in northern Italy, had asked Jerome to write the hymn of blessing, called the Exultet, he was to sing over the paschal candle at the Easter Vigil. Though Jerome declines to do so primarily because, he said, the Scriptures offer a dearth of material about wax and candles, he does positively attest to the existence of the ceremony at that time.

It is in Ennodius, Bishop of Pavia, 514 to 521,[176] that we find the oldest forms for this blessing.[177] His extant works include two blessings for the paschal candle.[178] Ennodius became deacon at Pavia c. 493 but moved to Milan c. 496.[179] Duschesne believes the two blessings are formularies drawn up for Ennodius's own use as a deacon of Pavia before he became its bishop.[180] It is of passing interest to note that Ennodius was the first to restrict the title of *papa* almost entirely to the Bishop of Rome.[181]

Did Deacons Preach?

It has sometimes been thought that preaching was a function of the diaconate in the early Church.[182] An examination of the evidence, however, would seem to make this conclusion highly questionable.

Since the time of Irenaeus, as we have noted, the Seven of Acts 6 were considered a model for the diaconate. Stephen and Philip, the only two mentioned again in the New Testament, have been thought of as evangelists, Philip being so described in Acts 21.[183] Though it is possible to argue with Brockman that the thing Stephen and Philip are doing in Acts "represents an essentially catechetical instruction" and that they are simply doing what any committed Christian would,[184] the picture there seems to be more than that. Their role appears to be one of leadership, and preaching is strongly implied.

Canon 2 of the Council of Ancyra, c. 314 A.D., has been interpreted to indicate that the deacon did preach at that time. The canon refers to lapsed deacons who had returned to the Church. It provides that they shall keep their office but specifies in this connection that they "shall abstain from making proclamations (*kerussein*)."[185] Hefele here translates this term as "preach" but adds in his commentary that other proclaiming functions of the deacon are also intended under the prohibition of this canon.[186] However, Bingham argues convincingly that "preaching" here is not correct but rather the term is to be understood to refer to the deacon as "the sacred crier of the congregation," citing others maintaining this view.[187] Henry Percival in his commentary on the canon supports Bingham and sees this as a reference to the reading of the Gospel and the numerous proclamations of the deacons at the Eucharist.[188]

Echlin quotes[189] the *Didache*:

> Elect therefore for yourselves bishops and deacons worthy of the Lord, humble men and not covetous, and faithful and well tested; for they also serve you in the ministry of the prophets and teachers. Do not, therefore, despise them, for they are the honored men among you along with the prophets and teachers.[190]

He rightly sees, as we have noted, that the bishops and deacons took over the function of the prophets and teachers. However, he argues that deacons as well as bishops assumed the function of both the prophets and teachers, and therefore of preaching:

> Deacons did by reason of their office what prophets and teachers did by reason of *their* charism which was itself becoming institutionalized. The task of prophets and teachers, therefore of *episcopoi* and deacons, was to preach. . . .[191]

Other evidence from the period would seem to indicate that the bishop was the one who assumed from the prophets the function of presiding at the Eucharistic assembly and preaching, and the deacons assumed other functions in the leadership of the local Church.[192] Brockman interprets the *Didache* to mean that the deacon's ministry of the word at this time was of a catechetical nature.[193] In light of the evidence it is more logical to interpret this passage to mean simply that the leadership of the Church was transferred in this period from the prophets and teachers to the bishops and deacons without any intention of meaning that either the bishop or the deacons took over *all* the functions of the prophets and teachers.

The letter of Ignatius of Antioch *To the Philadelphians* is also seen by Echlin to contain evidence that deacons preached at this early date. He translates the pertinent passage, "Philo, the deacon from Cilicia who has been so well spoken of, is at present giving me his help in preaching God's word."[194] However, Gerald Walsh in *The Fathers of the Church* renders the phrase in question, ". . . who is now ministering to me in the word of God . . .",[195] and the translator of this letter in the *Ante-Nicene Fathers* has ". . . who still ministers to me in the word of God. . . ."[196] Richardson translates the phrase ". . . he is helping me in God's cause. . . ."[197] Again, the weight of evidence seems to favor an understanding other than preaching.

In the fifth century there is one clear reference to a deacon preaching. The historian Philostorgius reports, c. 430, that Aetius, a deacon of Antioch, was allowed to preach publicly in the church by his bishop, the Arian Leontius.[198] Echlin cites this as evidence not only that the deacons "still preached" but also that the deacon Aetius "contributed to the demise of diaconal preaching" by preaching Arianism.[199] But it appears more probable that preaching by deacons is not to be found later because it was never a function of the order itself.

The great classic writer of the Syrian Church, Ephraem Syrus, d. 373, who remained a deacon throughout his life, is described by Altaner as "a brilliant exegete, controversialist, preacher, and poet."[200] His reputation as a preacher, however, may well be due to the excellence of his written compositions, which Jerome records were read in many churches immediately after the Scriptures, presumably as the sermon at the Eucharist.[201] The reading of such homilies by deacons is in accord with the legislation of the Second Council of Vaison (529). Canon 2 provides,

> Not only in the cities, but also in all rural churches the priests may preach. If the priest is hindered through sickness, a deacon should read a homily by a Father of the Church.[202]

However, even were it true that Ephraem preached, it would seem to be due more to his special charisma than to his office as a deacon.

In writing of the diaconate in the medieval Church, Brockman says that it is clear that deacons were "ordained to the ministry of the word" and that this ministry remains a major diaconal function in both the East and the West.[203] However, he sees it in a missionary context, envisioning the deacon in his ancient role as a kind of messenger of the bishop who sought out "those in need, prospective converts, and the poor" and brought word back to the bishop.[204] He does not mention liturgical preaching.

The assertion that deacons preached as a matter of office in the early Church would, then, seem to be highly unlikely in view of the lack of evidence. The function belonged ordinarily to the president of the Eucharistic assembly, and except when the deacon functioned in that capacity as an extraordinary act, there is very little reason to believe that he preached before the Church. It is probable that the deacon came to preach when licensed by his bishop in the medieval period when the diaconate had become largely an interim office on the way to the priesthood.[205]

A Permanent Vocation

There is one other major aspect of the diaconate which should be noted before we turn to the fourth century. In the Pre-Nicene Church the diaconate was conceived of as a permanent vocation. Deacons could become presbyters but usually did not.[206] The clerical offices were not yet regarded as grades through which one moved from the inferior to the superior. However, considerable development did take place after the emergence of the monepiscopate in the second century and its adoption throughout the Church.[207] It was natural that the bishop came to be considered the highest official because he was president of the local Church, presiding over both the presbyteral council and the Eucharistic assembly. Next would come the presbyters. They were normally older, and at least in those churches which had originally been governed by a council of presbyters, one of their number had presided. Their position and honored place is shown by their forming a semicircle on either side of the bishop at the Eucharist. The deacons, normally being younger and actively serving the Church in their distinctive functions both pastorally and liturgically, naturally came to be thought of as time went on as ranking after the bishops and presbyters. However, it would be a mistake to overemphasize the importance of the presbyters in relation to the deacons in this period, as we shall shortly see.

Certainly by the middle of the third century a developed conception of gradation with respect to the clerical offices is clearly in evidence. Cyprian can write at that time that Pope Cornelius

> was not one who on a sudden attained to the episcopate; but, promoted through all the ecclesiastical offices, and having often deserved well of the Lord in divine administrations, he ascended by all the grades of religious service to the lofty summit of the Priesthood.[208]

Cyprian, however, did not view the various offices of the Church as "steps" up a ladder in the sense that was to develop. This idea was not present except perhaps in embryonic form, as has been affirmed by Walter H. Frere:

> It is noticeable that the idea that "the Christian clergy consisted of a hierarchy of grades, through each of which it was *necessary* to pass in order to reach the higher offices," was not yet current.[209]

This idea was only to develop later, as we shall see when we turn to the fourth century. The various orders were still regarded as permanent vocations, baptism being the only sacramental prerequisite.

Whether or not presbyters ever later became deacons is an interesting subject and important only because the possibility of asking the question is indicative of the pre-Nicene conception of the Church's offices. There seems to be no recorded instance of this having happened, though that could be due to the sparsity of records in the very early period. However, if such ordinations did occur, they were rare. Presbyters were usually older and may have been allowed to function as deacons when necessity demanded from an early time, though it is perhaps more likely that someone from among the younger men of the local Church might have been pressed into service under such circumstances. As late as the *Apostolic Constitutions,* c. 380, it is stated that "it is not lawful for any one of the other clergy to do the work of a deacon."[210] However this may be, each order was viewed until the transition in the fourth century Church as a lifelong vocation.

In the eighth century the noted Alcuin provides an example of continuing lifelong diaconal vocations. Born c. 730 of a noble family near York in England, he was ordained deacon in 770.[211] A man of vast learning, Alcuin was persuaded by Charlemagne to join his court in 781, where he served as the Emperor's most distinguished advisor and rekindled the light of classical and biblical learning in the Frankish kingdom. He was made Abbot of Tours, to which he retired in 796. He died there on 19 May 804, still a deacon.[212]

In the eleventh century the Archdeacon of Rome was still in deacon's orders. Archdeacon Hildebrand would undoubtedly have remained a deacon had he not been elected to fill the papal throne in 1073.

Thomas of Celano, a contemporary of Francis of Assisi, who joined the Franciscan friars c. 1214, wrote the earliest biography of Francis, d. 1226, at the command of Pope Gregory IX in 1228.[213] In describing the Eucharist on Christmas Eve c. 1223 at Greccio, when Francis had a creche prepared and thus inaugurated the custom of putting nativity scenes in the churches at Christmas,[214] Celano says that Francis was a deacon. He writes, "The saint of God was clothed with the vestments of a deacon, for he was a deacon, and he sang the holy Gospel in a sonorous voice. . . . Then he preached to the people standing about."[215]

In the late fifteenth century Cardinal Piccolomini administered the Diocese of Siena as a deacon for forty years until his election to the papacy in 1503.[216] At the Council of Trent, 1545–1563, Cardinal Reginald Pole was one of its three presidents. He was in deacon's orders at that time and remained so until being made a bishop later.[217]

In the Church of England in the early seventeenth century Nicholas Ferrar demonstrates that there could still be a place for a lifelong vocation as a deacon. Coming from a family prominent in the affairs of the Virginia Company, he was ordained a deacon when that company was dissolved in order to establish a unique religious community in 1626 at Little Gidding.[218] There in a manor house he, his mother, his brother and sister with their spouses and nineteen children, and a number of servants formed a community for prayer, study, and service. Their discipline of prayer was rigorous. Their works included education of the children of the district and care of the poor and the sick.[219] Ferrar died in 1637, as a deacon, but the community continued until Little Gidding was sacked by the Puritans in 1646.[220] Inspired by this community, T. S. Eliot named the last of his *Four Quartets*, considered to be one of the great religious poems of the twentieth century, "Little Gidding."[221]

Brockman says that the diaconate as a permanent vocation remained at Rome in a curious form until nearly the turn of the twentieth century. There, certain members of the papal diplomatic corps were in deacons' orders until the dissolution of the Papal States in 1870, the last of them dying before the end of the century.[222]

The Subdiaconate and Minor Orders

Cyprian's reference to "all the grades of religious service" would include the minor orders which were in existence at the time.[223] The development of these orders was basically a true expression of the Church's ministry in that it showed and expressed the broadness and variety of that ministry much more than the three major orders alone do.

In the mid-second century Pope Cornelius wrote that there were then seven subdeacons, forty-two acolytes, and fifty-two exorcists, readers, and janitors or doorkeepers at Rome.[224] From Tertullian we know that the office of reader had come into existence a half century earlier.[225] Hippolytus mentions readers and subdeacons and specifies that hands shall not be laid upon them, since they are not ordained.[226] However, by c. 380 the *Apostolic Constitutions* direct that subdeacons and readers are to be ordained.[227] But as Bishop Wordsworth says in his translation of the collection of prayers of Serapion, Bishop of Thmuis in lower Egypt, dating probably from before 350, that the absence of ordination forms for the subdeacons, readers, and interpreters mentioned there indicates that only the bishops, presbyters, and deacons were ordained at that time in Egypt.[228] Cyprian himself mentions both subdeacons and acolytes in his letters.[229] Acolytes assisted at the Eucharist and appear to be found only in the West, where they became numerous.[230]

The existence of the subdiaconate is in itself evidence of the growing importance of the office of deacon in the late second and early third centuries. The office of subdeacon arose due to the need of releasing the deacon from some of his duties.[231] The subdeacon's primary work was to aid the deacons at the Eucharist and in their other functions.[232] Mention of the office in the Syrian *Didascalia*,[233] which probably dates from the first half of the third century, perhaps even its earlier decades,[234] is evidence that the subdiaconate had become widespread if not universal by the middle of the third century. In the fourth century the office is mentioned in the legislation of councils such as Elvira (c. 305), Canon 30;[235] Antioch (c. 341), Canon 10;[236] and Laodicea (343–381), Canons 20–22 and 25.[237]

NOTES

1. Edgar J. Goodspeed, *A History of Early Christian Literature*, rev. & enlarged Robert M. Grant (Chicago: University of Chicago Press, 1966), p. 103, for the date (hereafter cited *Early Christian Literature*).

2. Justin, *Apology* 65–67, "The First Apology of Justin, the Martyr," trans. Edward R. Hardy, in vol. 1: *Early Christian Fathers*, in Library of Christian Classics (Philadelphia: Westminster Press, 1953), 1:285–88.

3. Ibid., 65, 1:286.

4. Ibid., 67, 1:287.

5. Dom Gregory Dix, *The Shape of the Liturgy* (Westminster: Dacre Press, 1945), pp. 135–36.

6. John Bligh, "Deacons in the Latin West since the Fourth Century," in *Theology* 58 (London: 1955): 425. (Citation in Durandus, *Rationale*, 4, 54, 2.)

7. Justin, *Apology* 65, in *Early Christian Fathers*, 1:286.

8. A. Cleveland Coxe, Vol. 1, *The Apostolic Fathers with Justin Martyr and Irenaeus*, in *The Ante-Nicene Fathers: Translations of the Writings of the Fathers down to* A.D. *325*, ed. Alexander Roberts and James Donaldson, Amer. reprint ed. A. Cleveland Coxe (Grand Rapids, Mi.: William B. Eerdmans Publishing Co., 1956), 1:185 fn.

9. Edward R. Hardy, "Introduction," to "The First Apology of Justin, the Martyr," in *Early Christian Fathers*, 1:225–31.

10. Justin, *Apology* 67, *Early Christian Fathers*, 1:287. For the same reason he refers to "those whom *we call* deacons."

11. Massey H. Shepherd, "Introduction," to "The Letter of Polycarp," in *Early Christian Fathers*, 1:121–23.

12. Irenaeus, *Against Heresies* 3.3.4 and 3.4.3, in *Early Christian Fathers*, 1:374, 1:375.

13. Goodspeed, *Early Christian Literature*, p. 120, for date.

14. Irenaeus, *Against Heresies* 3.12.10, in *Ante–Nicene Fathers*, 1:434. Irenaeus makes an almost identical reference to Stephen in Book 4.15.1, in *Ante-Nicene Fathers*, 1:480. Echlin (Edward Echlin, *The Deacon in the Church Past and Future* [Staten Island, N.Y.: Alba House, 1971], p. 30) quotes the similar passage in Irenaeus (4.15.1) as, "Luke also has recorded that Stephen, who was first elected into the assembly by the apostles . . . ," but the text of his reference, an earlier edition of the *Ante-Nicene Fathers* (vol. 5: *The Writings of Irenaeus*, trans. Alexander Roberts and W. H. Rambout [Edinburgh: T & T Clark, 1868], 5:419), reads ". . . Stephen, who was first elected into the *diaconate* by the apostles . . ." (italics added).

15. Irenaeus, *Against Heresies* 1.26.3, in *Ante-Nicene Fathers* 1:352.

16. Richard B. Rackham, *The Acts of the Apostles* (London: Methuen [13th ed.], 1947), p. 84.

17. *Epistle of Clement to James* 12, in vol. 8: *Pseudo–Clementines, Homilies*, in *Ante-Nicene Fathers*, 8:220. This letter, ostensibly written by Clement of Rome to James of Jerusalem, along with another by Peter to James, was designed to give the *Homilies* credibility. The *Pseudo–Clementines* probably date from between 313–325 in their present form but were based on an earlier fictional work about Clement probably written c. 260, which in turn probably drew from two earlier sources: these two earlier documents are dated c. 160–220 (Goodspeed,

Early Christian Literature, pp. 83, 74, 78; and Berthold Altaner, *Patrology,* trans. Hilda C. Graef (New York: Herder and Herder, 1960), p. 105.

18. *Pseudo-Clementines, Homilies* 3.67, in *Ante-Nicene Fathers,* 8:250.

19. Goodspeed, *Early Christian Literature,* pp. 159, 163, for date.

20. Tertullian, *On Baptism* 17, in vol. 3: *Latin Christianity: Its Founder, Tertullian,* in *Ante-Nicene Fathers* (1956), 3:677.

21. Ernest Evans translates the expression as "high priest" (see *Tertullian's Homily on Baptism: The Text edited with an Introduction, Translation and Commentary* [London: S.P.C.K., 1964], p. 35). It represents *archiereus* in the Vulgate (J. M. Lupton, *Q. Septimi Florentis Tertulliani—De Baptisma* [Cambridge: University Press, 1908], p. 46). *Archiereus* is used to mean "high priest" in Mark 2:26; 14:47, and of Christ in Heb. 2:17; 3:1. In the plural it is used as "chief priests" in Matt. 2:4; Mark 8:31 (G. Abbott-Smith, *A Manual Greek Lexicon of the New Testament* [Edinburgh: T. & T. Clark, 1937], p. 62).

22. Lupton, p. 46 fn.

23. John Wordsworth, *The Ministry of Grace: Studies in Early Church History with Reference to Present Problems* (London: Longmans, Green & Co., 1901), p. 124.

24. Goodspeed, *Early Christian Literature,* p. 178.

25. Lupton, p. 46 fn. Cf. Wordsworth, p. 133. Cf. also Jean-Paul Audet, *Structures in Christian Priesthood: A study of home, marriage and celibacy in the pastoral service of the church,* trans. Rosemary Sheed (New York: Macmillan and Co., 1967), p. 83. He states that Cyprian's view, exemplified in his assertion that the clergy "ought to serve only the altar and sacrifices, and to have leisure for prayers and supplication," made in reference to a Christian's having appointed a presbyter guardian in his will (Epistle LXV.1), is "still a novelty upon the third-century scene, [and] undoubtedly marks a major change in the conception of the church's pastoral care."

26. Goodspeed, *Early Christian Literature,* p. 163, for date.

27. Tertullian, *Exhortation to Chastity* 7 in vol. 4: *Tertullian, Part Fourth: Minucins Felix; Commodian; Origen, Parts First and Second,* in *Ante-Nicene Fathers,* 4:54.

28. Digamy is "a second legal marriage; marriage to a second husband or wife after the death or divorce of the first" (*Webster's New World Dictionary of the American Language,* College Edition [1966]), s.v. "Digamy."

29. Goodspeed, *Early Christian Literature,* pp. 143, 149–50, for date.

30. Hippolytus, *Refutation of All Heresies* 9.6, in *Ante-Nicene Fathers,* 5:128.

31. *Prayer Book Studies VIII: The Ordinal,* prepared by The Standing Liturgical Commission of the Protestant Episcopal Church in the United States of America (New York: The Church Pension Fund, 1957), p. 5.

32. Lukas Vischer, "The Problem of the Diaconate," in *The Ministry of Deacons,* ed. Department of Faith and Order (Geneva: World Council of Churches, 1965), p. 22.

33. R. C. D. Jasper and G. J. Cuming (*Prayers of the Eucharist: Early and Reformed,* trans. and ed. R. C. D. Jasper and G. J. Cuming [New York: Oxford University Press (2nd ed.) 1980], p. 21) put the tradition represented here some fifty years earlier at Rome close to the time of Justin Martyr.

34. Hippolytus, *Apostolic Tradition* 9.1 and 2, trans. and ed. Burton Scott Easton, *The Apostolic Tradition of Hippolytus: Translated into English with Intro-*

duction and Notes (Cambridge: The University Press, 1934), pp. 38, 39 (hereafter cited *Apostolic Tradition of Hippolytus*).

35. Ibid., 9.2–4, p. 38.

36. Burton Scott Easton, *The Pastoral Epistles* (New York: Charles Scribner's Sons, 1947), p. 183.

37. Hippolytus, *Apostolic Tradition* 9.10–12, in Easton, *Apostolic Tradition of Hippolytus*, pp. 38–39.

38. The prayer for the ordination of the bishop refers to the bishops both in terms of "priests" and "high-priesthood." (Hippolytus, *Apostolic Tradition* 3.3 and 6, in Easton, *Apostolic Tradition of Hippolytus*, p. 34.)

39. Ibid., 10.1–2, p. 39.

40. Marion J. Hatchett, *Rites of Ordination*, lectures at the School of Theology, Sewanee, Tn., Summer, 1975.

41. Hippolytus, *Apostolic Tradition* 23.1, in Easton, *Apostolic Tradition of Hippolytus*, p. 48. Cf. Ibid., 4.2, p. 35, where the deacons bring the offering to the bishop at the Eucharist for the ordination of a bishop.

42. Dix, *Shape of the Liturgy*, p. 104.

43. Hippolytus, *Apostolic Tradition* 4.2, in Easton, *Apostolic Tradition of Hippolytus*, p. 35.

44. Ibid., 24.1, p. 58. Easton regards statute 24 as a later addition, but Dix is probably correct in maintaining otherwise in the "Textual Notes" appended to his translation of the *Apostolic Tradition, The Treatise on the Apostolic Tradition of St. Hippolytus of Rome*, ed. Dom Gregory Dix (London: S.P.C.K., 1937), p. 82 (hereafter cited as *Hippolytus*).

45. Hippolytus, *Apostolic Tradition* 23.4–7, in Easton, *Apostolic Tradition of Hippolytus*, p. 49.

46. Ibid., 24.2, p. 58.

47. T. G. Jalland, "The Parity of Ministers," in *The Apostolic Ministry: Essays on the History and Doctrine of Episcopacy*, ed. Kenneth E. Kirk (London: Hodder & Stoughton, 1946), p. 348.

48. Ambrose, *Duties of the Clergy* 1.41.214, in vol. 10: *St. Ambrose: Select Works and Letters*, trans. H. de Romestin, in *Nicene and Post-Nicene Fathers of the Christian Church*, Second Series, ed. Philip Schaff and Henry Wace, 14 vol. (Grand Rapids, Mi.: William B. Eerdmans Publishing Co., 1955), 10:35.

49. Ibid. The translator believes that the use of "consecration" here may be explained as due to either the close association of the deacon with the celebrant-bishop or to the sanctification of the faithful in receiving the sacrament. Massey Shepherd concurs with Jalland that it simply means Lawrence administered the chalice (personal communication to the author).

50. Jalland, "Parity of Ministers," p. 348.

51. Cyprian, *Treatise* 3.25, in *Ante-Nicene Fathers*, 5:444.

52. Jalland, "Parity of Ministers," p. 348.

53. "Notes," in Easton, *Apostolic Tradition of Hippolytus*, p. 91.

54. Ibid.

55. Ibid., p. 90.

56. Ibid., p. 93.

57. Hippolytus, *Apostolic Tradition* 21–22, in Ibid., pp. 45–47.

58. Ibid., 30, p. 53.

59. Ibid., 33.1, 2, p. 53.

60. Ibid., 35, 36.1, p. 54.

61. Ibid., 35.2, p. 54.
62. Ibid., 35.3, p. 54.
63. Ibid., 26.11, 12, p. 51.
64. Johannes Quasten, vol. 1: *Beginnings of Patristic Literature*, in *Patrology* (Westminster, Md.: Newman Press, 1950), 1:146–48.
65. *Apocalypse of Paul* 36, in vol. 9: *Documents, Remains of the First Ages: Biographical Synopsis, Index*, in *The Ante–Nicene Fathers* (1951), 9:160.
66. Bo Reicke, "Deacons in the New Testament and in the Early Church," in *The Ministry of Deacons*, ed. Department of Faith and Order (Geneva: World Council of Churches, 1965), p. 12.
67. Hans Lietzmann, *A History of the Early Church*, vol. 1: *The Beginnings of the Christian Church;* vol. 2: *The Founding of the Church Universal* (bound together), trans. Bertram Lee Woolf (New York: The World Publishing Co., Meridian Books, 1961), 2:249.
68. Leo Gillet, "Deacons in the Orthodox East," in *Theology* 58 (London: 1955): 416 fn.
69. R. P. Symonds, "Deacons in the Early Church," *Theology* 58:408.
70. Lietzmann, 2:249.
71. Dom Gregory Dix, "The Ministry in the Early Church c. A.D. 90–410," in *The Apostolic Ministry: Essays on the History and the Doctrine of Episcopacy*, ed. Kenneth E. Kirk (London: Hodden & Stoughton, 1946), p. 283.
72. Joseph Bingham, vol. 1: *The Antiquities of the Christian Church, Books I–III*, in *The Works of Joseph Bingham*, ed. R. Bingham (London: Oxford University Press [new ed.], 1855), 2.10.5, 1:109. The concept of the clerical offices as an hierarchial structure through which one must move to attain the higher rank develops later and is discussed in chap. 6.
73. It has sometimes been said that Heron, the successor of Ignatius of Antioch, was a deacon when elected bishop: e.g., John Mason Neale, vol. 2: *The Patriarchate of Alexandria*, in *A History of the Holy Eastern Church* (London: Joseph Masters, 1847), 2:21 (hereafter cited *Alexandria*), cites Eusebius (*H. E.* 3.36), but Eusebius does not say that Heron was a deacon here. *The Epistle of Ignatius to Hero* does say so, but it is spurious, dating from the fourth century (*Ante-Nicene Fathers*, 1:113–15).
74. John Mason Neale, vol. 3: *The Patriarchate of Antioch*, in *A History of the Holy Eastern Church* (London: Rivingtons, 1873), 3:54–55 (hereafter cited *Antioch*).
75. Eusebius, *Ecclesiastical History* 7.11.26, 32.5, in vol. 1: *Eusebius: Church History, Life of Constantine the Great, and Oration in Praise of Constantine*, trans. and ed. Arthur Cushman McGiffert, in *Nicene and Post-Nicene Fathers*, Second Series (1952), 1:302, 318, and 318 fn.
76. Optatus 1.16, *The Work of St. Optatus Bishop of Milevis Against the Donatists*, trans. O. R. Vassal-Phillips (London: Longmans, Green, & Co., 1917), p. 31.
77. Theodoret, *The Ecclesiastical History of Theodoret* 1.25, in vol. 3: *Theodoret, Jerome and Grennadius, Rufinius Historical Writings etc.* in *Nicene and Post–Nicene Fathers*, Second Series (1953), 3:60–61.
78. Ibid., 3:79. Cf. Socrates Scholasticus, *The Ecclesiastical History* 2.37, in vol. 2: *Socrates, Sozomenus: Church Histories*, in *Nicene and Post–Nicene Fathers*, Second Series (1952), 2:65.
79. In *Oxford Dictionary of the Christian Church*, ed. F. L. Cross and E. A.

Livingston (London: Oxford University Press [2nd ed.], 1974), p. 821 (s.v. "Liberius").

80. Altaner, p. 374, for date.

81. Socrates, *The Ecclesiastical History* 6:11, in *Nicene and Post-Nicene Fathers,* Second Series, 2:146.

82. Leo the Great, *Letter* 14.7, in vol. 12: *The Letters and Sermons of Leo the Great,* trans. Charles Lett Feltoe: *The Book of Pastoral Rule and Selected Epistles of Gregory the Great,* trans. James Barmby, in *Nicene and Post-Nicene Fathers,* Second Series (1956), 12:18.

83. Altaner, p. 557.

84. Neale, *Alexandria,* 2:55.

85. Ibid., 2:237.

86. Altaner, p. 56.

87. *Didascalia Apostolorum: The Syriac Version* 3.13, trans. R. Hugh Connolly (Oxford: Clarendon Press, 1929), p. 148.

88. Ibid., 2.44, p. 109.

89. Ibid., 3.13, p. 148.

90. Ibid., 2.44, p. 109.

91. Ibid., 2.28, p. 90.

92. Ibid., 2.26, p. 88.

93. Ibid., p. 88 fn.

94. Ibid. Cf. 3.6, pp. 133–34; 3.10, p. 143; 4.5, p. 156.

95. Ibid., 3.12, pp. 146–48.

96. Ibid., 3.12, pp. 146–47.

97. Ibid., 3.13, p. 148.

98. Ibid., 3.12, p. 146.

99. Cyprian, *Epistle* 64.3, in *Ante-Nicene Fathers,* 5:336.

100. Ibid., 67.4, 5, 5:370–71.

101. Ibid., 32.1, 5:311–12.

102. Symonds, p. 409.

103. *Didascalia Apostolorum* 2:28, p. 90.

104. Ibid., 2.47, p. 111.

105. Ibid., 2.26, p. 86.

106. Vischer, p. 23.

107. *Didascalia Apostolorum* 2.26, p. 86.

108. Ibid., 2.28, p. 90.

109. Cyprian, *Epistle* 33.5, in *Ante-Nicene Fathers,* 5:314.

110. *Didascalia Apostolorum,* "Introduction," p. xii.

111. Ibid., 2.54, p. 117.

112. Ibid., 2.57, p. 120.

113. In describing the pre-Nicene Eucharist Dix says that it was the function of the deacon to cover the altar with a linen cloth after the exchange of the kiss of peace, just prior to the Eucharist itself (*Shape of the Liturgy,* p. 104). However, his reference is from Optatus of Milevis, which he dates c. 360. Optatus states simply that the altar is covered and says nothing about the deacons: ". . . which of the faithful is there who is unaware that during the celebration of the Mysteries, the wood of the altar is itself covered with linen?" (Optatus, 6.1, p. 251, though Dix's reference is to 6.2, in which the cloth is not mentioned.)

114. *Didascalia Apostolorum* 2.58, p. 120.

115. Ibid., 3.12, pp. 146–47.

116. Easton, *Pastoral Epistles,* p. 183.

117. Marion J. Hatchett, "Seven Pre–Reformation Eucharistic Liturgies," in *St. Luke's Journal of Theology* 16 (June, 1973): 17 (hereafter cited "Seven Liturgies").

118. Easton, *Pastoral Epistles,* p. 183.

119. A. Cleveland Coxe, "Introductory Notice to Cyprian," in *Ante-Nicene Fathers,* 5:263.

120. Cyprian, *Elucidations* 2, in *Ante-Nicene Fathers,* 5:410.

121. Cyprian, *Epistle* 5.4, in *Ante-Nicene Fathers,* 5:283.

122. Ibid., 12.1, 5:293.

123. Herbert Thurston, "Deacons," in *The Catholic Encyclopedia,* ed. Charles G. Herbermann et al. (New York: The Encyclopedia Press, 1908), 4:649.

124. Symonds, p. 412.

125. Cyprian, *Epistle* 33.5, in *Ante-Nicene Fathers,* 5:313.

126. Altaner, p. 59, for date.

127. *Apostolic Constitutions* 11.57, in vol. 7: *Lactantius, Venantius, Asterius, Victorinus, Dionysius, Apostolic Teaching and Constitutions, Homily, and Liturgies,* in *Ante-Nicene Fathers* (1951), 7:421.

128. Jerome, *Letter* 147.6, in vol. 6: *St. Jerome: Letters and Select Works,* trans. G. Martley, in *Nicene and Post-Nicene Fathers,* Second Series (1954), 6:292.

129. Sozomen, *Ecclesiastical History* VII.19, in *Nicene and Post–Nicene Fathers,* Second Series, 2:390.

130. Marion J. Hatchett, *Sanctifying Life, Time and Space: An Introduction to Liturgical Study* (New York: Seabury Press, 1976), p. 45.

131. Dix, *Shape of the Liturgy,* p. 31. Cf. Hatchett, *Sanctifying Life,* p. 49.

132. Quasten, 3:82.

133. John Wordsworth, *Bishop Serapion's Prayer Book—An Egyptian Sacramentary Dated about* A.D. *350–356* (London: S.P.C.K. [2nd ed.], 1923), "Introduction," p. 24 and p. 86 fn. (hereafter cited *Serapion's P. B.*).

134. *Apostolic Constitutions* 8.2.5, 6, in *Ante-Nicene Fathers,* 7:483.

135. Ibid., 7:485ff.

136. Ibid., 8.2.11, 7:486.

137. Ibid., 8.2.12, 7:486.

138. Ibid., 8.1.14, 7:491.

139. Dix, *Shape of the Liturgy,* p. 35.

140. Theodore Klauser, *A Short History of the Western Liturgy: An Account and Some Reflections,* trans. John Halliburton (London: Oxford University Press, 1969), p. 15.

141. Quasten, 2:278.

142. Tertullian, *Tertullian's Homily on Baptism,* ed. with intro., trans., and comm. Ernest Evans (London: S.P.C.K., 1964), p. 35 (hereafter cited *Homily on Baptism*).

143. Quasten, 2:280, for date.

144. *Didascalia Apostolorum* 3.12, pp. 146–47.

145. Bingham, 2.20.9, 1:258.

146. Ibid.

147. Altaner, p. 470, for date.

148. Jerome, *Dialogue Against Luciferians* 9, in *Nicene and Post-Nicene Fathers,* Second Series, 6:324.

149. Cyril of Jerusalem, *Catech.* 17.35: "For, at the season of baptism, when thou art come before the Bishops, or Presbyters, or Deacons, (for its grace is everywhere, in villages and in cities, on them of low as on them of high degree, on bondsmen and on freemen, for this grace is not of men, but the gift is from God through men),—approach the Minister of Baptism but approaching, think not of the face of him thou seest, but remember this Holy Ghost of whom we are now speaking." (In vol. 7: *St. Cyril of Jerusalem: St. Gregory Nazianzen,* in *Nicene and Post-Nicene Fathers* Second Series, [1955], 7:132.)

150. Ignatius, *Smyrneans* 8, in *Early Christian Fathers,* 1:115 (italics added).

151. Canon 15, Arles, in Charles Joseph Hefele, vol. 1: *A History of the Christian Councils, from the Original Documents to the Close of the Council of Nicaea,* A.D. *325,* in *A History of the Councils of the Church,* trans. William R. Clark (Edinburgh: T. & T. Clark [2nd ed. rev.], 1894), 1:193. Bingham, 2.20.8, 1:255.

152. Edward Landon, *A Manual of Councils of the Holy Catholic Church* (London: Griffith Farrar & Co., n.d.), 1:45.

153. Early in chap. 6 consideration is again given to this and certain other evidence of the deacon presiding at the Eucharist.

154. Hefele, *History of the Councils,* 1:169.

155. Alfred W. W. Dale, *The Synod of Elvira and Christian Life in the Fourth Century* (London: Macmillan & Co., 1882), p. 70.

156. Hefele, *History of the Councils,* 1:170. Hefele includes the *chorepiscopoi* along with the presbyters and deacons as being put over these rural congregations.

157. Bingham, 9.8.4–5, 3:413–18. Canon 13 of Neocaesarea is also cited but only presbyters are mentioned in it in this connection.

158. *Testament,* trans. Wilhelm Schamoni, in *Married Men as Ordained Deacons* (London: Burns & Oates, 1955), p. 72. The *Testament* of the martyrs of Sebaste, in contrast to their *Acts,* is authentic. Altaner, p. 250.

159. Charles Joseph Hefele, vol. 2: *A History of the Councils of the Church, from the Original Documents,* A.D. *326 to* A.D. *429,* trans. Henry N. Oxenham, in *A History of the Councils of the Church* (Edinburgh: T. & T. Clark, 1876), 2:421. (Canon 20 of Toledo.)

160. Charles Joseph Hefele, vol. 3: *A History of the Councils of the Church, from the Original Documents,* A.D. *431 to* A.D. *451,* trans. "Editor of Hagenbach's *History of Doctrines,*" in *A History of the Councils of the Church* (Edinburgh: T. & T. Clark, 1883), 3:165.

161. Gregory of Tours, *De Gloria Confess.* Cap. 30, in *Patrologiae Latinorum,* ed. J. P. Migne, vol. 71 (Paris: n.p., 1879), 71:851.

162. Schamoni, p. 74. He also cites Canon 49 of Agde, 506, but Charles Joseph Hefele, vol. 4: *A History of the Councils of the Church, from the Original Documents,* A.D. *451 to* A.D. *680,* trans. William R. Clarke, in *A History of the Councils of the Church* (Edinburgh: T. & T. Clark, 1895), 4:84, does not regard this canon as genuine. Further, the pertinent part may be otherwise interpreted: "Deacons and priests who are appointed to a parish may not alienate anything of the ecclesiastical property entrusted to them . . . ," which does not necessarily imply that deacons were placed over parishes in the absence of priests. Schamoni would seem to press the evidence further than it will bear in light of the lack of other testimony.

163. Schamoni, p. 32.

164. W. J. O'Shea, "Easter Vigil," in *New Catholic Encyclopedia* (New York: McGraw-Hill Book Co., 1967), 5:10.

165. Eusebius, *Church History* 6.9.2, 3, in *Nicene and Post-Nicene Fathers*, Second Series, 1:255.

166. Eusebius, *Life of Constantine* 4.22, in *Nicene and Post-Nicene Fathers*, Second Series, 1:545.

167. Dix, *Shape of the Liturgy*, pp. 23, 24 fn.

168. O'Shea, 5:10.

169. J. N. D. Kelly, *Jerome: His Life, Writings, and Controversies* (New York: Harper & Row, 1975), p. 111 and 111 fn.

170. Augustine, *The City of God*, trans. Henry Bettenson (Hammondsworth, Middlesex, England: Penguin, 1971), p. 636 fn. (hereafter cited Bettenson).

171. Ibid., 15.22, p. 636.

172. Ibid., p. 636 fn. Bettenson here also says that the chant of the Easter Vigil called the *Exultet* has sometimes been attributed to Augustine "without good reason."

173. Augustine, *City of God*, in vol. 2: *St. Augustin's City of God and Christian Doctrine*, trans. Marcus Dods, in *Nicene and Post-Nicene Fathers of the Christian Church, A Select Library of the*, First Series, ed. Philip Schaff, 14 vol. (Grand Rapids, Mi.: William B. Eerdmans Publishing Co., 1956), 2:303. John Healy's translation reads "Creator" with no alternative (Augustine, *The City of God*, ed. R. V. G. Trasker [London: J. M. Dent & Sons, 1945], 2.89). J. W. C. Wand, abridg. and trans., reads "Paschal Candle" but gives "Creator" as alternate (*St. Augustine's City of God* [London: Oxford University Press, 1963], p. 258).

174. Kelly, *Jerome*, p. 111, for date.

175. Jerome, *Epistle* 28, *Ad Praesidium, De Cereo paschali*, ed. Jacques Paul Migne, *Patrologia cursus completus*, Series latina, Tomus 30, S. *Hieronymi, Tomus undecimus* (Paris: n.p., 1846), pp. 182–88, published on Microcards, 1960, Fo–60, M359–2, vol. 30, card 1 (of 6), pp. 1–88. Duschene mentions this letter in a footnote and dates it in 384, but in accord with the assumption that it was apocryphal he says that it is "attributed" to Jerome (L. Duchesne, *Christian Worship, Its Origin and Evolution: A Study of the Latin Liturgy Up to the Time of Charlemagne* [London: S.P.C.K. (5th ed.), 1923], p. 253 fn.).

176. Altaner, p. 572, for date.

177. Tyrer says that the oldest witness to the blessing of the paschal candle is the two blessings in Ennodius, but as we have seen the earliest reference is in Jerome. Tyrer probably still assumes this work of Jerome to be spurious (*Historical Survey of Holy Week: Its Services and Ceremonial* [London: Oxford University Press, 1932], p. 150).

178. Ennodius, *Opuscula miscella* 9 and 10, "Benedictio Cerei," in vol. 6: *Magni Felicis Ennodii: Opera Omnia*, in *Corpus Scriptorum Ecclesiasticorum*, recensuit et commentario, Guilelmus Hartel (Vindobonae: Apud C. Geroldi Filium Bibliopolam Academiae, 1882), pp. 415–22.

179. Altaner, p. 572.

180. Duchesne, p. 253 fn.

181. Altaner, p. 574.

182. Echlin, pp. 17, 21, 76. Cf. Schamoni, p. 15, and Urban T. Holmes III, *The Future Shape of Ministry: A Theological Projection* (New York: Seabury Press, 1971), p. 25 (hereafter cited *Future Shape*). Bingham, 2.20.11, 1:260–61, says that deacons preached but only with the license of the bishop.

183. Acts 21:8.

184. Norbert Brockman, *Ordained to Service: A Theology of the Permanent Diaconate* (Hicksville, N.Y.: Exposition Press, 1976), p. 8.

185. *The Council of Ancyra,* in vol. 14: *The Seven Ecumenical Councils,* ed. Henry R. Percival, in *Nicene and Post-Nicene Fathers,* Second Series (1956), 14:63.

186. Hefele, *History of the Councils,* 1:202–03.

187. Bingham, 2.20.10, 1:260.

188. See Percival's commentary on Canon 2, in *The Council of Ancyra,* in *Nicene and Post-Nicene Fathers,* Second Series, 14:64.

189. Echlin, p. 16.

190. *The Didache or Teaching of the Twelve Apostles* 15.1, 2, trans. Francis X. Glimm, in vol. 1: *The Apostolic Fathers,* in *The Fathers of the Church* (New York: Cima Publ. Co., 1947), 1:183.

191. Echlin, p. 17.

192. Fuller, *Early Catholicism.*

193. Brockman, p. 21.

194. Echlin, p. 21. The citation is *To the Philadelphians* 11.

195. *The Letters of St. Ignatius of Antioch, To the Philadelphians* 11, trans. Gerald G. Walsh, in vol. 1: *The Apostolic Fathers,* in *The Fathers of the Church* (New York: Cima Publ. Co., 1947), 1:117.

196. *Ignatius, To the Philadelphians* 11, in *Ante-Nicene Fathers,* 1:85.

197. Ignatius, *To the Philadelphians* 11, in *Early Christian Fathers,* 1:111.

198. Philostorgius, *Ecclesiastical History* 3.17, in *Patrologiae Cursus Completus Omnium SS. Patrum, Doctorum Scriptorumque Ecclesiasticorum Sive Latinorum, Sive Graecorum,* ed. J. P. Migne (Turnholt, Belgium: Brepols, n.d.), 65:508–09.

199. Echlin, p. 76.

200. Altaner, p. 401.

201. Jerome, *De Scriptor. Eccles.* 115, in Bingham, 1:262 fn. The Greek text, in which Photius says that Ephraem composed several excellent sermons that were translated into other languages after his death, is also given in Bingham, 1:262 fn.

202. Hefele, *History of the Councils,* 4:170.

203. Brockman, p. 28.

204. Ibid.

205. Cf. Hardy, "Deacons," p. 29.

206. Symonds, p. 412.

207. Cyprian, *Epistle* 5.4, in *Ante-Nicene Fathers,* 5:283.

208. Ibid., 51.8, 5:329.

209. Walter Howard Frere, "Early Forms of Ordination," in *Essays on the Early History of the Church and the Ministry by Various Writers,* ed. H. B. Swete (London: Macmillan & Co. [2nd ed.], 1921), pp. 263–312 and 226 fn.

210. *Apostolic Constitutions* 8.28, in *Ante-Nicene Fathers,* 7:494.

211. *The Proper for the Lesser Feasts and Fasts together with the Fixed Holy Days* (New York: Church Hymnal Corp. [3rd ed.], 1980), p. 220.

212. L. Wallach, "Alcuin," *New Catholic Encyclopedia,* 1:279.

213. In *The Oxford Dictionary of the Christian Church,* 2nd ed., p. 1373.

214. John R. Moorman, *Saint Francis of Assisi* (London: S.P.C.K., 1963), p. 101.

215. Thomas of Celano, *The First Life of St. Francis* 30.86, trans. in Marion A. Habig, *St. Francis of Assisi: Writings and Early Biographies: English Omnibus of the Sources for the Life of St. Francis* (Chicago: Franciscan Herald Press, 1972), p. 301. Though it is possible to interpret this text and later references, which are

dependent upon it, to mean that Francis was deacon at the Eucharist without having been ordained to the office, the interpretation given by the translator is more probable. Conrad L. Harkins, Director of the Franciscan Institute, St. Bonaventure University, St. Bonaventure, New York, and an expert on the life of Francis, states that in his opinion "it is morally certain that Francis was a deacon." (Personal communication to the author.) Cf. André Callebaut, "Saint Francois lévite," *Archivum Franciscanum Historicum,* 20 (1927), pp. 193–96.

216. Brockman, p. 30.

217. Ibid.

218. *The Proper for the Lesser Feasts and Fasts,* p. 80.

219. John R. H. Moorman, *A History of the Church in England* (New York: Morehouse-Barlow Co. [2nd ed.], 1967), p. 236.

220. Ibid.

221. *The Proper for the Lesser Feasts and Fasts,* p. 80.

222. Brockman, pp. 30, 31.

223. Cyprian, *Epistle* 51.8, in *Ante-Nicene Fathers,* 5:329.

224. Eusebius, *Church History* 6.43.11, in *Nicene and Post-Nicene Fathers,* Second Series, 1:288.

225. Tertullian, *On Prescription Against Heretics* 41, in *Ante-Nicene Fathers,* 3:263.

226. Hippolytus, *Apostolic Tradition* 12, 14, in Easton, *Apostolic Tradition of Hippolytus,* pp. 40–41.

227. *Apostolic Constitution* 8.3.21, 22, 26, in *Ante-Nicene Fathers,* 7:492–93.

228. Wordsworth, p. 87 fn.

229. Cyprian, *Epistle* 27.3, in *Ante-Nicene Fathers,* 5:306.

230. A. J. Maclean, "Ministry (Early Christian)," in *Encyclopedia of Religion and Ethics,* ed. James Hastings (New York: Charles Scribner's Sons, 1916), 8:668.

231. Frere, p. 305.

232. Maclean, 8:668.

233. *Didascalia Apostolorum* 2.34, p. 96.

234. Altaner, p. 56.

235. Hefele, *History of the Councils,* 1:149.

236. In *Nicene and Post-Nicene Fathers,* Second Series, 14:113.

237. Ibid., 14:144.

CHAPTER 6

The Radical Transition of the Fourth Century

The Importance of the Deacon

The deacon enters the fourth century as a person of considerable importance and prestige in the Church. We have already noted how often a deacon was elected bishop. He was not only the executive assistant of the bishop but represented him on occasion at councils. Pope Sylvester sent two presbyters and two deacons to represent him at the Council of Arles, c. 314, where the British Church was represented by three bishops and a deacon.[1]

The deacon Athanasius was perhaps the most notable example of the period. He played a leading role in the first ecumenical council, in 325. Theodoret tells us that while "a very young man, although he was the principal deacon" of Alexandria, he attended the Council of Nicaea in the retinue of its bishop Alexander.[2] There, he "so defended the doctrines of the apostles, that . . . he won the approbation of all the champions of the truth."[3] Though no minutes of Nicaea have survived, it is likely that the influence of Athanasius was exercised from the sidelines, since the records of all later ecumenical councils and ancient synods of bishops indicate that advisors brought by bishops may exercise great influence but did not sit, speak, or vote in formal council sessions. Shortly after the council adjourned, Alexander died and Athanasius succeeded him as bishop of that great city.[4]

Other testimony to the importance of the deacon at this time, particularly in relation to the presbyter, is seen in the repeated reminders to the deacons regarding the limits of their functions and their "inferiority" to the presbyters.

Canon 18 of Arles, 314, is directed against "city deacons," who have apparently assumed prerogatives belonging to the presbyters, though the exact application is uncertain:

> Concerning the city deacons, that they take not so much upon themselves but preserve to the presbyters their order, that they do nothing without the presbyters' knowledge.[5]

As noted in the previous chapter, Canon 15 of Arles forbids deacons to offer (celebrate or preside at) the Eucharist, which in many places seems to have been allowed, probably during the Diocletian persecution when no bishops or presbyters were available.[6] This practice may not have been so much a presumption as a reflection of the importance of the diaconate and the old "organic" theology wherein the priesthood belonged to the whole people of God and distinctions between orders were not so clearly drawn. It is in fact in the third century that "the line between clergy and laity was only beginning to be defined."[7]

The matter of deacons presiding as Eucharistic celebrants was definitely settled in 325 by Canon 18 of Nicaea, which states that according to neither canon nor custom do the deacons have any right "to offer" the Eucharist and should not, therefore, administer to presbyters, who do offer, nor touch the Eucharist before the bishop. Further, the canon provides, the deacons are not to sit among the presbyters whose "inferiors" they are, the legislation itself attesting by its protest to the high esteem in which the diaconate was held. As we have seen already, the practice of deacons administering the Eucharist to the presbyters, now condemned and forbidden at Nicaea, was the practice of the earlier period. It is the reflection of the more organic concept of the Church in the pre-Nicene age, where office was not so much a matter of rank and status but rather of function. It was only natural that the deacons administer the Eucharist to the "*liturgically non-participant* but revered and seated" presbyters of the congregation.[8]

The importance of the diaconate in this early period is to be seen as much as anything else in its lingering eminence, even as it slowly declined. Ambrosiaster, in the time of Pope Damasus (366–384), was moved to write "On the Boastfulness of the Roman Deacons," because the deacons there attempted to take precedence over the presbyters.[9] Jerome tells us that at Rome a presbyter is only ordained on the recommendation of a deacon and that "their paucity makes deacons persons of consequence, while presbyters are less thought of owing to their great numbers."[10] The position of the deacons, especially at Rome, was enhanced by their close association with the bishop and their responsibility in administering large funds and great estates.[11] Jerome wrote his letter to Evangelus in reference to the latter's inquiry regarding Ambrosiaster's observations about the deacons at Rome, though Jerome is more interested in showing that presbyters and bishops are the same than that the deacons there are arrogant. However, Jerome continues regarding deacons:

> But even in the Church of Rome the deacons stand while the presbyters seat themselves, although bad habits have by degrees so far crept in that I have seen a deacon, in the absence of the bishop, seat himself among the presbyters, and at social gatherings give his blessing to them.[12]

The history of the diaconate prior to Jerome's time indicates that what Jerome supposes to be newly acquired "bad habits" are but a reflection of the traditional prestige and place of the deacon in the early Church, especially before Nicaea. It was the presbyters who were increasing in importance as they assumed the place and functions of the pre-Nicene bishops.

We see the importance the deacons still retained in the seventh century when the Council of Toledo, 633, directs that deacons "are not to raise themselves above the presbyters, and stand in the first choir whilst the priests are in the second."[13]

Dix remarks that

> no deacon ever played again quite the sort of part which Athanasius seems to have played at Nicaea as the right-hand man of Bishop Alexander, though at Rome the archdeacon (who was still a man in deacon's orders) could still be a most important functionary as late as the eleventh century, as the Archdeacon Hildebrand was to show.[14]

Hildebrand was appointed Archdeacon of Rome in 1059. He was elected pope and enthroned still in deacon's orders on 22 April 1073, being ordained priest on May 22 and bishop on June 29 of that year.[15] Ariald, another deacon of the eleventh century, demonstrates that Hildebrand was not simply an isolated case. He achieved prominence as leader of a reform party in the Church at Milan, protesting against what had been termed the dissolute life of the clergy there, so many of the clergy including the archbishop being married at that time.[16]

A Constitutional Change?

However, radical changes in the Church's ministry came in the fourth century with the entrance of unprecedented numbers into the Church following the adoption of the Constantinian policy of toleration for Christianity and equality for all religions by the emperors at Milan in 313.[17] The transition in the diaconate can only be understood in relation to the episcopate and presbyterate as the three orders together underwent a marked transformation. Dix argues that the change is "administrative" and not "constitutional" and is possibly correct, particularly in the way he defines these terms.[18] However, the transition of the fourth century is one so profound and far-reaching that it would seem to come very close, at the least, to being constitutional.

It is Canon 18 of Nicaea which seems to sum up in many ways the developments within the ministry in the second and third centuries which made possible the transformation of the fourth century.[19] Canon 18 decrees:

> It has come to the knowledge of the holy Synod that in certain places and cities, the deacons give the Eucharist to the presbyters, whereas neither canon nor custom allows that they who have no authority to offer should give the Body of Christ to those who do offer. It has also been made known that now some of the deacons receive the Eucharist even before the bishops. Let all such practices be done away, and let the deacons keep within their proper bounds, knowing that they are the ministers of the bishop and inferior to the presbyters. Let them, therefore, receive the Eucharist, according to their order, after the presbyters, either the bishop or presbyter administering it to them. Further, the deacons are not to be allowed to sit among the presbyters; for this is done contrary to the canon and due order. But if any one even after this decision will not obey, let him be put out of the diaconate.[20]

This canon of Nicaea does demonstrate that the Church is in the process of assimilating the social order's pretentions of rank and status. It is emerging as a major religion with considerable prestige in the fabric of the Roman Empire. The emperor, Constantine the Great, had embraced Christianity and had contributed large sums to enable the Church to erect fine buildings. The number of Christians had rapidly increased following adoption of the policy of toleration in 313 and had forced organizational changes upon the Church, which increasingly looked to the Empire as its model.

Not long after Nicaea the Council of Antioch in 341 ordered that the bishop in the chief city or metropolis of each province would have precedence over the other bishops of the province. Though the Council thought it was acting in accord with traditional practice of long standing, it was rather confirming this relatively recent development.[21] Creation of metropolitans or archbishops was one phase in the creation of a hierarchy of graded ranks as the Church restructured its offices along the lines of the Roman Empire in the fourth century.

Even though in places there may have been deacons whose conduct was presumptuous, the legislation of Nicaea in this respect is primarily due to the transition occurring in the Church. Time honored customs, such as deacons administering the Eucharist to presbyters and even non-presiding bishops, are mistakenly assumed by Nicaea to be prideful innovations and condemned. The declaration that deacons are "inferior" not only reflected the change taking place but served to further it.

The Presbyter Gains Liturgical Function

The primary though by no means the only development to be noted in Canon 18 has to do with the exchange of function between the bishop and the presbyters. As we have noted, the bishop of the later New Testament period and the sub-apostolic age had or came to have the liturgical monopoly emphasized by Dix.[22] The "special place" of the presbyters was simply to sit in a semicircle beside the bishop at the Eucharist, denoting their honored place as elders of the Church and members of the ruling presbyteral council, but without liturgical function. However, by Nicaea the presbyter had acquired as a prerogative of his office the right "to offer" (preside at the celebration of) the Eucharist in the place of the bishop. The council now confirmed this right. Following the adoption of the policy of toleration for the Church by the co-emperors at Milan in 313 and the ensuing growth in numbers of Christians and of church buildings, the bishop could no longer function as the pastor and normal president of the Eucharistic assemblies in all the churches of the local Church, which had begun to take on some characteristics of the later diocese. He remained pastor of his own church but most of his liturgical functions were delegated to presbyters for the surrounding churches.[23] Dix writes,

> The history of the episcopate is in one sense the history of the steady breaking down of its primitive liturgical monopoly. It was inevitable that as the Church grew this should be so by the mere necessity of numbers. By the fourth century only the power of ordaining remains a strictly episcopal preserve. . . .[24]

The change was gradual. Between Clement (c. 96) and Hippolytus (c. 215), presbyters began to participate liturgically by joining the bishop in laying hands on the oblations, which were probably held in front of them by deacons, thus concelebrating with the bishop, becoming "co-consecrators" with him as he said the Thanksgiving.[25] We must not forget that in this early period consecration in the Eucharist was not viewed in terms of a personal possession. The priesthood belonged to the Church, and the Church as a body, Christ's body, offered the Eucharist, led by its officers.[26] Therefore, it was a natural development for the presbyter to join the bishop in this way. But the presbyter could only concelebrate with the bishop and join in the laying on of hands in the ordination of a presbyter, this being due to the original nature of the presbyterate as a corporate body which rules the local Church.[27] However, the distinctiveness of the concelebrating aspect is somewhat blurred by the fact that the deacons, who probably held the bread on patens before the presbyters during the Thanksgiving, themselves broke eucharistized Bread that was on the altar before the bishop, joined in the administration of the Bread, if needed, and administered the chalice.

Though the date when presbyters first offered the Eucharist apart from the bishop is uncertain, the practice apparently had come about by the latter part of the third century. The Council of Ancyra, held in the capitol of Galatia, c. 314, gives clear testimony to the transformation which had taken place in the office of presbyter, especially in light of the acceptance of these canons by Nicaea. Canon 1 is concerned with the restoration of lapsed presbyters. It provides, "Nevertheless it is not lawful for them to make the oblation, nor to preach, nor in short to perform any sacerdotal function."[28] The fact that these presbyters are now inhibited from offering the Eucharist (oblation) and preaching and performing any priestly function demonstrates that these functions had now not only been delegated to the presbyterate but were considered theirs as a matter of course, at least in this region. Canon 18 of Nicaea demonstrates that by 325 the prerogative was considered to be inherent in the office throughout the Church, indicating that it had long been so.

It may well have first come about as a result of the bishop's absence in the persecutions, and Dix sees the first reference to the practice in a letter of Cyprian during the Decian persecution.[29] He believes, however, that at least by the third century the number of Christians in a few of the great cities had resulted in the delegation of the presidency of the Eucharist to presbyters.[30] Though it has frequently been said that this delegation was made by the bishop, it is probable that it was originally the decision of the presbyteral council, presided over by the bishop, and only later, in retrospect as the monarchial episcopate flourished, came to be thought of as the delegation of the bishop.

Perhaps the most ironic aspect of the delegation of functions is to be seen in the fact that it was only possible because of the old organic concept of the Church. While it was logical to delegate to the older and more respected presbyters, who had come to concelebrate with the bishop, the function of presiding at the Eucharist, the delegation was theologically possible only because of the earlier concept of the Church as an organic society which as a whole possessed the priesthood of Christ and which could delegate and authorize those whom it chose to exercise these functions. (It could as well have selected deacons as presbyters to preside at the Eucharist.) Thus, the irony is that with the transition which came about partially as a result of this delegation, the organic understanding, which had made the delegation possible, was largely lost.

The principle, which is clearly evident here, has the most profound and fundamental implications for us today. The Church, ever seeking the guidance of the Holy Spirit, has the plentitude of authority from its Lord to structure its life and order as it sees fit in striving to fulfill its task in the world. Understanding of this principle gives Catholicism—Roman, Anglican, or Orthodox—far greater breadth than it has had in centuries and brings it to a new vision of its internal life and a new charity in its appreciation of other Christians.

The Presbyter Becomes a "Priest"

The presbyter has become a priest. Tertullian and Hippolytus were the first to use the words "priests" and "high priest"' in reference to officers of the Church.[31] Though the term "priest" was originally applied to presbyters as well as bishops in the middle of the third century, Dix says that the change of language regarding the office of the presbyter does not become general until the latter half of the fourth century.[32] The priesthood, which had originally belonged to the whole Church with the bishop coming to be called "high priest," now increasingly came to be thought of as associated with the bishops and presbyters.[33] The presbyter is termed a "priest," a *sacerdos* or *hiereus*, instead of "presbyter" or "elder." It is instructive to note that the English word "priest" is derived from the Greek term *presbyteros*, meaning elder, and not from the Latin *sacerdos* or Greek *hiereus*, which are now translated "priest."[34]

Dix says that Optatus, Bishop of Milevis, is the first in the West to apply the term *sacerdos* and then with qualification (*sacerdos secundi ordinis*) to presbyters. He reports that c. 360 *hiereus* is found on gravestones of presbyters in Asia Minor.[35] Optatus, writing c. 365, even terms deacons a third degree of the priesthood (*sacerdotium*), though this seems to be the only reference of its kind in antiquity and perhaps reflects the older idea of priesthood in the Church.[36] The presbyter is not called "high priest" (*archiereus* or *sacerdos* without qualification) due to the long association of that term with the bishop, who had been "the 'high-priest' in the midst of the whole 'priestly' People of God."[37] "Priesthood" now is thought of as belonging to the presbyterate instead of being "the function of all members of the church with the bishop as 'high-priest,' " an important impoverishment.[38]

The Diocese Emerges

With the delegation of the bishop's liturgical functions to the presbyter and the latter's assumption of the bishop's pastoral role, the city "parish" was acquiring characteristics of what later was to be called a diocese.

Though the bishop continued his role in his own church, he also headed the churches of the city and the surrounding communities, which were becoming "parishes" as the word later came to be used.[39] The country churches were still under rural bishops who were called *chorepiscopoi* in the fourth century.[40]

The first reference to them by this name is in the canons of the Councils of Ancyra and Neocaesarea, c. 314.[41] Already they were being suppressed and becoming almost a separate class between the bishops of the cities and the presbyters.[42] Canon 13 of Ancyra declares it to be unlawful for them to ordain presbyters and deacons without the consent of the (city) bishop,[43] and Canon 8 of Nicaea provides for the demotion of Novatian bishops who "come over" to the Catholic Church in a place where there is a Catholic bishop, to the position of a "Chorepiscopus, or presbyter,"[44] putting them almost on a par with the presbyter. As the number of *chorepiscopoi* diminished, presbyters are for the first time put in charge of local communities, except perhaps in Egypt.[45]

The peculiar situation we find in Egypt until the middle of the third century is probably reminiscent of the time of presbyter-bishops in the post-apostolic age as seen in 1 Clement. Jerome says that down to the episcopates of Heraclas (233–249) and Dionysius (249–265), the presbyters of Alexandria elected the bishop and implies that they also ordained him:

> For even at Alexandria from the time of Mark the Evangelist until the episcopates of Heraclas and Dionysius the presbyters always named as bishop one of their own number chosen by themselves and set in a more exalted position, just as an army elects a general, or as deacons appoint one of themselves whom they know to be diligent and call him archdeacon.[46]

Lightfoot maintains that the inference may be made that the presbyters themselves ordained the Alexandrian bishops up to this time, citing Ambrosiaster[47] and the testimony of Eutychicus, Patriarch of Alexandria, 933–940, who says the custom continued until the time of Alexander, patriarch from 313–326.[48] Eutychicus also states that the only bishop in Egypt up to the time of Demetrius (190–233), who appointed three others, was at Alexandria.[49] Demetrius's successor Heraclas (233–249) added twenty more. In this case presbyteral ordination would have been a virtual necessity.[50] With this increase in the number of bishops in Egypt, what appears to have been the last vestige of the presbyter-bishop disappeared. The presbyter-bishop of the late first century, who had functioned as a bishop, lost these functions finally, but by Nicaea presbyters generally had acquired the functions of bishops, with the probable exception of ordination.

The Presbyter Becomes a Bishop (Almost?)

THE BISHOPS ASSUME RULE FROM PRESBYTERS

As the presbyter assumes the role of the bishop in the local congregation, the presbyterate loses its corporate character and function. As has been noted, there is an exchange. The bishop at the same time assumes much of the rule of the Church that had formerly been exercised by the corporate presbyterate acting as a council of the Church with the bishop as its president. We remember that in Hippolytus the bishop is not called the "ruler" of the Church. The presbyter, not the bishop, is ordained "that he may sustain and govern thy people."[51] The bishop has given up his liturgical and sacramental monopoly to the presbyters but in the process has assumed the government of the Church in large measure.

In the pre-Nicene Church the clergy, including the bishops, were thought of primarily as *belonging to the local Church.* This is seen in various canons of the fourth century. Canon 2 of Arles provides that "ordained clerics," which probably refers to minor orders, are to stay in the places of their ordination.[52] Canon 21 provides that presbyters and deacons who leave the places of their ordination and wish to be transferred are to be deposed.[53] Canon 15 of Nicaea, 325, repeated at Antioch in 341, prohibited any bishop, presbyter, or deacon from moving from one city to another, decreeing that any such act would be "totally annulled."[54] However, the focus was moving away from the local Church. Later in the century, as the organic character of the Church was eroded, the idea of clergy belonging first to the Church at large and, therefore, being free to move, was fostered theologically by Augustine's development of a theology of order, during the Donatist controversy, which conceives of the validity of the sacraments and the ministerial orders virtually apart from the context of the Church.[55]

The bishop, who in the period before Nicaea had to get the consent of the presbyteral council for all that he did regarding policy, now increasingly took over the rule of the Church both as an individual and, meeting with his fellow bishops, as a corporate body in synods and councils. Synods become frequent: Canon 5 of Nicaea provides that there be two in every province each year to deal with disciplinary matters.[56] Even though the Syrian *Apostolic Constitutions,* c. 380, still speaks of presbyters as constituting "the sanhedrin and senate of the Church,"[57] the presbyteral council is now replaced by a council of bishops as the decision-making body of the Church. A. G. Hebert well observes that one important result of this process was that "the check upon episcopal autocracy which had previously existed had now largely disappeared."[58]

In the exchange of function between the bishop and the presbyter the bishop retained exclusively but a single liturgical and sacramental right—control over ordination of the clergy.[59] However, the distinction was sufficiently blurred between the bishop and the presbyter by the late fourth century that some of the fathers assert that the two are essentially the same. The presbyter, Jerome, says in a letter to Evangelus:

> I am told that someone has been mad enough to put deacons before presbyters, that is, before bishops. For when the apostle clearly teaches that presbyters are the same as bishops, must not a mere server of tables and widows be insane to set himself up arrogantly over men through whose prayers the body and blood of Christ are produced?

He cites Titus 1:5–7 as a "passage which clearly proves a bishop and a presbyter to be the same," though he asks rhetorically, "For what function excepting ordination, belongs to a bishop that does not belong to a presbyter?"[60] Chrysostom in his homily on 1 Timothy 3:8–10 says that Paul discusses the character and qualities bishops should have and then passes over presbyters to deacons because

> between Presbyters and Bishops there was no great difference. Both had undertaken the office of Teachers and Presidents in the Church, and what he [Paul] has said concerning Bishops is applicable to Presbyters. For they are only superior in having the power of ordination, and seem to have no other advantage over Presbyters.[61]

Though the equating of presbyters with bishops is not generally to be found in the fathers of this period,[62] Lightfoot says that Pelagius, Theodore of Mopsuestia, and Theodoret also acknowledge it.[63] The emergence of such an equation does illustrate the extent to which presbyters have assumed the functions of bishops and the importance they have gained during the course of the century. It further and more importantly indicates the radical transformation that occurs as the old organic conception and structure of the Church broke down.

In Ambrosiaster we find further evidence of the breakdown of the idea of a functional ministry and new teaching which facilitates the transformation to a "vertical" structure of hierarchy. Like Jerome and Chrysostom, the bishop and the presbyter are one:

> The Apostle Paul proves that a presbyter is a bishop when he instructs Timothy, whom he had ordained as a presbyter, what sort of person he is to create a bishop. For what is a bishop but the first presbyter, that is, the highest priest? Finally, he calls these men none other than fellow presbyters and fellow priests. Does a bishop call his minister fellow deacons? No, for they are much inferior, and it is a disgrace to mix

them up with a judge (?). For in Alexandria and throughout Egypt, if a bishop is lacking a presbyter confirms (ordains?—*consignat*).[64]

Not only do we see here the fact that in the author's eyes the presbyter is a bishop, probably even ordaining in Egypt, but also that the diaconate has become "much inferior." However, of more importance is Ambrosiaster's assertion that "the greater order contains within itself the lesser."[65] It is at this point that we see the extent of the change that has taken place, for now there not only are "greater" and "lesser" offices but the greatest contains them all.

The Diaconate Declines: A Third Order

With the steady transformation of the presbyterate and the increasing importance of the presbyter as an individual apart from the corporate presbyterate, the diaconate begins to decline, though deacons continue, as we have noted, for a long time as men of importance.

By the latter part of the fourth century the deacons had ceased to form the bishop's personal staff. As the presbyters take the place of the bishop in the churches of the "diocese," the deacons become their assistants as well, though this is not documented until about 500.[66] However, their relationship with the presbyters was never clearly defined. Vischer observes that this lack of definition caused repeated difficulties and rightly sees it as one of the major reasons for the decline of the diaconate in the middle ages.[67] With their increase in numbers and subordination to the presbyterate, deacons became a third order.

Cursum Honorum

FROM "HORIZONTAL," ORGANIC, TO "VERTICAL," HIERARCHICAL, STRUCTURE

By the end of the fourth century there was an extension of the clerical ministry above the level of diocesan bishop, together with an increase of the "minor orders." The earliest use of the term "metropolitan" is found in the fourth century.[68] Canons 4 and 6 of the Council of Nicaea mention them.[69] The suppression of the *chorepiscopoi*, mentioned earlier, is indicative of the developing status of the urban bishops. Canon 10 of Antioch, 341, provides that the *chorepiscopoi*, once on a par with other bishops, may ordain presbyters and deacons only with the consent of the bishop of the city to which he and his district are subject.[70] Bishops of provincial capitals developed status as metropolitans with the right of presiding in provincial councils and increasingly disassociated themselves from the local presbyteries, developing a sense of collegiality.[71] Canon 24 of Laodicea, 343–381, lists subdeacons, readers, singers, exorcists, and door-keepers as belonging to the "minor orders."[72] Natural to such a structure is the idea of a succession of grades onto which one moves from lower to higher.

The decline of the diaconate springs more from the development of the idea of *cursus honorum* than from any other single factor.[73] The model used by the Church would seem to be that of the organization of the Roman Empire.[74] The transformation here stands in marked contrast to the old organic structure of the Church and its ministry of the pre-Nicene period. Prior to the fourth century, as we have seen, the Church's ministry was one in which every person had a part and each functioned for the benefit of the whole. Offices were not thought of in terms of orders but in terms of functions, each related to the other. But by the end of the fourth century a radical transition has taken place in the structure of the Church's ministry, which has affected the basic character of the Church itself. The old "horizontal" concept and structure were replaced by one that is "vertical" and hierarchical. This structure has continued to the present time essentially unchanged, at least in Catholic Christendom.

It has been maintained that from the late fourth century onwards ordination to each of the successive offices was required. Bligh says that popes Siricius, Innocent I, and Zosimus "insisted on adherence to this orderly progressing through the lesser orders to the higher."[75] C. H. Turner states that a serious development of the fourth century was the idea "that the Christian clergy consisted of a hierarchy of grades through each of which it was *necessary* to pass in order to reach the higher offices."[76] However, the evidence does not support these views. It is true that the idea of *cursus honorum* grew up in the fourth century, and many, perhaps most, probably did go through the succession of grades. But it appears to have been a long time before the rule became binding.

Among the earliest references to holding the various offices in succession is that given by Cyprian. He writes regarding the character of Pope Cornelius, 251–253, that he "was not one who on a sudden attained to the episcopate; but, promoted through all the ecclesiastical offices, . . . he ascended by all the grades of religious service to the lofty summit of the Priesthood."[77] He then records that the episcopal office was forced upon him, refuting the detractors of Cornelius. Cyprian's point here is clearly to show that Cornelius had demonstrated his ability and his fitness for the office. Cyprian speaks of "grades of religious service," the context giving an entirely different perspective from that of rank, each of which was required in succession to reach the top, though the idea of a succession of grades is now present. We would recall that Cyprian himself had not so moved through each office.

Turner points to an inscription of Pope Damasus, 366–384, referring either to himself or his father as the earliest known case in point of *cursus honorum.*[78] However, the inscription simply reads, "Exceptor, lector, levite, sacerdos," which indicates no more than that he did hold these various offices. There seems to be no evidence to support the theory that he held these offices in succession because that was required.

Pope Siricius does state in a letter to Himerius, Bishop of Tarragona, c. 385, that those ordained are to go through the offices in succession. However, it is clearly not because there is any necessity for one to hold the various offices in themselves but rather "that through these periods the integrity of his life and of his faith has gained approbation."[79] The point is even clearer in Zosimus's letter to Hesychius, Bishop of Salonae, c. 418. Speaking of the widespread practice in Gaul, Africa, and Spain of admitting laymen to the priesthood in ways "contrary to the precepts of the Fathers," without spending sufficient time and undergoing discipline in the lower orders, he continues:

> For if secular offices bestow high position not on those who have just entered the vestibule of action but on the one who through time has been tested on very many levels, who can be found so arrogant, so impudent as, in the service of heaven (which should be given greater weight and, like gold, should be tested repeatedly in the fire), to desire to be a leader immediately when he has not previously been a recruit and to wish to teach before he learns?[80]

Pope Innocent I writes in a similar vein to Felix, first Bishop of Nuceria, c. 402:

> Let no one become lector, acolyte, deacon, or priest rapidly, for if they perform for a long time in the minor offices and their lives and their obedience are equally approved, thereafter let them come to the priesthood when the merits of their duties have been measured, and let them not carry off prematurely what an upright life deserves to receive.[81]

The evidence from these sources does not then indicate that a new sacramental requirement has been added. Baptism is still the only sacramental prerequisite for ordination to any office in the Church. The principle involved in the advice of these popes writing to their fellow bishops was not that of *cursus honorum* proper but rather that of fitness for office as set forth by Cyprian and stated in the conciliar decrees of the fourth century.

The first conciliar legislation on this point is that of the Council of Sardica, 343 or 344. Canon 2 of Nicaea legislated against recent converts who with little instruction are "straightway brought to the spiritual laver, and as soon as they have been baptized, are advanced to the episcopate or the presbyterate."[82] Canon 10 of Sardica develops this idea:

> If some rich man or professional advocate be desired for bishop, he be not ordained until he have fulfilled the ministry of reader, deacon, and presbyter, in order that, passing by promotion through the several grades, he may advance (if, that is, he be found worthy) to the height of the episcopate. And he shall remain in each order assuredly for no brief time, that so his faith, his reputable life, his steadfastness of character and considerateness of demeanour may be well-known, and that he, being deemed worthy of the divine sacerdotal office (sacerdotium, i.e., the episcopate) may enjoy the highest honour.[83]

The canon is directed against an abuse that had arisen and attempts to insure that only men qualified by service in the Church are ordained to positions of leadership. Wealth and success in other fields are inadequate qualifications for offices in the Church.

Ordination to the episcopate without passing through the "successive grades" apparently continued for a long time. Frequently deacons were ordained bishops without ever having been made presbyters, and the rule of Nicaea against ordaining recently baptized converts to the episcopate seems to have been frequently broken. Joseph Bingham observes that in the time of Gregory Nazianzus, made Bishop of Constantinople in 381 (d. c. 390), "this rule was frequently transgressed, without any reason or necessity."[84] Gregory, in his oration on Basil the Great, Bishop of Caesarea, d. 379, says that when Basil was made a bishop

> it was not by suddenly advancing him, nor by cleansing [baptising] and instructing him in wisdom at the same time, as is true of the majority of those today who aspire to the episcopate. He received the honour according to the law and order of spiritual advancement. [He explains that] the same holds true in military affairs: one is soldier, captain, general. This order is the best and most advantageous for subordinates. If the same system were in force in our case, it would be of great value.[85]

It is apparent that the system of *cursus honorum* was not yet in effect.

In 381 Nectarius was named successor to Gregory of Nazianzus as Patriarch of Constantinople.[86] Sozomen records that he was nominated by the Emperor when still unbaptized, though this fact seems to have been generally unknown until after the nomination. Nectarius was then baptized and apparently ordained bishop without intermediate orders:

> When at last consent had been given to the imperial mandate, Nectarius was baptized, and while yet clad in his white robes was proclaimed bishop of Constantinople by the unanimous voice of the synod.[87]

By being "proclaimed bishop" Sozomen apparently means that he was ordained, since he had just referred to the bishop's consent and he afterwards speaks of "the ordination of Nectarius."[88] Further, Socrates records that Nectarius was "seized upon by the people, and elected to the episcopate, and was ordained accordingly by one hundred and fifty bishops then present" at Constantinople.[89] It is worth noting that the Church of the third century or before would hardly have elected an unbaptized person bishop.

The fact that Ambrose, who was governor of Milan, was unbaptized when elected bishop of that city in 374 is well known. His former secretary and biographer, the deacon Paulinus,[90] tells us that when Ambrose finally agreed to the election he demanded baptism by a Catholic bishop and records,

> Thus, when he was baptized, he is said to have fulfilled all the ecclesiastical offices, so that he was consecrated bishop on the eighth day with the greatest favor and joy on the part of all.[91]

Ambrose himself says that his ordination as bishop was not according to the prescribed rule prohibiting a new convert being ordained to the episcopate:

> How I fought against being ordained! And, finally, when I was compelled, I tried at least to have the ordination deferred! But the prescribed rule did not avail, pressure prevailed. Yet the Western bishops approved my ordination by their decision, and the Eastern bishops, too, by their examples. Yet the ordination of a new convert is prohibited lest he be lifted up by pride. If the ordination was not postponed it was because of constraint, and if humility which is becoming to the priesthood is not wanting, where there is no cause, blame will not be imputed.[92]

Nowhere from the period does there seem to be any record of Ambrose having passed through each office on succeeding days or at all.

The most probable interpretation of this record in light of the evidence generally from the period would seem to be that baptism was still considered to be the only prerequisite for ordination to the episcopal office. Socrates says that the bishops present at Ambrose's election baptized him "for he was then but a catechumen" and were about to ordain him but he refused. The matter was referred to the Emperor Valentinian who sent word that they should "do the will of God by ordaining him. . . . Ambrose was therefore ordained."[93] Similar evidence is found in Theodoret's *Ecclesiastical History.*[94] To deduce from the evidence that after Ambrose was baptized he was consecrated bishop after "passing through various stages of the ecclesiastical hierarchy," as his recent biographer Angelo

Paredi and others do,[95] is reading back into the fourth century what was to become the custom. Neither Socrates nor Theodoret seems to be aware that intermediate steps are necessary in this case or others. Elsewhere, for example, Theodoret seems to make a special point of commending Athanasius for having done an admirable job in offices he had filled before election as a deacon to the see of Alexandria, again asserting the principle of fitness for office.[96]

John Chrysostom reports that Philogonius, Bishop of Antioch, 324, was "taken from the court of judicature and carried from the judge's bench to the bishop's throne."[97] Augustine in a letter, 423, describes how a young man, Antonius, who was only a reader and without experience in the "labours pertaining to the various degrees of rank in the clerical office," was accepted on his suggestion by the people of Fussala and apparently made bishop immediately without any other prior office.[98] In a letter to the Bishop of Thessalonica, c. 444, Pope Leo continues to teach the desirability though not the necessity of men proving themselves by serving in the various offices:

> After a lapse of time he who is to be ordained a priest or deacon *may* be advanced through all the ranks of the clerical office, and thus a man may have time to learn that of which he himself also is one day to be a teacher.[99]

Leo himself was apparently ordained bishop of Rome directly from the diaconate. Prosper of Aquitaine records that after the death of Bishop Sixtus IV the Church of Rome awaited the return of the "Deacon Leo" from a diplomatic mission to reconcile Aetius and Albinus in Gaul. "Then," he writes, "the Deacon Leo having performed his public commission, being presented with praise by his countrymen, was ordained 43rd Bishop of the Church of Rome."[100] Trevor Jalland in his biography of Leo is apparently unable to find any evidence for Leo's ever having been ordained presbyter. He described his election while still in deacon's orders and then says he "was consecrated Bishop of Rome on September 29th, A.D. 440."[101]

This custom apparently continued at Rome until at least the time of Gregory the Great, who succeeded Pelagius II in 590.[102] Gregory, a deacon, was chosen by "all the people" to succeed Pelagius. But Gregory strove to avoid the high office. Gregory of Tours recounts the ordination of the deacon Gregory like this:

> And when Gregory was making ready to go to a hiding place he was seized and brought by force to the church of the blessed apostle Peter and there he was consecrated to the duties of bishop and made pope

> of the city. Our deacon did not leave until Gregory returned from the port to become bishop; and he saw his ordination with his own eyes.[103]

James Barmby in the "Prolegomena" to his translation of Gregory's works also says that, after the Emperor's confirmation of Gregory's election had arrived in Rome and Gregory had been found, he was brought "to the church of St. Peter, and there at once ordained, on the 3rd of September, A.D. 590."[104]

Sixth century inscriptions on towers and some literary references record that deacons died in Gaul at sixty, seventy, or eighty years.[105] Alcuin, who was ordained deacon when about 35 years old and who died in the year 804 at about 75, was never ordained priest.[106] But such men increasingly become the exception. Orders gradually came to be regarded by and large as "rungs" in the clerical ladder through which one must go to attain the "full ministry" of the priesthood, with some few being "advanced" to the episcopate. It is to be noted that even this terminology of "full ministry" and "advanced," which we take for granted today, was foreign to the spirit of the pre-Nicene Church, though the idea of "advancing" began to develop in the latter part of this period.

Joseph Bingham appears to be correct in asserting that the practice of going through the several orders on successive days was a practice virtually unknown until the time of Photius, who became Patriarch of Constantinople in 858.[107] David Nicetas in his *Life of Ignatius* records that Photius was made a monk the first day, a reader the second, a subdeacon the third, a deacon on the fourth, a presbyter the fifth, and a patriarch on the sixth.[108] Bingham rightly points out that this practice was contrary to the true intent and meaning of the ancient canons "that men should continue some years in every order, to give some proof of their behaviour to the Church."[109]

Even though the requirement of passing through the various offices as a succession of grades appears to have come long after the fourth century, its basis was established in that century. The older practice simply seems to have lingered on. In the pre-Nicene Church the organic idea of the Church determined the procedure. The bishop was not conceived to be one who had all the powers and functions of the Church's ministry, "the full ministry." The Church and its Lord had these powers and functions. The bishop had his function in the body of the Church and was ordained to it, just as presbyters and deacons had theirs. In that age, though less so in the late third century, it would have seemed as much a violation of the principle of "order" for the deacon to fulfill the function of a presbyter as for the presbyter to act as a deacon,[110] though as we have seen the lines were not so clearly drawn and in urgent necessity deacons or presbyters sometimes assumed the function of the bishops. Even in the late fourth century the *Apostolic Constitutions* declares, "It is not lawful for any one of the other clergy to do the work of a deacon."[111]

The Profound Consequences

The shaping of the Church through a hierarchical structure in its clerical ministry from the plentitude of the greatest to the paucity of the least on the basis not of *diakonia* or service but of office has obscured the essential nature of the Church, so much so that we hardly comprehend the admonition that other clergy are not permitted to do the work of a deacon. The fundamental change was from the principle of organism to that of hierarchy in which the greatest is the sum of all its parts. The organic wholeness of the ministry of the local church was destroyed.[112]

Clericalism developed, bringing about such a distinction between the clergy and the laity that the latter have very little ministry and what there is seems to be derived from the clergy. The subtle but insidious nature of the transition is to be seen in the use of the adjective *laikos*. Originally in the New Testament, as we saw earlier, it meant "one of the people of God" and included all members of the Church. As a general term, it had come by the third century to mean "one of the people of God" who was not a clergyman. But by the fifth century it meant "profane."[113]

The Church which had affirmed the goodness of all creation and chosen words without sacred connotations to designate its officers in its primitive period now created a dichotomy. Illustrative of the distinction which arose between the sacred and the profane are the decrees of the Council of Laodicea, 343–381. Canon 24 provides

> No one of the priesthood, from presbyters to deacons, and so on in the ecclesiastical order to subdeacons, readers, singers, exorcists, doorkeepers, or any of the class of Ascetics, ought to enter a tavern.[114]

Canon 54 of the same council directs that "members of the priesthood and of the clergy must not witness the plays at weddings or banquets; but, before the players enter, they must rise and depart."[115]

The sacralization of the clergy in contrast to the laity is clearly in evidence by the middle of the fourth century. The clergy were set apart from the *laos* as "sacred" persons for whom the ordinary amusements of society are not appropriate. Lay persons apparently could freely enjoy such activities, but the clergy had become "holy" people in a world which was no longer seen to be unified by the immanence of God's presence permeating all things.

Celibacy

Celibacy and continence of the clergy is another manifestation and contributing cause of this distinction with its implied dualism. It is important not only due to its implication regarding the distinction between the sacred and the profane but because it was a major cause of the decline of the diaconate, as it became obligatory, particularly in the West.

When we look for Jewish antecedents in the Old Testament we find no instance of anyone voluntarily embracing a life of celibacy.[116] Celibacy is virtually unknown among the Jews. Marriage was a sacred duty in obedience to the command "increase and multiply."[117] The rabbis taught that men should marry by the age of about 18, and the Hebrew language does not even contain a word for "bachelor." Indeed, continence is permitted by the rabbinical schools for periods of only one to two weeks unless it is necessitated by a particular occupation.[118] When continence is practiced during military campaigns or by the Essenes, there seems to have been no suggestion that coitus was intrinsically evil.[119]

The author of the Pastoral Epistles expressly puts the prohibition against marriage in the class of "subversive doctrines inspired by devils" and describes it as a denial of the goodness of creation.[120] Nevertheless, there was a growing though not unanimous tendency in the early centuries in favor of continence or celibacy.

Clement of Alexandria, writing c. 200, sees the ideal of the Christian Gnostic as one who marries and has children, because he conquers more temptation and so comes to a higher excellence.[121] Though probably apocryphal, Clement also records Peter's last words to his wife as she was being led to martyrdom:

> They say, accordingly, that the blessed Peter, on seeing his wife led to death, rejoiced on account of her call and conveyance home, and called very encouragingly and comfortingly, addressing her by name, "Remember thou the Lord." Such was the marriage of the blessed, and their perfect disposition towards those dearest to them.[122]

Eusebius says that Clement wrote regarding the marriage of the apostles "on account of those who rejected marriage." He quotes Clement: "Or will they reject even the apostles? For Peter and Philip begat children; and Philip also gave his daughters in marriage."[123]

Tertullían agrees that marriage is good but maintains that celibacy is better.[124] In an apparent reference to 1 Timothy 2:2 and Titus 1:6 he says that Paul does not permit men "twice married" to preside over the Church.[125] In his work *On Monogamy* after his break with the Church, c. 207, he protests against Catholic clergy who are digamists, indicating that many clergy have been married a second time:

> Why, how many digamists, too, preside in your churches; insulting the apostle [Paul], of course; at all events, not blushing when these passages are read under their presidency.[126]

Hippolytus gives other evidence that digamy was not uncommon at that time but indicates it was contrary to the tradition. He writes unfavorably of Pope Callistus, 217–222:

> About the time of this man, bishops, priests, and deacons, who had been twice married, and thrice married, began [to be allowed] to retain their place among the clergy. If also, however, any one who is in holy orders should become married, [Callistus permitted] such a one to continue in holy orders as if he had not sinned.[127]

Clearly, Hippolytus believes that such marriages are sinful. But Hippolytus was dissenting from Callistus's teaching that a bishop who is guilty even of "[a sin] unto death" is not to be deposed. While Hippolytus does say that Callistus allowed those in orders to marry and retain their places "as if they had not sinned," it is not clear whether this is a reference to digamy or to the later requirement that men ordained before marriage must remain celibate.[128]

The Council of Elvira, c. 305, decreed the most ancient command of celibacy or, technically, continence for the clergy.[129] Its 33rd canon declared:

> Bishops, presbyters and deacons—indeed, all clerics who have a place in the ministry [of the altar]—shall abstain from their wives and shall not beget children—this is a total prohibition: whoever does so, let him forfeit his rank among the clergy.[130]

Schillebeeckx affirms that the question for many centuries was actually that of continence. He observes that the law of celibacy dates only from the twelfth century.[131] The requirement of Elvira is that the clergy are to "abstain from their wives" and "not beget children." The motivation lying behind the legislation not only of Elvira but of succeeding councils was "the unsuitability of sexuality for someone who stands at the altar, that is, the ancient motive of 'cultic purity'; the sacred and the 'impure' are mutually exclusive."[132] This is also the reason increasingly given in the writings of the fathers of the fourth century relating to continence of the clergy in contrast to that of monks, virgins, and widows.[133]

The implications here set the clergy apart as those who are distinct from and superior to others in the Church, those ordained being closest to God. Further, "cultic purity" brought about by continence ultimately carries with it the implication that sexual intercourse is in some way tainted. These ideas stand in marked contrast to those of the New Testament and generally of the pre-Nicene Church.

Conciliar decrees continue to legislate in a similar vein. Canon 10 of the Council of Ancyra, 314, provided that deacons who are unmarried at the time of their ordination but who state that they must marry "because they are not able to abide so" shall continue in their office after marrying, because the bishop had conceded it to them. But if any were silent on this and later marries, he shall "cease from the diaconate."[134]

A proposal was made at the Council of Nicaea, 325, forbidding bishops, presbyters, deacons, and possibly subdeacons who had been married at the time of their ordination from having intercourse with their wives.[135] The similarity of this proposal with Canon 33 of Elvira would lead to the conclusion that it was made by the Spanish bishop Hosius.[136] However, Bishop Paphnutius of a city in Upper Thebes, a confessor who had lost an eye in one of the persecutions and who had never been married, argued that marriage is honorable and that intercourse of a man with his wife is chaste. He thought it would be sufficient for those who had been unmarried when ordained to remain so according to what both Socrates and Sozomen report was said "to be the ancient tradition of the Church." The counsel of Bishop Paphnutius prevailed, and no law prescribing continence for the clergy was enacted at Nicaea.[137].

The anathema of the Council of Gangra, variously dated from 340 to 376, upon those maintaining that it is not lawful to partake of the Eucharist when the presbyter is married indicates the growing tendency towards clerical celibacy.[138] In this period Athanasius also defends the married state or at least optional celibacy when he writes to Dracontius, c. 355, contrasting first of all many bishops who have not married with monks who are the fathers of children and conversely bishops who are fathers of children and monks who are apparently celibate ("of the completest kind").[139]

Digamy is prohibited for bishops, priests, and deacons in the *Apostolic Constitutions* and the *Apostolic Canons*, both c. 375, and later at the Council of Orleans, c. 537.[140] Each of these also provides that one unmarried at the time of ordination must remain celibate.[141] However, the *Apostolic Canons* do not allow a bishop, priest, or deacon to "cast off his wife under pretense of piety."[142] A few years later, c. 413, Augustine teaches that second marriages are lawful for any, terming Tertullian and others heretical for teaching otherwise.[143]

Married bishops, priests, and deacons are required to refrain from intercourse with their wives under the penalty of deposition by the Councils of Carthage, 401; Orange, 441; and Orleans, c. 537.[144] However, though the historian Socrates is an Easterner, he does mention among the unusual customs of which he has heard that in Thessaly "if a clergyman in that country, after taking orders, should sleep with his wife, whom he had legally married before his ordination, he would be degraded." In the East he tells us that all clergy abstain from their wives, but they "do so of their own accord." He adds that there are many bishops among the clergy who have had children by their legal wives during their episcopates.[145]

The Eastern Church retained the fourth century practice regarding clerical celibacy. Celibacy there was gradually limited to bishops, who were usually chosen from among the monks. The rule of a single marriage for the other clergy was adhered to, the marriage taking place before ordination.[146] The final legislation in the Eastern Church on this subject was that of the Council of Trullo, 692.[147] Canon 13 of that Council explicitly states that presbyters, deacons, and subdeacons are not to be deprived of cohabitation and intercourse with their lawful wives and that no presbyter or deacon may dismiss his wife on the pretense of piety. It also refers to the rule of the Western Church regarding continence of married clergy, saying that lawful marriage by men in holy orders is "the ancient rule and apostolic perfection and order."[148]

It should not be assumed that the enforcement of celibacy was due solely to theological or ascetic reasons. In the sixth century, a decree by the Emperor Justinian prohibiting a man who had children from becoming a bishop and directing that a married cleric who became a bishop must live in continence gives evidence of a sociological reason—the problem of the Church's property being inherited by a cleric's children.[149] We see this again in the refusal of Pope Pelagius I, 557, to consent to the ordination of a bishop because the man was married and had children, who might inherit Church property. His consent was granted only with the provision that adequate security be provided for the Church's property.[150]

By the tenth century the problem had become far more acute. Lea, in his detailed history of celibacy, tells us that at this time "all possessions previously held by laymen on precarious tenure were rapidly becoming hereditary."[151] Society was in a chaotic transition period in which there was virtually universal disorder.[152] As centralized power eroded, property and offices became the property of those who held them, even though it may have been given to the Church. Under the feudal benefice system married clergy were succeeded in the benefice by their sons, who may have no interest in the welfare of the parish.[153] In addition, property formerly belonging to the Church also might be appropriated under the system by the clergy for such purposes as providing dowries for their daughters.[154]

The problem was far from theoretical. In 925 the Council of Tours decided in favor of two priests, Ronald and Raymond, father and son, in reference to their complaint against another priest for certain tithes. The Council awarded these tithes to them and their successors forever.[155] In the same century a bishop of Verona, Rathenius, implies that his clergy were all married[156] and objects to successive priest-fathers making their sons priests, begging them to rear their sons as laymen in order to protect the Church's property.[157] We see the extent of the laxity in society generally when the bishop says that were the canon on repeated marriages enforced only boys would remain in the Church.[158]

Pope Benedict VIII attempted to bring about reform c. 1018 through legislation aimed at preventing the alienation of Church property by the families of priests.[159] Under these canons marriage was forbidden to priests, deacons, and subdeacons, and they were not to cohabit with a woman. Children born to offenders were "declared to be forever serfs of the Church and could not be freed or granted rights of property inheritance."[160] However, in spite of this attempt at reform, Desidenius, Abbot of Monte Cassino who became Pope Victor III, reports that under Benedict IX, who was made pope in 1032 when reportedly only ten or twelve years old and brought the papacy to its lowest depths of degredation,[161] all clerical orders lived openly in marriage throughout Italy.[162] Conditions elsewhere in the West appear to have been similar so far as clerical marriage was concerned.

The papacy, especially under Hildebrand, became determined to free the Church from the feudal benefice system as well as to enforce the law of celibacy for ascetic or theological reasons.

Following the marked success of Hildebrand as Pope Gregory VII, 1073–1085, in enforcing celibacy among the clergy, the final stage in the struggle for celibacy in the West came when the First and Second Lateran Councils of 1123 and 1139 declared clerical marriage invalid instead of only illicit.[163] The Reformation of the sixteenth century ended celibacy in the West in those churches not adhering to Rome. But only in our own time has the Roman Catholic Church begun to relax the rule. The Second Vatican Council provided:

> With the consent of the Roman Pontiff, this diaconate will be able to be conferred on men of more mature age, even upon those living in the married state. It may also be conferred upon suitable young men. For them, however, the law of celibacy must remain intact.[164]

Celibacy, then, began as a voluntary act for the sake of the Kingdom of God. Gradually, it was reinterpreted to be a superior state. In the fourth century restrictions began to be placed on clerical marriage, which eventually in the West developed into compulsory celibacy and were an important factor contributing to the decline of the diaconate in the Middle Ages. In writing of the change in the diaconate from an office which he sees to have been more important than the priesthood in many respects in the early centuries to one that was "merely a step on the way to the priesthood," Vischer states,

> One essential feature of the transformation of the office of deacon was that celibacy became a binding rule for deacons—at any rate in the Western Church.[165]

With the development of an hierarchical structure in which the "higher" order contained within itself the "lower," what point was there for men who had to commit themselves in either case to abstain from one of the strongest and most fundamental of all human desires, that of sex and procreation, to aspire only to the "lower?" Celibacy was no doubt not the only cause for the diaconate to wane and probably not so important as the change in the theology of the nature of the Church, but certainly it was a major factor. Without this rule married men would have continued to offer themselves to the Church for this office and would almost certainly have enabled it to retain at least many of the distinctive functions which are essential to its integrity and vitality. Even today, the Roman Catholic Church has tacitly recognized the importance of celibacy as a deterrent to the diaconate by relaxing the rule of celibacy in the restoration of the office of deacon as a "permanent" vocation. It could do so because celibacy has always been a matter of discipline and not of doctrine in the Church. Pope Paul VI in his encyclical on celibacy, *Sacerdotalis caelibatus*, 24 June 1967, reaffirmed the traditional position regarding the celibate state but conceded that celibacy is not demanded by the nature of the priesthood.[166]

Theological Implications of Celibacy

The development of compulsory celibacy for the clergy was inseparably related to the breakdown of the old organic concept and structure of the Church. It appears to be in part a result but also a facilitating factor in this breakdown. So long as all the people of God were seen to possess and together constitute the Church's ministry, the kind of distinctions we have discussed between members of the Church (clergy and laity) were unlikely to occur. However, as the ministry came increasingly to be conceived in terms of the clergy, it became far easier to draw lines and set some people, places, and things aside as being more sacred. Compulsory clerical celibacy is one of the major ways in which such distinctions were made. In light of this it is not difficult to see why the old functional idea of the Church's ministry being shared by all the people of God would give way to one in which it is summed up in, if not possessed by, the clergy.

But the implications are much broader for the Church and its ministry today. The Church, which had at the outset affirmed the inherent goodness and unity of all creation, gradually adopted a dualistic distinction between the sacred and the profane. The clergy who were once laity like any others, though with distinct functions, became sacred persons apart from the laity. The inherent goodness of at least parts of the material world was denied. By implication spiritual things were the things which were good and not simply of a higher order and of prime importance. Much of the material world and many of the concerns of daily life were relegated to the realm of the profane.

The implications of this dualistic position gradually came to fruition as the centuries passed. The effect of the clergy and "religious" being considered to belong to the "sacred," marked off particularly by celibacy, and the laity to the "secular" or "profane," was to degrade the laity and implied for them a lower standard of morality, particularly one which allowed marriage. The counsels of perfection seemed to apply essentially to the clergy and the "religious." Still today in the minds of many Christians full commitment to Christ means joining the ranks of the clergy or the "religious." Even the use (or misuse?) of the word "religious" in this way implies this kind of attitude.

In American Christianity in general the ultimate conclusion of the subtle change which took place in the early Church is perhaps to be seen in the puritanism of the Victorian era. The modern concept of God as one who is concerned with "spiritual things" is perhaps the most tragic result of this course, because God is left out of most of real life. This divorce of God from "non-spiritual" things is directly related to human sexuality, marriage, and intimacy.

In the Christian West the best and highest kind of life came to be seen as that of the priest or those belonging to monastic or "religious" orders. Such vocations were to "sacred" callings, which were set in contrast to "secular" vocations. And it is noteworthy that the one way in which these vocations were always different from those of others is that they did involve a commitment to celibacy. Celibacy seems to be the primary thing symbolizing an inherent or implicit denial of the goodness of the physical world.

Celibacy thus became a great symbol of the ideal regarding human sexuality. Symbol is used here as defined by Urban Holmes, as a powerful representation that has many meanings and evokes many feelings.[167] Gibson Winter emphasizes the importance of symbols:

> . . . Man is the symbolic being who is shaped by symbol and, in turn, reshapes symbols and thus remakes his world. The power of symbol rests, however, on the power of sociality, which it expresses, extends, and serves to renew. Participating in symbols, sharing a world through them, means participating in the relational character of man's being which has been expressed, enriched, and empowered through these symbols.[168]

Sexuality itself can be classified as an archetypal symbol and is among the most powerful for humanity.[169]

In a very real sense celibacy became the symbol of sexuality in the concept of the "fully committed," which was looked upon as the "ideal" Christian life in Western civilization. Though the reformers of the sixteenth century abolished compulsory celibacy, the influence of tradition and the continuing practice of the Roman Catholic Church rendered their efforts only partially successful. An important strain of Anglican spirituality in the nineteenth century, and up into the 1950s at least, tended to regard the monastic or "religious" life as in some sense an ideal. The existence of its married clergy and Article 32 of its 39 Articles of Religion, which declared that "Bishops, Priests, and Deacons, are not by God's Law, either to vow the estate of single life, or to abstain from marriage" but shall at their own discretion "judge the same to serve better to godliness,"[170] served to mute overt teaching exalting celibacy as the preferred way. But Protestantism along with Anglicanism did do away with the symbol of celibacy, which was important and in the long run has worked towards correcting the problem.

However, the sixteenth century reformers failed to recognize and correct the underlying dualistic attitudes separating the "sacred" and the "secular," the "spiritual" and the "material," which we saw emerging in the early Church. Calvinism, which heavily influenced all of Western Christianity and especially American Christianity, in fact broadened this cleavage. The puritanical attitudes, which came to prevail in American Christianity and culture and reached their zenith in the nineteenth and early twentieth centuries, by implication denied the goodness of much that was beautiful or pleasurable. Though the symbol of celibacy was abandoned, the content was retained.

The Diaconate: A Vestigial Remnant

As the diaconate lost its importance, it was increasingly restricted to liturgical functions.[171] A detailed history of its decline over the centuries to become a vestigial remnant in modern times of the great diaconate of the early Church is of slight interest and has little relevance for today or implication for renewal. Therefore, after a brief summary of diaconal functions we will turn to consider the restoration of the diaconate in the Church of the late twentieth century as the separate and equal order it was originally. The implications of such a restoration are broad and important for the total life of the Church, far more extensive than would appear initially.

A Summary of Diaconal Functions with Date and Source

The functions of the diaconate as that office developed in the Church, along with the date and source of the earliest reference, are listed below. It is to be remembered that generally the function was exercised by the deacon prior to the reference, sometimes probably considerably earlier.

PRE-NICENE

	1.	*Symbolize the servant-ministry of the Church.*
c. 95	2.	Possibly constitute with the bishops the ruling council in some churches. (*Didache*, also Ignatius and Polycarp)
c. 96	3.	Administer the distribution of alms to the poor and needy. (*Shepherd of Hermas*)
c. 115	4.	Symbolize Jesus Christ. (Ignatius)
c. 115	5.	Be the Servant of the *Church*. (Ignatius, also Polycarp)
c. 115	6.	Function liturgically at the Eucharist. (Clear in Ignatius, though probable in the *Didache*, c. 95)
c. 150	7.	Administer the Eucharistic Bread and Wine to *all* present. (Justin Martyr)
c. 150	8.	Take Eucharistic Bread and Wine to absent. (Justin Martyr)
c. 200	9.	Be the "eye" of the bishop in all matters but especially in discovering the pastoral needs of the people. (*Pseudo-Clementines*)
c. 200	10.	Keep order in the Christian meetings. (*Pseudo-Clementines*)
c. 200	11.	Report the sick to the *congregation* for their visits and help. (*Pseudo-Clementines*)
c. 200	12.	Baptize on a par with presbyters with the bishop's authorization. (Tertullian)
c. 215	13.	Instruct the people at weekday non-Eucharistic assemblies. (Hippolytus)
c. 215	14.	Assist with the oils of exorcism and thanksgiving at baptism. (Hippolytus)
c. 215	15.	Bring the people's oblations to the bishop and probably arrange them at the Eucharist. (Hippolytus)

c. 215 16. Bless non-Eucharistic bread at Christian fellowship meals in the bishop's absence. (Hippolytus)

c. 215 17. Administer the chalice *only* in Hippolytus, but probably in most places continues to administer the Bread also until sometime in the fourth century. (Hippolytus)

c. 215 18. Be the servant of the bishop. (Hippolytus)

c. 235 19. Guard the doors and keep order among the people at the Eucharist. (*Didascalia*)

c. 235 20. Announce a bidding to the people at the Eucharist. (*Didascalia*)

c. 235 21. Judge disputes with the presbyters between members of the Church. (*Didascalia*)

c. 235 22. Function as full-time, paid servants of the Church. (*Didascalia*)

c. 306 23. On occasion, head small, rural congregations. (Elvira)

c. 314 24. On occasion, preside at the Eucharist, probably under extraordinary circumstances and in the absence of a bishop (or presbyter?). (Forbidden at Arles)

AFTER NICAEA

c. 380 25. Announce various stages of the Eucharist. (*Apostolic Constitutions*)

c. 380 26. Read the Gospel at the Eucharist. (*Apostolic Constitutions*)

c. 380 27. Bid the prayers of the people at the Eucharist. (*Apostolic Constitutions*)

c. 380 28. Announce the kiss of peace. (*Apostolic Constitutions*)

c. 384 29. Bless the paschal candle. (Jerome)

These functions are pastoral, charitable, and liturgical, connecting and illustrating the interrelation of these activities of the Church in its ongoing life. The deacon is par excellence the embodiment of the ministry of Christ in the world.

NOTES

1. Edward Landon, *A Manual of Councils of the Holy Catholic Church* (London: Griffith Farrar & Co., n.d.), 1:44.

2. Theodoret, *Ecclesiastical History* 1.25, in vol. 3: *Theodoret, Jerome and Grennadius, Rufinius Historical Writings etc.*, in *Nicene and Post-Nicene Fathers*

of the Christian Church, Second Series, ed. Philip Schaff and Henry Wace, 14 vol. (Grand Rapids, Mi.: William B. Eerdmans Publishing Co., 1953), 3:61.

3. Ibid.

4. Ibid., 3:60–61.

5. J. Stevenson, ed., *A New Eusebius: Documents Illustrative of the Church to* A.D. *337* (New York: Macmillan, 1957), p. 324. Cf. Charles Joseph Hefele, vol. 1: *A History of the Christian Councils, from the Original Documents to the Close of the Council of Nicaea,* A.D. *325,* trans. William R. Clark, in *A History of the Councils of the Church* (Edinburgh: T. & T. Clark [2nd ed., rev.], 1894), 1:194.

6. Hefele, *History of the Councils,* 1:193. Stevenson (*A New Eusebius,* p. 324) numbers this Canon 16. R. P. Symonds, "Deacons in the Early Church," *Theology* 58 (London: 1955): 412, supports deacons so offering by stating that Tertullian in *De exhort. Cast.* 7 taught that laymen could offer the Eucharist under exceptional circumstances: "Accordingly, where there is no joint session of the ecclesiastical Order, you offer and baptize, and are priest, alone for yourself. But where three are, a Church is, albeit they be laics. . . . Therefore, if you have the *right* of a priest in your own person, in cases of necessity, it behoves you to have likewise the discipline of a priest wherever it may be necessary to have the right of a priest." (*On Exhortation to Chastity,* in vol. 4: *Tertullian, Part Fourth; Minucius Felix; Commodian; Origen, Parts First and Second,* in *The Ante-Nicene Fathers: Translations of the Writings of the Fathers down to* A.D. *325,* ed. Alexander Roberts and James Donaldson, Amer. rep. ed. A. Cleveland Coxe (Grand Rapids, Mi.: William B. Eerdmans Publishing Co., 1956), 4:54. However, *On Exhortation to Chastity* was probably written shortly before Tertullian's conversion to Montanism. Earlier, in his pre-Montanist *The Prescription against Heretics* 41, he forcibly rejects the idea.

7. Walter Howard Frere, "Early Forms of Ordination," in *Essays on the Early History of the Church and the Ministry by Various Writers,* ed. H. B. Swete (London: Macmillan & Co. [2nd ed.], 1921), p. 304.

8. George H. Williams, "The Ministry of the Ante-Nicene Church (c. 125–325)," in *The Ministry in Historical Perspective,* ed. H. Richard Niebuhr and Daniel D. Williams (New York: Harper & Brothers, 1956), p. 58 (hereafter cited "Ante-Nicene").

9. Ambrosiaster (Pseudo-Augustini), *Quaestiones Veteris et Novi Testamenti CXXVII 101,* trans. Alexander Souter, in *Corpus Scriptorum Ecclesiasticorum Latinorum,* vol. 50 (1908) (New York: Johnson Reprint Corp. [reprint], 1963), 50:193–98.

10. Jerome, *Letter* 146.2, in vol. 5: *Early Latin Theology,* trans. S. L. Greenslade, in Library of Christian Classics (Philadelphia: Westminster Press, 1956), 5:388. The number of deacons at Rome had been fixed at seven in accord with Acts 6.

11. John Bligh, "Deacons in the Latin West since the Fourth Century," *Theology* 58 (London: 1955): 423. Cf. "Introduction," to Jerome, *Letter* 146, in *Early Latin Theology,* 5:384.

12. Jerome, *Letter* 146, in *Early Latin Theology,* 5:384.

13. Charles Joseph Hefele, vol. 4: *A History of the Councils of the Church, from the Original Documents,* A.D. *451 to* A.D. *680,* trans. William R. Clark, in *A History of the Councils of the Church* (Edinburgh: T. & T. Clark, 1895), 4:454.

14. Dom Gregory Dix, "The Ministry in the Early Church c. A.D. 90–410," in

The Apostolic Ministry: Essays on the History and Doctrine of Episcopacy, ed. Kenneth E. Kirk (London: Hodden & Stoughton, 1946), p. 283.

15. A. J. MacDonald, *A Life of Gregory VII* (London: Methuen & Co., 1932), pp. 58, 89, 92, 95.

16. John William Bowden, *The Life and Pontificate of Gregory the Seventh* (New York: J. R. Dunham, 1845), p. 89. It is of interest to note that the controversy centered on marriage of the clergy and money, the Archbishop Guido and many of the clergy of Milan being married.

17. Dom Gregory Dix, *The Shape of the Liturgy* (Westminster: Dacre Press, 1945), p. 34. Cf. Dix, "Ministry in the Early Church," pp. 283–85, and George H. Williams, "The Ministry in the Later Patristic Period (314–451)," in *The Ministry in Historical Perspective,* p. 60 (hereafter cited "Later Patristic"). Also, Massey H. Shepherd, *The Church in the Fourth Century,* lectures at the Graduate School of Theology, Sewanee, Tn., 1970.

18. Dix, "Ministry in the Early Church," pp. 187–90, 291–95. Cf. A. G. Hebert, *Apostle and Bishop: A Study of the Gospel, the Ministry and the Church-Community* (New York: Seabury Press, 1963), p. 66.

19. Williams, "Ante-Nicene," p. 58.

20. Stevenson, *A New Eusebius,* p. 363. It might also be noted that there seems to be little concept of the indelibility of orders here, the offending deacon to be "put out of the diaconate."

21. Kenneth Scott Latourette, *A History of Christianity,* vol. 1: *To* A.D. *1500* (New York: Harper & Row [paperback], 1975), p. 185.

22. Dix, *Shape of the Liturgy,* p. 33.

23. Ibid., pp. 33–34.

24. Dom Gregory Dix, ed., "Textual Materials," in *The Treatise on the Apostolic Tradition of St. Hippolytus of Rome* (London: S.P.C.K., 1937), p. lxxx (hereafter cited *Hippolytus*).

25. Dix, *Hippolytus,* 24.2, p. 44; Cf. "Textual Notes," in Dix, *Hippolytus,* p. 82.

26. Dix, *Shape of the Liturgy,* p. 29.

27. Dix, *Hippolytus,* p. lxxx. Dix states that the *only* difference in liturgical function between the presbyters and deacons in this document which he can see is in the presbyters' joining in the laying on of hands at ordination. This seems an overstatement in view of his maintaining that in Hippolytus the presbyters did concelebrate, which deacons are not allowed to do. See also in his edition of *Hippolytus,* "Textual Notes," p. 82, and in *Shape of the Liturgy,* p. 34, where the same point is made.

28. In vol. 14: *The Seven Ecumenical Councils,* ed. Henry R. Percival, in *Nicene and Post-Nicene Fathers,* Second Series (1956), 14:63.

29. Dix, *Shape of the Liturgy,* p. 34, finds the first reference to the practice in Cyprian, *Epistle* 5.2. But Cyprian is here addressing both his presbyters and deacons from his retirement in the Decian persecution of 250, and directs only that they "should in my stead discharge my duty, in respect of doing those things which are required for the religious administration." This certainly is not a clear reference.

30. Dix, "Ministry in the Early Church," p. 281.

31. Massey H. Shepherd, Jr., "Priests in the NT.," in *The Interpreter's Dictionary of the Bible,* ed. George A. Buttrick, 4 vol. (New York: Abingdon Press,

1962), 3:891; Tertullian, *On Baptism* 17, in vol. 3: *Latin Christianity: Its Founder, Tertullian,* in *Ante-Nicene Fathers* (1957), 3:677; Hippolytus, *Refutation of All Heresies* 1."Preface," in vol. 5: *Fathers of the Third Century: Hippolytus, Cyprian, Caius, Novation, Appendix,* in *Ante-Nicene Fathers* (1951), 5:10.

32. Dix, "Ministry in the Early Church," p. 282. Cf. Williams, "Ante-Nicene," p. 29, and Dix, *Shape of the Liturgy,* p. 34.

33. Dix, *Shape of the Liturgy,* pp. 29–34.

34. See *Webster's New World Dictionary,* s.v. "Priest."

35. Dix, "Ministry in the Early Church," p. 282 fn.

36. Optatus, *Against the Donatists* 1.13, in *The Work of Optatus, Bishop of Milevis, Against the Donatists,* trans. O. R. Vassall-Phillips (London: Longmans, Green & Co., 1971), p. 26.

37. Dix, "Ministry in the Early Church," p. 282 fn.

38. Dix, *Shape of the Liturgy,* p. 34.

39. Williams, "Later Patristic," p. 60.

40. Hefele, *History of the Councils,* 1:17–18.

41. Arthur W. Haddan, "Chorepiscopus," in *A Dictionary of Christian Antiquities,* ed. William Smith and Samual Cheetham (Hartford: J. B. Burr, 1880), 1:354. In the West they are not mentioned until the next century at the Council of Riez.

42. Williams, "Ante-Nicene," pp. 57, 59.

43. *Council of Ancyra,* in *Nicene and Post-Nicene Fathers,* Second Series, 14:68. See also Canon 14 of Neocaesarea, in *Nicene and Post-Nicene Fathers,* Second Series, 14:85.

44. *Council of Nicaea,* in *Nicene and Post-Nicene Fathers,* Second Series, 14:19–20.

45. J. W. C. Wand, *A History of the Early Church to* A.D. *500,* (London: Methuen & Co. [3rd ed.], 1949), p. 119. Hefele (*History of the Councils,* 1:18) says the office of *chorepiscopus* had been abolished by the Council of Chalcedon in 451 but was reestablished in the middle ages in the form of bishops without dioceses. However, Hadden (1:354) believes the office continued until the ninth century in the East and the tenth in the West. George Williams says that the earliest reference to rural *presbyters* is in Dionysius of Alexandria (d. c. 265), preserved in Eusebius's *Church History* 7.24.6 (in *Nicene and Post-Nicene Fathers,* Second Series, 1:309), but that, though probable, it is not certain that they had only *ad hoc* sacerdotal powers (Williams, "Ante-Nicene," p. 57).

46. Jerome, *Epistle* 146 *To Evangelus,* in vol. 6: *St. Jerome: Letters and Select Works,* trans. G. Martley, in *Nicene and Post-Nicene Fathers,* Second Series (1954), 6:288.

47. See this chap., "The Presbyter Becomes a Bishop (Almost?)."

48. J. B. Lightfoot, *St. Paul's Epistle to the Philippians* (Grand Rapids, Mi.: Zondervan Publishing House, 1963 [reprint of 1913 ed.]), p. 231.

49. Lightfoot, p. 232. Massey Shepherd wrote in a personal communication to the author, "To my knowledge the only bishop in Egypt until the second half of the third century was that of Alexandria. The Bishop of Alexandria was a peculiarly 'pope-patriarch' who ruled as a monarch over his domain of Egypt and Libya, ordaining bishops for churches as he willed."

50. Ibid.

51. Hippolytus, *Apostolic Tradition* 8, in Burton Scott Easton, trans. and ed.,

The Apostolic Tradition of Hippolytus: Translated into English with Introduction and Notes (Cambridge: The University Press, 1934), p. 37 (hereafter cited *Apostolic Tradition of Hippolytus*).

52. Hefele, *History of the Councils*, 1:185.

53. Ibid., 1:185, 1:195.

54. Ibid., 1:422–23. Though this canon was adopted as Canon 21 of Antioch in 341, Hefele observes that it was frequently broken.

55. Augustine, *On Baptism, Against the Donatists* 1.1.2, in vol. 4: *St. Augustin: The Writings Against the Manichaeans and Against the Donatists*, in *Nicene and Post-Nicene Fathers of the Christian Church, A Select Library of the*, First Series, ed. Philip Schaff, 14 vol. (Grand Rapids, Mi.: William B. Eerdmans Publishing Co., 1956), 4:411–12.

56. *Council of Nicaea*, in *Nicene and Post-Nicene Fathers*, Second Series, 14:13.

57. *Apostolic Constitutions* 2.28, in vol. 7: *Lactantius, Venantius, Asterius, Victorinus, Dionysius, Apostolic Teaching and Constitutions, Homily, and Liturgies*, in *Ante-Nicene Fathers* (1951), 7:411.

58. Hebert, p. 67. Cf. Dix, *Shape of the Liturgy*, p. 34.

59. *Apostolic Constitutions* 8.46, in *Ante-Nicene Fathers*, 7:499; Jerome, *Epistle to Evangelus* 146.1, in *Nicene and Post-Nicene Fathers*, Second Series, 6:289; John Chrysostom, *Homily* 11, 1 Tim. 3:8–10, in vol. 13: *Saint Chrysostom: Homilies on Galatians, Ephesians, Philippians, Colossians, Thessalonians, Timothy, Titus, and Philemon*, in *Nicene and Post-Nicene Fathers*, First Series, 13:441.

60. Jerome, *Epistle to Evangelus* 146.1, in *Nicene and Post-Nicene Fathers*, Second Series, 6:288–89.

61. Chrysostom, *Homily* 11, 1 Tim. 3:8–10, in *Nicene and Post-Nicene Fathers*, First Series, 13:441.

62. Williams, "Later Patristic," p. 62.

63. Lightfoot, p. 99. References are to Pelagius on Phil. 1:1; 1 Tim. 3:12; Tit. 1:7; Theodore of Mopsuestia on Phil. 1:1; Tit. 1:7; and especially 1 Tim. 3; and Theodoret on Phil. 1:1; 1 Tim. 3:1f; and Tit. 1:7.

64. Ambrosiaster, 101.5, *Pseudo-Augustini, Quaestiones Veteris et Novi Testamenti* CXXVII, trans. Alexander Souter, in *Corpus Scriptorum Ecclesiasticorum*, vol. 50 (New York: Johnson Reprint Corp. [reprint of 1908 ed.], 1963), 50:196.

65. Ibid., 101.4, 50:195–96.

66. Williams, "Later Patristic," p. 63. Cf. T. G. Jalland, "The Doctrine of the Parity of Ministers," in *The Apostolic Ministry: Essays on the History and the Doctrine of Episcopacy*, ed. Kenneth E. Kirk (London: Hodden & Stoughton, 1946), p. 347.

67. Lukas Vischer, "The Problem of the Diaconate," in *The Ministry of Deacons*, ed. Department of Faith and Order (Geneva: World Council of Churches, 1965), p. 25.

68. A. J. Maclean, "Ministry (Early Christian)," in *Encyclopedia of Religion and Ethics*, ed. James Hastings (New York: Charles Scribner's Sons, 1916), p. 666.

69. *Council of Nicaea*, in *Nicene and Post-Nicene Fathers*, Second Series, 14:11, 15.

70. In *Nicene and Post-Nicene Fathers*, Second Series, 14:113.

71. Williams, "Ante-Nicene," p. 59.

72. *Council of Laodicea,* in *Nicene and Post-Nicene Fathers,* Second Series, 14:144.
73. Dix, "Ministry in the Early Church," p. 284.
74. Frere, p. 306.
75. Bligh, pp. 421–22.
76. C. H. Turner, "The Organization of the Church," in *The Cambridge Medieval History,* ed. H. M. Gwatkin (Cambridge: University Press, 1936), 1:150. (Italics added.)
77. Cyprian, *Epistle* 51.8, in *Ante-Nicene Fathers,* 5:329.
78. Turner, p. 151.
79. Siricius, *Ep. 1 to Himerius* 13, 14 (Cap. 9 and 10), in *Patrologiae Latinorum,* ed. J. P. Migne (Paris: n.p., 1845), 13:1142–43.
80. Zosimus, *Ep. 9 to Hesychius* 2 (Cap. 1), in *Patrologiae Latinorum,* 20:671.
81. Innocent 1, *Ep. 37 to Felix* 6 (Cap. 5), in *Patrologiae Latinorum,* 20:604–05.
82. *Council of Nicaea,* in *Nicene and Post-Nicene Fathers,* Second Series, 14:10. It may be noted that Canon 80 of the *Apostolic Canons,* probably c. 550, is similar to this canon of Nicaea (*Ante-Nicene Fathers,* 7:505).
83. *Council of Sardica,* in *Nicene and Post-Nicene Fathers,* Second Series, 14:424–25. Canon 20 of the disciplinary canons of the Council of Braga, 563, also described the rule of going through successive offices (Hefele, *History of the Councils,* 4:386).
84. Joseph Bingham, vol. 1: *The Antiquities of the Christian Church, Books I–III,* in *The Works of Joseph Bingham,* ed. R. Bingham (London: Oxford University Press [new ed.], 1855), 2.10.4, 1:127.
85. Gregory Nazianzen, *Oration on St. Basil the Great* 25, 26, in vol. 22: *Funeral Orations by St. Gregory Nazianzen and St. Ambrose,* trans. Leo P. McCauley, in *Fathers of the Church* (New York: Fathers of the Church, Inc., 1953), 22:50.
86. The manner of his election is uncertain. Theodoret says he was selected by the members of the Council of Constantinople meeting in 381 (*Ecclesiastical History* 5.8, in *Nicene and Post-Nicene Fathers,* Second Series, 3:136). Socrates refers to his having been elected by the people themselves (*Ecclesiastical History* 5.8, in vol. 2: *Socrates, Sozomenus: Church Histories,* in *Nicene and Post-Nicene Fathers,* Second Series [1952], 2:121).
87. Sozomen, *Ecclesiastical History, A History of the Church in Nine Books from* A.D. *324 to* A.D. *440,* trans. (not given), in *The Greek Ecclesiastical Historians of the First Six Centuries of the Christian Era* (London: Samuel Bagster & Sons, 1846), p. 333.
88. Ibid.
89. Socrates, *Ecclesiastical History* 5.8, in *Nicene and Post-Nicene Fathers,* Second Series, 2:121.
90. Altaner dates Paulinus's biography c. 422 (in Berthold Altaner, *Patrology,* trans. Hilda C. Garef [New York: Herder and Herder, 1960], p. 445). Cf. John A. Lacy, "Introduction," to "Life of St. Ambrose by Paulinus," in vol. 15: *Early Christian Biographies,* in *The Fathers of the Church,* 15:27, 28.
91. Paulinus, *Life of St. Ambrose* 3.9, in *The Fathers of the Church,* 15:38.
92. Ambrose, *Epistle* 59, *To the Church at Vercelli,* in vol. 26: *Saint Ambrose Letters,* trans. Mary Melchior Beyenka, in *The Fathers of the Church,* 26:345.

The translator indicates that Ambrose probably has Nectarius's ordination as Bishop of Constantinople in mind by his reference to the examples of the Eastern bishops, Ambrose having mentioned this in his *Epistle* 42, *To Theodosius*, given on 26:220.

93. Socrates, *Ecclesiastical History* 4.30, in *Nicene and Post-Nicene Fathers*, Second Series, 2:113–14.

94. Theodoret, *Ecclesiastical History* 4.6, in *Nicene and Post-Nicene Fathers*, Second Series, 3:111.

95. Angelo Paredi, *Saint Ambrose His Life and Times*, trans. M. Joseph Costelloe (Notre Dame, In.: University of Notre Dame Press, 1964), p. 124. Others maintaining this are: Frederick W. Farrar, *Lives of the Fathers* (Edinburgh: Adam and Charles Black, 1884), 2:120; Dix, "The Ministry in the Early Church," p. 284.

96. Theodoret, *Ecclesiastical History* 1.25, in *Nicene and Post-Nicene Fathers*, Second Series, 3:61.

97. John Chrysostom, *Contra Anomoeos*, "De Beato Philogonio" 6, in *Patrologia sive Latinorum sive Graecorum*, 48:752.

98. Augustine, *Epistle* 209.3, in vol. 1: *St. Augustine's Prologemena, Confessions, Letters*, in *Nicene and Post-Nicene Fathers*, First Series, 1:560.

99. Leo, *Epistle* 6.6, *To Anastasius*, in vol. 12: *The Letters and Sermons of Leo the Great*, trans. Charles Lett Feltoe: *The Book of Pastoral Rule and Selected Epistles of Gregory the Great*, trans. James Barmby, in *Nicene and Post-Nicene Fathers*, Second Series (1956), 12:6.

100. Prosper of Aquitaine, *Chronicon*, A.D. 440, in *Monumenta Germaniae Historica*, ed. G. H. Pertz et al. (Berlin and Hanover: n.p., 1826), 1:478.

101. Trevor Jalland, *The Life and Times of St. Leo the Great* (London: S.P.C.K., 1941), pp. 37–38. Charles Feltoe in his "Introduction" (in *Nicene and Post-Nicene Fathers*, Second Series, 12:vi) says that Leo was ordained both priest and Bishop of Rome on 29 September 440. However, no reference is given, and it would appear this is a supposition.

102. Altaner, pp. 556–57.

103. Gregory, Bishop of Tours, *History of the Franks*, trans. Ernest Brehaut (New York: Columbia University Press, 1916), pp. 227–28.

104. James Barmby, "Prolegomena," to *The Book of Pastoral Rule and Selected Epistles of Gregory the Great*, in *Nicene and Post-Nicene Fathers*, Second Series, 12:xvi, xvii.

105. Bligh, p. 422. Bligh says (p. 421) that "at the beginning of the 4th century the diaconate had already become a step in the ecclesiastical *cursus honorum*," but this appears to be almost a century too early as a widespread practice and even much more than that as a sacramental requisite.

106. Eleanor Shipley Duckett, *Alcuin, Friend of Charlemagne* (New York: Macmillan Co., 1951), pp. 26, 304.

107. Bingham, p. 131.

108. David Nicetas Paphlago, *Vita s. Ignatii*, in *Patrologiae sive Latinorum, sive Graecorum*, ed. J. P. Migne (Belgium: Brepols, n.d.), 105:511–12.

109. Bingham, p. 132.

110. Dix, "Ministry in the Early Church," p. 284.

111. *Apostolic Constitutions* 8.28, in *Ante-Nicene Fathers*, 7:494.

112. Williams, "Ante-Nicene," p. 29.

113. Dix, "Ministry in the Early Church," p. 285.

114. *Council of Laodicea,* in *Nicene and Post-Nicene Fathers,* Second Series, 14:144. Canon 21 of Laodicea (ibid., 14:140) states that "the subdeacons have no right to a place in the Diaconicum, nor to touch the Lord's vessels." Hefele (Charles Joseph Hefele, in vol. 2: *A History of the Councils of the Church, from the Original Documents,* A.D. *326 to* A.D. *429,* trans. Henry N. Oxenham, in *A History of the Councils of the Church* [Edinburgh: T. & T. Clark, 1876], 2:313) believes *diaconicum* refers to the place where the sacred vessels and vestments were kept and the prohibition against touching the sacred vessels refers to the deacon's duties, the meaning of the canon being that the subdeacons are not to assume the functions of the deacons.

115. *Council of Laodicea,* in *Nicene and Post-Nicene Fathers,* Second Series, 14:157.

116. J. Massingberd Ford, *A Trilogy on Wisdom and Celibacy,* The Cardinal O'Hara Series: Studies and Research in Christian Theology at Notre Dame (Notre Dame, In.: University of Notre Dame Press, 1967), pp. 23–24.

117. Joseph Blenkinsopp, *Celibacy, Ministry, Church* (New York: Herder and Herder, 1968), p. 27.

118. Ford, pp. 43, 49. Ford also records (p. 49) that the Mishnah and Gemara direct that coitus shall be "every day for them that are unoccupied; twice a week for labourers; once a week for ass drivers; once every thirty days for camel drivers; and once every six months for sailors."

119. Ibid., pp. 52–58. Cf. 1 Sam. 21:5.

120. 1 Tim. 4:1–5.

121. Clement of Alexandria, *Miscellanies* 7.12, in vol. 2: *Fathers of the Second Century: Hermas, Tatian, Athenagoras, Theophisbus, and Clement of Alexandria (entire),* in *Ante-Nicene Fathers* (1956), 2:543. Cf. Philip Schaff, in vol. 2: *Ante-Nicene Christianity* A.D. *100–325,* in *History of the Christian Church* (New York: Charles Scribner's Sons, 1924), pp. 406–07.

122. Clement of Alexandria, *Miscellanies* 7.11, in *Ante-Nicene Fathers,* 2:541.

123. Eusebius, *Church History* 3.30, in *Nicene and Post-Nicene Fathers,* Second Series, 1:161–62. The thing illustrated here is the tradition of the Church, not the historicity of the statement. The quotation is from *Miscellanies* 3.6.

124. Tertullian, *To His Wife* 1.2, 3, in *Ante-Nicene Fathers,* 4:39–40.

125. Ibid., 1.7, 4:43.

126. Tertullian, *On Monogamy* 12, *Ante-Nicene Fathers,* 4:69.

127. Hippolytus, *The Refutations of All Heresies* 9.8, in *Ante-Nicene Fathers,* 5:131.

128. Schaff seems to believe Hippolytus opposed the marriage of clergy after ordination (2:409).

129. Hefele, *History of the Councils,* 1:150.

130. Council of Elvira, in Stevenson, *New Eusebius,* p. 307.

131. E. Schillebeeckx, *Celibacy,* trans. C. A. L. Jarrott (New York: Sheed and Ward, 1968), p. 40.

132. Ibid., p. 58.

133. Ibid.

134. *Council of Ancyra,* in *Nicene and Post-Nicene Fathers,* Second Series, 14:67.

135. Socrates, *Ecclesiastical History* 1.11, in *Nicene and Post-Nicene Fathers,* Second Series, 2:18. Sozomen, *Ecclesiastical History* 1.23, Ibid., 2:256. Sozomen adds subdeacons to the list of orders included.

136. Hefele, *History of the Councils*, 1:436.

137. Socrates, *Ecclesiastical History* 1.11, in *Nicene and Post-Nicene Fathers*, Second Series, 2:18; Sozomen, *Ecclesiastical History* 1.23, Ibid., 2:256.

138. Canon 4, Council of Gangra, in J. Stevenson, ed., *Creeds, Councils and Controversies: Documents Illustrative of the History of the Church* A.D. *337–461* (London: S.P.C.K., 1966), p. 4.

139. Athanasius, *To Dracontius* 9, in vol. 4: *St. Athanasius: Select Works and Letters*, trans. Archibald Robertson, in *Nicene and Post-Nicene Fathers*, Second Series (1953), 4:560.

140. *Apostolic Constitutions* 6.17, in *Ante-Nicene Fathers*, 7:457. *Apostolic Canons*, Canon 17, in *Ante-Nicene Fathers*, 7:501, which also includes "any one of the sacerdotal catalogue." Council of Orleans, Canon 6, in Hefele, *History of the Councils*, 4:205–06.

141. *Apostolic Constitutions* 6.17, in *Ante-Nicene Fathers*, 7:457. *Apostolic Canons*, Canon 27, Ibid., 7:501, which permits only readers and singers among the clergy to marry after ordination. Council of Orleans, Canon 7, in Hefele, *History of the Councils*, 4:206.

142. *Apostolic Canons*, Canon 6, in *Ante-Nicene Fathers*, 7:500.

143. Augustine, *On the Good of Widowhood* 6, in vol. 3: *St. Augustin: On the Holy Trinity, Doctrinal Treatises, Moral Treatises*, in *Nicene and Post-Nicene Fathers*, First Series, 3:443. Cf. Augustine, *De haeresibus ad Quodvultdeum* 86.

144. *Council of Carthage*, Canon 4, in Hefele, *History of the Councils*, 2:424. *Council of Orange*, Canon 22 and 23, in Charles Joseph Hefele, vol. 3: *A History of the Councils of the Church, from the Original Documents*, A.D. *431 to* A.D. *451*, trans. "the Editor of Haggenbach's *History of Doctrines*," in *A History of the Councils of the Church* (Edinburgh: T. & T. Clark, 1883), 3:4. Though only deacons are named, the bishops and priests are implied. Canon 24 of Orange excepts those previously ordained but prohibits such deacons from being made priests or bishops. The *Council of Arles* (c. 450) permits the wife of a cleric to live in the house of her husband only if she also has taken a vow of chastity (Canon 3: Ibid., 3:168).

145. Socrates, *Ecclesiastical History* 5.22, in *Nicene and Post-Nicene Fathers*, Second Series, 2:132.

146. Schaff, p. 412.

147. P. Delhaye, "History of Celibacy," in *New Catholic Encyclopedia*, 3:371.

148. *Council of Trullo*, Canon 13, in *Nicene and Post-Nicene Fathers*, Second Series, 14:371.

149. Schillebeeckx, pp. 35–36, 65. Cf. Henry C. Lea, *The History of Sacerdotal Celibacy in the Christian Church* (New York: Russell & Russell, 1957 [First published under the title *An Historical Sketch of Sacerdotal Celibacy in the Christian Church* (Philadelphia: J. B. Lippincott & Co., 1867]), p. 57.

150. Lea, p. 40.

151. Ibid., pp. 114–15.

152. Latourette, pp. 365–66.

153. Lea, 114f. Cf. Schillebeeckx, pp. 60–61.

154. Lea, p. 116.

155. Ibid.

156. Ibid., p. 118.

157. Ibid., p. 116.

158. Ibid., p. 118.

159. Delhaye, 3:372.
160. Ibid.
161. J. J. Fox, "Papacy," *The Encyclopedia Americana* (New York: Americana Corp., 1938) 21:253.
162. Lea, pp. 145–46.
163. Delhaye, 3:373.
164. Constitution of the Church 3.29, in *Documents of Vatican II—All Sixteen Official Texts Promulgated by the Ecumenical Council 1963–65*, ed. Walter M. Abbott (New York: Guild Press, 1966), p. 56.
165. Vischer, p. 25.
166. Bernardino M. Bonansea, "Celibacy," in *The Encyclopedia Americana*, International Edition (New York: Americana Corp., 1977), 6:131.
167. Urban T. Holmes III, *Ministry and Imagination* (New York: Seabury Press, 1976), p. 46.
168. Gibson Winter, *Elements for a Social Ethic—Scientific Perspectives on Social Process* (New York: Macmillan Co., 1966), p. 227.
169. Holmes, *Ministry and Imagination*, p. 48, with references to its power and importance at numerous other points in this book.
170. *The Book of Common Prayer and Administration of the Sacraments and Other Rites and Ceremonies of the Church* (New York: Church Hymnal Corp. and Seabury Press, 1979), p. 874.
171. Vischer, p. 25.

PART TWO

THE RENEWAL OF THE DIACONATE IN THE CHURCH TODAY

CHAPTER 7

Organism as the Principle of Renewal

The stage was set in the Renaissance with its new insights into the Scriptures and the life of the early Church for the recovery of a pre-Nicene concept of the Church's organic character and total ministry. Even with the extremes and errors in both directions we may see the first stages of the fruition of this renewal in the developments of the sixteenth century. However, the reformers of the sixteenth century, whether of the Reformation or of the Counter-Reformation, were men of their own times and subject to the limitation imposed by the tradition and culture of the age, as are we. It is too much to expect that they would have been able at that point to have seen and augmented the full implications of their insights. Such a radical change as would then have occurred might have, in addition, proven to be a disaster for the Church.

But now in the late twentieth century as the Church disengages itself from an identification with the whole of society in the West, it is again examining its life in the light of scriptural truths, particularly as they are illuminated by the practice of the early period and the writings of the fathers, that the Holy Spirit may guide it to renewed life and vigor.

On the most fundamental level, it is apparent that there are two basic ways to think of the Church's nature and function. First, the Church can be seen as an institution governed and directed by the clergy, who "shape the policy and make the plans for implementing it, and then *enlist recruits*, the laity, to assist them in carrying out these plans."[1] Or second, the Church can be viewed as the people of God in which "every member has a share in a common, though differentiated, responsibility."[2] The analogy in the first instance is that of employers and employees. In the second it is that of a team.

A. T. Hanson says that, even in the Protestant traditions which have maintained in theory that the clergy are only part of a corporate ministry, this is not true in practice and that in Catholic traditions even the theory has been discarded. In the latter, even in theory, the bishop is not head of a team but superintendent over an area. A presbyter or priest has similar oversight in a town where there is but one parish. In larger places there may be many presbyters but they do not usually work as a group.[3] Today, however, a consensus seems to be emerging, at least in the West among the major churches, that the New Testament picture is of a corporate ministry of the whole people, each of whom has an important function and who together constitute the ministry of Christ and his Church.

It is most encouraging to note that a report prepared by Richard L. Rashke under the sponsorship of Pro Mundi Vita, the international research and information center in Brussels, states

> [American Roman] Catholics are beginnning to realize that the full impact of Vatican II lies . . . in a shift in the very understanding of the Church itself from a hierarchical institutional model to a community people-of-God model.[4]

In writing about the growing interest in the Roman Catholic Church in team ministry in the United States, the report records that "team ministry is a logical application of a theological principle: ministry belongs to all Christians, not just to the ordained."[5]

The Church needs the functions of rule, of preaching, of healing, of teaching, of visiting the sick; of caring for the poor, the lonely, the troubled, and the depressed; of praying, of administering the sacraments, and of ministering in other ways to the lives of people in a broken world. And the other side of the coin is that the Church's people need to do these things—all need to minister. So great is the task of ministry and so great is our need to minister that it can only be accomplished by recovering the fullness of an organic ministry constituted by no less than all the people of God. Obviously the primary meaning of a corporate conception of the ministry has to do with the local church. This is where it must be recovered if it is to have reality.[6]

In our complex world it is widely recognized that the priest or pastor of a local church can do only a very limited part of what is needed even in relatively small parishes. But there exist within these Christian communities ample numbers of people capable of meeting the challenges to ministry, just as there were in the early Church. Each congregation should be able to raise up from its own membership those whom it needs. But how is this to be done?

The Organic Principle

In recent years much emphasis has been placed on lay ministry, and rightly so. However, because the organic principle of the pre-Nicene

Church has not been properly understood, there has been a "confusion of orders." Laity have been delegated functions traditionally belonging to another order.[7] Pope Paul VI pointed this out in his apostolic letter, *General Norms for Restoring the Permanent Diaconate in the Latin Church,* issued *motu proprio,* saying that some functions of deacons have been given to lay persons but suggesting that these lay persons performing a diaconal ministry would benefit by the grace of ordination to the office.[8]

There is no question of authority here. As we noted in a previous chapter, the Church has broad authority to structure and change its forms of ministry. This position is supported by a committee of the Catholic Theological Society of America in "A Report on the Restoration of the Office of Deacon as a Lifetime State" made at the request of the Bishops' Committee on the Permanent Diaconate in the U.S. In speaking of the members of this committee the report states,

> Their studies, discussions, and reflections have led them to the conviction that the Church is free—much freer than is often recognized—to shape the structures of its various ministries, including the traditional triadic structure of episcopate, presbyterate, and diaconate, for the good of men.
>
> In the process of discerning which are the most apt structures and functions, tradition must be reverenced. But tradition itself has no clearer and stronger word to say to us than that, as a matter of fact, the Church has frequently exercised great freedom in adapting form to purpose, structure to mission.[9]

The question then becomes not so much what the Church can do but rather what the Church should do to meet the needs of people in our world.

The problem with "confusion of orders" is that the organic nature of the Church is in some sense negated. In a physical body a particular organ, such as the eye, has been created to fulfill a certain function. It is true that the hands can fulfill some of the functions of the eyes, but never so well as the eyes themselves. Though a lay person may assume functions of a clerical office, such as that of the deacon, it does make a significant difference that such a person has neither the authorization nor the grace of the office itself. And we see another aspect of the problem of "confusion of orders" in the attempt, for whatever reason, of one order to assume almost the totality of ministry. Many of the problems of the Church today in relationship to ministry are due to the priests or pastors assuming, or trying to assume, all the functions of the ministry.

The "General Instructions of the Roman Missal" today attempt to restore the ancient practice of the Church by directing that each take only his or her rightful part in the Eucharistic Liturgy. The instruction states,

> Everyone in the eucharistic assembly has the right and duty to take his own part according to the diversity of orders and functions. In exercising his function, everyone, whether minister or layman, should do that and only that which belongs to him, so that in the liturgy the Church may be seen in its variety of orders and ministries.[10]

This provision has ended the abuse of priests serving as deacons at the Eucharist according to a study prepared by the American Roman Catholic Bishops' Committee on the Liturgy.[11] It has also served to encourage broad lay participation.

The Episcopal Church has also moved towards restoration of the reality and integrity of the several orders within the Church. Its 1979 *Book of Common Prayer* directs,

> In all services, the entire Christian assembly participates in such a way that the members of each order within the Church, lay persons, bishops, priests, and deacons, fulfill the functions proper to their respective orders, as set forth in the rubrical directions for each service.[12]

The proper liturgical role of the deacon is set forth in the several liturgies. Though extensive lay participation has become the rule in Episcopal parishes in recent years, few have as yet been enriched by the presence of deacons.

The lack of in-depth comprehension of the nature of the Church and its various orders is illustrated much too frequently on parish and diocesan levels when genuine deacons are present yet their special functions are assigned to lay people or priests. This has been witnessed all too often by the author and others knowledgeable about and sensitive to this problem. No doubt, the motivation to involve the laity is good, but there are ample opportunities for lay people to function in nondiaconal roles. Authorization for the laity to perform functions historically belonging to the deacon has been given only because there is a real need for the function and deacons have not been and are not usually available. A notable example of this is lay administration of the Eucharistic elements when deacons are present in sufficient numbers. Another is a priest or bishop reading the Gospel lesson at the Eucharist with a deacon standing by.

In an age such as ours which values and utilizes specialization of function far beyond any society of the past, the Church should be all the more attuned to the need and advantage of differentiation of function provided by many offices. This is true especially in light of the New Testament emphasis on differing gifts of the Spirit. Some fall into the category of the ordained ministry, some lay ministry, when we see in these terms differentiation of function and also of the manner and nature of authorization for ministry. Donald Tytler well observes,

> What is needed is nothing less than a revolution of thought and feeling on the part of laity and clergy towards one another. It is not just a matter of straightening out the theology of ministry, if by that phrase is meant chiefly the intellectual acceptance of certain right (i.e., biblical) ideas of ministry. There is required a radical change of ideas between the body of the clergy and the mass of laity and between individual clergy and laymen.[13]

The crux of the radical change required is to see again the fact that all are *laos*, all are ministers of Christ, sharing in his ministry and priesthood, though in different ways.

NOTES

1. F. A. Cockin, "Ministers of the Priestly People," *Theology* 65 (January 1962): 7.
2. Ibid.
3. A. T. Hanson, "Shepherd, Teacher and Celebrant in the New Testament Conception of the Ministry," in *New Forms of Ministry,* ed. David M. Patton, Research Pamphlets No. 12, World Council of Churches Commission on World Missions and Evangelism (London: Edinburgh House Press, 1965), p. 31.
4. Richard L. Rashke, *The Deacon in Search of Identity* (New York: Paulist Press, 1975), p. 5.
5. Ibid., p. 13. The report records that in 1972 team ministries had been created or their feasibility studied in half of the dioceses in America. In 1974 one diocese had 30 teams (p. 13). There were at least four team pastoral training centers being operated in the United States at that time along with a national placement agency for those in the field (p. 15).
6. Hanson, p. 31.
7. Massey H. Shepherd, Jr., *Prayer Book Revision,* lectures at the Graduate School of Theology, Sewanee, Tn., Summer, 1970. Dr. Shepherd specifically termed the Episcopal Church's authorizing lay administration of the chalice a "confusion of orders," stating that the function properly belongs to the diaconate.
8. Pope Paul VI, *General Norms for Restoring the Permanent Diaconate in the Latin Church* (*Motu Proprio*), United States Catholic Conference, Washington, D.C., 18 June 1967 (hereafter cited *Permanent Diaconate*).
9. "A Report on the Restoration of the Office of Deacon as a Lifetime State," a Committee of the Catholic Theological Society of America, chair. Edward Echlin, made at the request of the Bishops' Committee on the Permanent Diaconate (Roman Catholic), published in *The American Ecclesiastical Review* (March 1971) 164:3, par. 8, p. 192.
10. "General Instructions of the Roman Missal," No. 58, in *The Roman Missal, the Sacramentary* (New York: Catholic Book Publishing Co., 1974), p. 28.
11. In *The Deacon, Minister of Word and Sacrament,* Study Text VI, prepared by the Bishops' Committee on the Liturgy (Washington: United States Catholic Conference, 1979), p. 14.
12. *The Book of Common Prayer and Administration of the Sacraments and*

Other Rites and Ceremonies of the Church (New York: Church Hymnal Corp. and Seabury Press, 1979), p. 13.

13. Donald Tytler, "Each in His Own Order," in *New Ways with the Ministry*, ed. John Morris (London: Faith Press, 1960), p. 25.

CHAPTER 8

The Deacon as Symbol

Perhaps the most misunderstood idea relating to the diaconate is the fact that its primary significance does not lie in any of its functions, whether pastoral, charitable, or liturgical. The origin of the diaconate and its development in the first centuries reveals above all the deacon as symbol. He is the symbol par excellence of the Church's ministry. In the deacon is seen the indelible character of *service* Christ put on his ministry and of *servant* on those who minister. He is the embodiment of the first principle of this ministry which is *sent* to *serve*.

As we have already noted in another connection, a symbol in the sense in which we are using the word is a powerful representation that has many meanings and evokes many feelings. We would recall that *man* is a symbolic being who is formed and molded by symbol and who, himself, reshapes symbols and thereby shapes his world.[1] Though it would be perhaps simplistic to see in the decline of the diaconate the cause of the Church's losing *diakonia* as the primary thrust of its ministry, it is true that this primary symbol of the early Church was degraded and essentially lost over the centuries as service to others became less and less central in Christian ministry. It is reasonable to conclude that the loss of the deacon as symbol was at least a highly significant factor in the reshaping of the Church's ministry.

The deacon above all epitomizes within his or her office the ministry Christ has given to his Church, the servant ministry to which we are all called and commissioned in our baptism. The particular functions are, of course, important. They give meaning and content to the symbol a deacon is. However, as Article 16 of the guidelines of the Roman Catholic Bishops' Committee on the Permanent Diaconate states, the deacon's "overall symbolizing of the service is more meaningful than his specific functions."[2]

The need for a powerful symbol to proclaim that the ministry of the

Church is *diakonia* is indeed great. It is all too apparent that Christian congregations generally tend to be self-centered and self-serving, though not so much as a matter of deliberate intent as of inheriting a form of Christianity which conceives of ministry essentially in spiritual terms of bringing personal salvation to people's souls. The social unrest, demonstrations, and strife of the 1960s in the United States was certainly in part at least due to the failure of the Church in recent generations to be concerned about and to serve the poor and powerless in the face of gross economic and social injustice in the midst of an affluent and professed democratic society. The Church needs to heed the advice of a Lutheran leader, Thure-Gengt Molander, who urges the recovery of the fundamental nature of Christian ministry. "The Church," he said, "must become a diaconal Church in the deepest and most forward-looking sense, or it will not be the Church."[3]

Other Ministries Enhanced

Though we shall deal separately with the relationship between the deacon and other orders of the clergy, it is appropriate that we consider here briefly the idea that the diaconate is not needed on the one hand because lay people today can do virtually all that the deacon can do and on the other that priests can do all the deacons can do and much more.

The crux of this problem allowing such a fundamental "confusion of orders" lies, first of all, in a failure to understand the organic nature of the Church as it was founded by Christ, with which we have already dealt. However, beyond this, there is the underlying idea that the primary function of the deacon is to do something. But as we have seen, his or her first reason for being is *to be* something. H. Boone Porter, Jr., astutely observes that bishops are not ordained primarily in order to do the few distinctive things that are unique to their order. Rather he says, bishops are ordained "*primarily* to preach the Gospel and to unify, lead, and oversee the church."[4] Most of their time is spent in doing things like reading the daily office, answering mail, seeing visitors, and attending meetings, which lay people can also do. The special functions of a bishop, notably ordaining, "belong to the bishop because he is the authoritative spokesman of the church, not *vice versa.*"[5]

In turning to the question of why deacons are ordained, Porter sees their role to be uniquely Christian with no real counterpart in secular organizations:

> Their mandate, some of us believe, is to give sacramental embodiment to our Lord's teaching that the greatest shall be servant of all, and to lead the church as a whole in implementing this teaching. To the sec-

> ular world, this does not, and cannot make sense. Even for us Christians, it is not easily understood.[6]

Deacons then are not ordained essentially in order that they may perform the distinctive functions of their order but to hold up *diakonia* as central to all Christian ministry.

Restoration of a true diaconal ministry will enhance the other ministries of the Church. In relationship to lay ministry "A Report on the Restoration of the Office of Deacon as a Lifetime State," by a committee of theologians of the Catholic Theological Society of America, to the Bishops' Committee on the Permanent Diaconate, states that "far from rivaling or inhibiting the ministry of laymen, the ministry of deacons, when it is judiciously exercised, will powerfully promote that ministry. . . ."[7] The deacons envisioned here will live like lay people with jobs, families, and social responsibilities as before but yet will be ordained to the diaconate and minister in their special ways liturgically, pastorally, and charitably. Their ministries will almost inevitably bring new dimensions to the ministry of the laity.

This diaconal ministry will serve to complement and enlarge the ministry and effectiveness of bishops and more especially of parish priests and pastors, with whom they would generally be serving. The enhancement of the other orders by a restored diaconate will be more apparent as we go on to consider its renewal.

NOTES

1. Gibson Winter, *Elements for a Social Ethic—Scientific Perspectives on Social Process* (New York: Macmillan, 1966), p. 227.
2. In Bishops' Committee on the Permanent Diaconate, *Permanent Deacons in the United States: Guidelines on their Formation and Ministry* (Washington: United States Catholic Conference, 1971), p. 8.
3. Minutes of the *Fifth Biennial Convention of the Lutheran Church in America*, Minneapolis, Mn., 25 June–2 July 1970 (Philadelphia: Board of Publication of the Lutheran Church in America, 1970), p. 449.
4. H. Boone Porter, Jr., "Ordained Ministers in Liturgy and in Life," in *The Living Church*, 9 January 1977: 13.
5. Ibid.
6. Ibid., 14.
7. "A Report on the Restoration of the Office of Deacon as a Lifetime State," a Committee of the Catholic Theological Society of America, chair. Edward Echlin, made at the request of the Bishops' Committee on the Permanent Diaconate (Roman Catholic), published in *The American Theological Review* (March 1971) 164:3, par. 23, p. 198.

CHAPTER 9

A Full and Equal Order

In our consideration of the development of the Church's ordained ministry we found that the greatest single cause of the decline of the diaconate was the development of *cursus honorum.* There is, of course, nothing detrimental in one person holding various offices requiring differing and increasing responsibility in the Church. As the ancient councils and the fathers saw, it was good for one to demonstrate by service in the Church proper qualifications for positions of leadership entailing greater responsibility. However, to see the ministry of the Church essentially as a graded succession of offices does contradict the organic character with which the Church was originially endowed by Christ and his Spirit. Such a view sees the ministry largely in terms of power and honor, not of service. The ministry is properly *diakonia,* service, a truth needing reiteration just because it has been so neglected, if not forgotten. Lampe affirms that

> . . . the study of the New Testament gives us the assurance that, so long as a commissioning and *diakonia* are its keynotes, the essentials of the apostolic ministry of the first century are present and operative in our totally different world. . . .[1]

The first step in the restoration of the essential character of the ministry of the pre-Nicene Church is the reassertion of the principle that each order and office is a distinct and distinctive vocation to which the Holy Spirit calls the various members of the Church as he wills. As this principle comes alive, increasingly the ministry will include and utilize all the people of God.

A necessary part of any profound renewal of the ministry must include abandoning all requirements of passing through successive orders or offices. Baptism must be restored as the only sacramental prerequisite for ordination and/or commissioning to any office in the Church. Of course, the ancient concern that those chosen for positions of leadership will have first demonstrated their fitness for the office by their service *in the Church* is still valid. Success in other fields fits one no better today than in ancient times for stepping directly into positions of leadership and responsibility in the Church, a fact to be especially noted at a time when secularism has made considerable inroads into the thinking of some Christian leaders. There have been exceptions like Ambrose of Milan and Thomas Becket of England, but they are notable just because they are rare. However, it is one thing to test people with the criteria of committed service in the Church and another to require a succession of offices, which is no guarantee in itself of genuine *diakonia*.

Karl Rahner in his *Theological Investigations* relating to the restored diaconate regards the requirement for ordination of "absolute" (life long) deacons to the minor orders as "superfluous."[2]

A Plan of Union for the Church of Christ Uniting, published in 1970, sets forth a most enlightened proposal for a diaconate under this scheme. The diaconate is to be a "distinctive vocation" with the emphasis on service restored to the ministry of the deacon. It is *not* to be a stage of preparation of presbyters.[3] Since the plan was not accepted by the participating churches, the proposal was not put into practice.

In the Roman Catholic Church the Council of Trent, 1545–1563, directed the restoration of the diaconate, including it in a decree relating to the minor orders. On 15 July 1563 the council fathers decreed

> That the function of holy orders from the deacon to the porter, which have been laudably received in the Church from the times of the Apostles, and which have been for some time discontinued in many localities, may again be restored to use in accordance with the canons, and may not be derided by the heretics as useless, the holy council burning with desire to restore the ancient usage, decrees that in the future such functions shall not be exercised except by those constituted in these orders, and it exhorts in the Lord each and all prelates of the churches and commands them that they make it their care to restore these functions, so far as it can be conveniently done, in cathedral, collegiate and parochial churches of their diocese, if the number of people and the revenues of the church are able to bear it.[4]

The decree apparently contemplates principally liturgical functions. The council had rejected a proposal on July 6th of that year setting forth a diaconate specifically mandating a ministry to the poor.[5] However, the decree approved did show some appreciation for the Church as a corporate body whose members had distinctive functions. Unfortunately, it was never implemented.[6]

The renewal in the Roman Catholic Church, begun in the pontificate of John XXIII, has moved it noticeably in the direction of recovering the Church's organic character. A part of this at least has been steps taken to restore the diaconate as a distinctive order, a process begun by the Second Vatican Council in its Constitution on the Church (*Lumen Gentium*) promulgated by Pope Paul VI in 1964.[7] The council fathers spoke of the need for the diaconate in the future to be "restored as a proper and permanent rank of the hierarchy."[8] The Roman pontiff implemented this decree in 1967 by publication of *General Norms for Restoring the Permanent Diaconate in the Latin Church.* We may consider his declaration that the diaconate "is not to be considered as a mere step towards the priesthood, but it is so adorned with its own indelible character and its own special grace" that it is to be considered a "permanent" vocation[9] as not only providing for the restoration of a true diaconate but also as taking the first step towards abolishing its interim character.

The National Conference of Catholic Bishops in the United States approved the restoration of the diaconate for this country in 1968[10] and requested permission for this restoration from the Vatican "both to complete the hierarchy of sacred orders and to enrich and strengthen the various diaconal ministries at work in the United States with the sacramental grace of the diaconate."[11] The request was approved the same year, marking the beginning of a program which has flourished. By the end of 1976 there were 1,875 permanent deacons in the Roman Catholic Church in North America out of 3,125 in the world.[12] By 31 October 1980 the diaconate in the United States alone numbered 4,656 with 2,514 diaconal candidates.[13]

However, a graded hierarchical structure is very much in evidence in the Roman Church. Paul VI in his Apostolic Constitution on *Approval of a New Rite for the Ordination of Deacons, Priests and Bishops* calls special attention to this graded structure by first stating that priests do not possess the "highest degree" of the ministry and then reiterating the statement of Vatican II:

> In the lower grade of the hierarchy are deacons on whom hands are imposed "not for the priesthood, but for the ministry" (Constitutions of the Church of Egypt, III, 2). Strengthened by sacramental grace, they serve the People of God in the *diaconia* of liturgy, word, and charity, in communion with the bishop and his presbytery.[14]

Direction was also given by Paul VI in the *General Norms* issued 18 June 1967 that "present discipline be observed until it is revised by the Holy See" in conferring "those orders which precede the diaconate" as well as the diaconate itself.[15] On 15 August 1972 Paul VI issued an apostolic letter, *Laying Down Certain Norms Regarding the Sacred Order of the Diaconate, motu proprio,* requiring all diaconal candidates to receive the minor orders of lector and acolyte.[16] The letter also provides for the introduction of a new rite of admission for candidates to the diaconate or priesthood by which the aspirant publicly manifests his desire for ordination to a "sacred order," replacing the rite of first tonsure.[17] A publication of the Archdiocese of Omaha states that directives from Rome set the interval between lector and acolyte at six months, though "the order of reception does not seem to matter."[18]

It is encouraging that Echlin refers to the mention by Vatican II of deacons being of "lower grade" but says that this "does not imply an ascending theology of ministry," since they are servants of Christ and the Church.[19] In his conclusion he writes,

> The deacon's role is not "lower than" nor "inferior to" the priest's, he is not a potential rival; his charism is *different* than any other charism in the Church including that of the priest.[20]

Here we see asserted the pre-Nicene organic conception of the Church and its ministry. However, the documents themselves do very definitely envision a vertical, hierarchical structure of ministry and tend to perpetuate the false dichotomy between clergy and laity. By implication the laity is not a "sacred order." The new rite for admission for candidates to the diaconate and priesthood specifically states the candidate is to declare publicly his "will to offer himself to God and the Church, so that he may exercise a sacred order."[21] By ordination they enter "the clerical state"[22] with the implication of becoming "sacred persons."

In Anglicanism the same problems prevail. The Canons of the Episcopal Church in America frequently imply that the clergy constitute the totality of the Church's ministers,[23] and its forms of intercessory prayer for the Eucharist reinforce this concept by the use of such phrases in some of them as those bidding prayer "for all bishops and other ministers, *and* for all the holy people of God."[24] Common terminology used to designate all three of its clerical offices at once is the "Sacred Ministry," implying that lay ministries are at least less sacred, if at all. A hierarchical structure remains with laity, deacons, priests, and bishops following in ascending order. The three orders continue to constitute a class of "sacred persons."

However, the Episcopal Church has also moved in the direction of recovering the New Testament concept of ministry as belonging to all the people. This is expressed in various ways in its revised Prayer Book of 1979, and the catechism of that book specifically asserts that "the ministers of the Church are lay persons, bishops, priests, and deacons" and includes a description of "the ministry of the laity" along with and equal to those of the clerical orders.[25]

Though there are differences, the situation in the Lutheran, Presbyterian, United Methodist, United Church of Christ, Baptist, Christian, and other churches seems to be fundamentally parallel. The clergy generally are sacralized as against or apart from the laity. Theologically the "full ministry" is only in the office of the presbyter, priest, pastor, or "minister." The diaconate ranks second best and the lay order a poor third. Sociologically the "real" clergy, the priests and pastors, and their wives, if any, are isolated from full social involvement even with their parishioners.

Though too much can be made of terminology, it is often of considerable importance due to the subtle implications it conveys unconsciously. Here, in connection with the diaconate it would seem that the need for any modifying term to describe a permanent vocation is essentially degrading to the office. In the Episcopal Church the term "*perpetual* deacon" has been used. Roman Catholics generally prefer "*permanent* deacon." Elsewhere we noted Karl Rahner uses "*absolute* deacon." One seems little better than the other. The term "deacon" should stand alone, having integrity of its own as a separate and equal office. The need to use these adjectives is itself indicative of the denigration of the office. The words, "perpetual" and "permanent," have to do with the nature of the vocation itself. They are not comparable to the use of "nonstipendiary" or "worker" priest, since such terms have to do with the manner or source of compensation and the nature of the vocation. The difference is to be noted in the "stepping-stone" character of the transitional diaconate.

In the Anglican Communion the Lambeth Conference, the worldwide council of its bishops, adopted an important resolution regarding the diaconate at its 1958 meeting. Resolution 88, "The Office of the Deacon," stated,

> The Conference recommends that each province of the Anglican Communion shall consider whether the office of Deacon shall be restored to its primitive place as a distinct order of the Church, instead of being regarded as a probationary period for the priesthood.[26]

This statement served to call the attention of Anglicanism to the office of deacon with the implication that restoration was in order. Though the conference has no legal authority, it carries great moral weight throughout Anglicanism.

The statement of Lambeth 1958 is further to be interpreted in light of the report of its committee, which stated that in recent years the offices of reader and catechist have grown in the Anglican Communion and have largely taken over the traditional functions of the deacon. The report said that part of the problem stemmed from the fact that the Anglican diaconate required the dedication of the whole of the deacon's life to this vocation. But of prime importance, the committee concluded that the Anglican Church needs to decide either to restore the diaconate or to give it up.[27]

The problem referred to by the Lambeth committee, that the Anglican deacon was required to dedicate the whole of life to this vocation, was and probably still is the case in various provinces of the Anglican Communion but not in the Episcopal Church in the United States. The canons of the Episcopal Church had been changed previously to allow for a diaconate which would be regarded as a permanent vocation and in which those entering it could continue to support themselves in their previous occupations. Such deacons were ordained in a number of dioceses, but attendant problems led rather quickly to the disuse of this form of the diaconate in most dioceses.

However, the experience of the Episcopal Church in this respect can be valuable. The problems seemed to manifest themselves particularly in two areas. Many who were ordained deacon under this program soon were unsatisfied with the diaconate and sought to go on and be ordained priest. This was perhaps made easier in the 1950s by the Episcopal Church's need for priests in considerably greater numbers than were then available to meet its rapid growth. A considerable number of these deacons were ordained to the priesthood without adequate training, going in through what was termed "the back door." In addition, the relationship between the deacon and the priest was not sufficiently clear, so that at times a priest moving to a new parish with a "perpetual" deacon felt threatened,[28] though the number of cases where this was an actual problem has undoubtedly been highly overestimated.

Akin to this is another problem which had a part in the reluctance of some Episcopal bishops to ordain these nonstipendiary (nonsalaried) deacons, who earn their own living in other work. In our highly mobile society deacons may often be transferred to other parishes or dioceses, where there may not be a place or even a welcome for their ministries. Though this sociological problem will be considered in the next chapter, might we not ask at this point if there is any inherent reason why a deacon moving to another place should create a greater problem than a lay person? Does not the lay person also have a ministry that will be available and might not be accepted in another place?

The underlying problems appear to be more fundamental, however. At that time the Episcopal Church still considered the office of deacon "an inferior" order both in theory and in practice. The ordinal of the 1928

Book of Common Prayer concluded with a prayer that the newly ordained deacons "may so well behave themselves in this *inferior* Office, that they may be found worthy to be called unto the higher Ministries. . . .[29] The ministry was still conceived of largely in terms of graded ranks, not in terms of members of an organic society. The diaconate was the first step up the major ladder to the top, so that it seemed to be only logical that one go on to the priesthood.[30] This thinking was perhaps strengthened by training which tended to imply that these deacons would be semi-professionals. Preparation was somewhat modified for such a deacon from that required of the "transitional" deacon but was essentially a lesser version of the training needed for the priesthood.[31]

These deacons were seen largely in terms of unpaid assistants to the clergy of a parish. The Church's canon provided that he "shall exercise his Ministry as *assistant* in any parish or parishes" to which he is assigned[32] and until 1964 could not be put in charge of a congregation.[33] The deacon was not viewed as a servant of the Church whose ministry was service to the Church, but as an assistant to the priest. Further, and of great importance, the ministry of such deacons was often primarily liturgical. Typically, pastoral and charitable functions for these deacons were all but nonexistent.

The experience of the Episcopal Church with this type of diaconate has resulted in its making major changes both in its liturgical forms and canon law. In writing of the Church's 1979 *Book of Common Prayer*, Marion Hatchett states,

> The rites recover for us the traditional liturgical and pastoral functions of the various orders of ministers. The bishop takes his place as chief pastor and minister of Word and Sacraments. The ministry of the deacon is set forth as a distinctive servant-ministry rather than as an internship or stepping stone. The ministry of the presbyter is depicted as a collegial ministry. The participation of the laity is broadened and increased.[34]

The canons on the ministry adopted at the Church's General Convention in 1973 provide for the implementation of such a recovery. These canons provide for a "diaconate with new expectations of how this order of ministry might be utilized in evangelism, pastoral care, and liturgy."[35]

There is widespread and renewed interest in the restoration of the diaconate in the Episcopal Church today. At the request of the Episcopal House of Bishops, the Church's Council for the Development of Ministry prepared a report in 1979 describing, analyzing, and interpreting the Episcopal diaconate.[36] At that time there were more than 500 deacons in the Episcopal diaconate in the United States, about 420 to 450 of whom were classified as active. The study reports that 94% of Episcopal bishops believe the Church should have a vital diaconate, but the need to clarify the role and duties of the diaconate and its effect on other ministries, especially lay ministries, before expanding diaconal programs was expressed.[37] The report also calls for new models for the selection, training, and examination of diaconal candidates to equip them to carry out a servant ministry.[38]

Organizations such as the National Center for the Diaconate and the Associated Parishes, Inc. actively support and encourage renewal of the diaconate in the Episcopal Church.

Widespread publicity has been given in the Episcopal Church to "The Wewoka Statement," adopted by the Council of Associated Parishes at its annual meeting in April 1977 at Wewoka, Oklahoma, boldly advocating abandonment of the interim diaconate. The statement declares,

> The Associated Parishes Council is committed to the renewal of the order of deacon as a full, normal ministry in the Church, alongside the priesthood. The diaconate is not properly a stepping-stone or a back door to the priesthood. It is not an auxiliary ministry. Deacons and priests have equal but different ministries whose functions are clearly outlined in the new ordinal of the Proposed Book of Common Prayer.
>
> In an effort to clarify the distinctive character and importance of each order, as well as the ministry of the laity, we feel that candidates for the priesthood should be ordained directly to that order. Deacons should be eligible to be elected bishop and ordained directly to that order.
>
> The ministry of lay persons, bishops, priests, and deacons is one in the Body of Christ our great high priest who came as one who serves.[39]

The national Conference of Liturgy and Music Commissions of the Episcopal Church in America at its 1980 meeting, attended by the author, adopted a resolution urging the restoration of the diaconate in every congregation and passage of "the necessary legislation so that for an experimental period the Episcopal Church may cease the practice of ordaining candidates for the priesthood as deacons." Abandoning the transitional diaconate is the logical conclusion of steps taken in both the Anglican Communion and the Roman Catholic Church to recover the diaconate and the wholeness of the organic ministry of the early Church.

The Eastern Orthodox Church has retained the diaconate to a greater degree than either the Latin or Anglican Churches, though it has ceased to have any charitable functions.[40] Interestingly, among the Orthodox, only one person may be ordained at a single liturgy, and each ordination requires the consent at least in theory of the whole people of God given by the acclamation *Axios!* ("He is worthy!") at one point in the service. In mentioning this, Ware notes that during the present century congregations in Constantinople or Greece have on several occasions shouted their disapproval with *Anaxios!*, but to no avail.[41]

Among the Orthodox churches the diaconate is largely restricted to liturgical functions in the Eucharist.[42] The deacon is the leader of the choir and directs the movements of the Liturgy. He offers certain prayers himself and calls on the priest to utter his prayers.[43] In the Byzantine liturgies he is called "concelebrant" twice by the priest. After the entrance the priest returns the censer to the deacon and addresses him, "Remember me, O my brother and concelebrant."[44] The Byzantine ordination rite does not present the office as transitional, though the Armenian and Coptic rites do.[45] Many Orthodox deacons regard their vocation today as lifelong.[46]

From time to time Orthodox deacons share in the pastoral and administrative work of the Church, but this appears to be inconsequential generally. In Russia in the 1880s the diaconate was reinstituted in parishes of over 700 members and given responsibility for education, both religious and general.[47] Both Coptic ordination rite and canon law retain the pastoral and social admonitions to the deacon from the ancient Church: To visit widows, orphans, and the afflicted; to bring the afflicted to the attention of the bishop or priest; and to minister to the poor. But charitable concern has disappeared from their ministries.[48]

Though some Protestant churches do have the office of deacon, Protestantism in general does not have the diaconate as a separate order of the ordained ministry.[49] The office historically has not been a part of either Lutheranism or Methodism.[50] The Presbyterians, Reformed, Congregationalists, Baptists, and Disciples have a diaconate which generally would appear to be a lay ministry.[51] However, there is considerable interest in these churches in renewal or recovery of the office. For example, a plan for establishing the diaconate in the Lutheran Church in America was presented to its 1976 convention but due to the press of business was made a "document for study" until its next meeting.[52] The plan, however, was dropped at its 1978 convention.

In European Lutheranism there is, however, a nonordained ministry which is composed of those called deacons. Johann Hinrich Wickern is considered to have founded this diaconate in 1840 in Hamburg by forming a community with true pastoral and charitable ministries, which worked with youth "in moral danger," as "home missioners," in Prussian prisons, and as wartime military medical orderlies or assistants to army chaplains.[53] Other communities were founded for varied purposes. The type of ministry done by the members of these communities includes nursing, social welfare, education, and parish work.[54] In the 1960s there were fifteen *Brudenhäuser* communities in Germany numbering some 4,550 deacons with several hundred more in Scandinavia.[55] They are not ordained and have no liturgical function.

The Reformed tradition today embodies a large number of deacons and deaconesses, though they are not ordained and do not hold an official office in their churches.[56] The ministry performed by the men and women in these diaconal communities is that of parish workers, missionaries, social and medical workers, educators and teachers, and other similar types of service.[57]

The practice of American Presbyterian congregations has varied regarding the diaconate for historical reasons. A "collegiate" diaconate existed in some of their churches early in American history but many had none.[58] Their General Assembly repeatedly urged the adoption of the diaconate in the early and mid-nineteenth century. The term "board" came into use in connection with the Presbyterian diaconate before the Civil War and has largely replaced the use of "diaconate."[59]

Following the schism occurring due to the Civil War, the Southern Church (the Presbyterian Church in the U. S.) increasingly entrusted to the deacons the management of the congregations' temporal affairs, the delegation becoming statutory after 1922.[60] In the Northern branch (the Presbyterian Church in the U. S. A.) the temporalities were committed to trustees, and the Board of Deacons continued to minister pastorally and charitably to various human needs.[61] This diaconate is corporate in nature, though members are elected by the congregation and are ordained deacons. It is also optional. Some congregations, formerly having Boards of Deacons, have instead instituted "deacons' committees" appointed from the ordained ruling elders of their governing councils, called sessions. Ordination to either the office of deacon or ruling elder is for life, though deacons when elected to the session are ordained ruling elders. It has been said that the Northern churches have "few deacons but rather many Boards of Deacons."[62] Since the uniting of the Northern and Southern Churches in 1958, efforts have been made to "recognize" those in some specialized ministries as deacons.[63]

There is considerable variation among Baptist churches regarding their diaconate. The most common structure today is that of one elder and a number of deacons who together form a kind of executive committee, the German Baptists using the term *Vorstand*, meaning "executive committee."[64] However, there are some Baptist churches, especially in Germany, which have a threefold structure of a pastor with a single elder and a board of deacons.[65] Baptist deacons at one time were customarily elected by their congregations for life but now serve for a limited period such as three years. In Great Britain they are no longer ordained, but there are Baptist churches elsewhere where the custom has survived.[66] John McBain, writing in the Southern Baptist magazine, *The Deacon*, speaks of Southern Baptist deacons as being ordained and also calls them "ordained laymen," using quotation marks.[67] Baptist "lay-preachers" usually are deacons and are allowed to officiate at baptism and the Eucharist.[68]

In America the diaconate of Baptist churches in the nineteenth and earlier part of the twentieth century had been largely concerned with the business affairs of the congregations, though in a number of places their responsibility was larger, functioning more as a board of directors.[69] In recent years strong emphasis has been placed on encouraging a fuller diaconate with pastoral and charitable concerns in both the Southern and American Baptist churches.[70]

The Christian Church (Disciples of Christ) does have the office of deacon/deaconess as provided in its "provisional Design for the Christian Church (Disciples of Christ)," adopted in 1968.[71] Their duties may include pastoral, charitable, liturgical, and administrative functions, such as visiting the sick, serving as ushers, caring for the poor, administering the Lord's Supper, and looking after parish property and finance.[72] Deacons may be ordained by the laying on of hands with prayer, and ordination may be repeated as often as an individual is elected to the office.[73]

The United Methodist Church in the United States has a "transitional" diaconate for those seeking to be ordained elder. In addition, *The Book of Discipline of the United Methodist Church* provides for the office of "diaconal minister" exemplifying the servanthood of all Christians[74] for those who wish to enter the diaconate as a lifelong vocation. Those holding the office, however, are not referred to as deacons. This "diaconal ministry" is regarded as a "called-out" and "set-apart" ministry including pastoral, charitable, and liturgical functions, though these are not specifically enumerated.[75] An "act of consecration," which may be combined with an ordination service, establishes the relationship of the diaconal minister with the United Methodist Church.[76]

The practice of the United Church of Christ with its congregational polity varies regarding diaconal ministries. Some congregations have boards of deacons and deaconesses, which may meet as one group. Where such groups exist, their duties range from responsibility for worship and membership in some churches to care of benevolences in others. This diaconate is more corporate than individual, and individuals involved in it are not regarded as holding the office of deacon in the historic sense.

There is, then, wide variation among the Churches of the late twentieth century in their understanding of and commitment to the historic diaconate. However, the Church has moved a long way towards the restoration of the office. It needs now to complete the task.

As the idea of *cursus honorum* was the greatest single factor in bringing about the decline of the office, nothing would help to restore its integrity more than to return to the original practice of the pre-Nicene Church by ordaining only those to the diaconate who intend to make it a permanent vocation. Others, notably those seeking the priesthood or selected for the episcopate, would be ordained directly to those orders. Baptism would become the essential *sacramental* prerequisite for ordination to any office in the Church.

Such a return to the original concept of order in the Church would help each of the orders and ministries within the Church regain its distinctive character. The ministry would be immeasurably enriched particularly by recognizing the diaconate as the specific form of ministry which embodies and exemplifies the work Christ sent his Church into the world to do. Then, it can rightly be described as a vocation symbolizing Christ himself in a unique way. The ministry of the Church will more readily be seen for what it is truly meant to be—*diakonia,* service.

NOTES

1. G. W. H. Lampe, *Some Aspects of the New Testament Ministry* (London: S.P.C.K., 1949), p. 20 (hereafter cited *N. T. Ministry*).
2. Karl Rahner, vol. 5: *Later Writings,* trans. Karl H. Kruger, in *Theological Investigations* (Baltimore: Helicon Press, 1966), 5:314.
3. Consultation of Church Union, *A Plan of Union for the Church of Christ Uniting* (Princeton, N. J.: n.p., 1970), p. 53.
4. Session 23, "Decree Concerning Reform," in chap. 17, "In What Name the Exercise of the Minor Orders is to be restored," in *Canons and Decrees of the Council of Trent,* trans. H. J. Schroeder (St. Louis: B. Herder Book Co., 1941), p. 174.
5. *The Deacon, Minister of Word and Sacrament,* Study Text VI, prepared by the Bishops' Committee on the Liturgy (Washington: United States Catholic Conference, 1979), p. 13.
6. Edward Echlin, *The Deacon in the Church Past and Future* (Staten Island, N. Y.: Alba House, 1971), p. 105.
7. *De Ecclesia, The Constitution on the Church of Vatican Council II Proclaimed by Pope Paul VI November 21, 1964,* ed. Edward H. Peters (Glen Rock, N. J.: Paulist Press, Deus Book, 1965), pp. 122–23, par. 29.
8. Ibid.
9. Pope Paul VI, *General Norms for Restoring the Permanent Diaconate in the Latin Church* (*Motu Proprio*), United States Catholic Conference, Washington, D. C., 18 June 1967, p. 2 (hereafter cited *Permanent Diaconate*).
10. Richard L. Rashke, *The Deacon in Search of Identity* (New York: Paulist Press, 1975), p. 23.

11. Bishops' Committee on the Permanent Diaconate, *Permanent Deacons in the United States: Guidelines on their Formation and Ministry* (Washington: United States Catholic Conference, 1971), p. 1, par. 1.

12. *Diaconal Quarterly* 2.1 (Winter, 1977): 8, Bishops' Committee on the Permanent Diaconate (1312 Massachusetts Ave., N. W., Washington, D. C., 20005). Deacons in Europe totaled 722 and in Central and South America 389.

13. *Diaconal Quarterly* 7.1 (Winter, 1981): 35.

14. Pope Paul VI, *Approval of a New Rite for the Ordination of Deacons, Priests and Bishops*, Apostolic Constitution, 18 June 1968, United States Catholic Conference, Washington, D. C.: 5. He quotes here the Constitution on the Church, par. 29.

15. Pope Paul VI, *Permanent Diaconate*, p. 10.

16. Pope Paul VI, *Laying Down Certain Norms Regarding the Sacred Order of the Diaconate* (*Ministeria Quaedom*), issued *motu proprio*, 15 August 1972, printed in *The Deacon, Minister of Word and Sacrament*, pp. 6, 8.

17. Ibid., pp. 6–9.

18. "The Basic Philosophy of the Permanent Diaconate Program for the Archdiocese of Omaha" (Mineographed, n.d.), p. 5.

19. Echlin, p. 116. Echlin translated the term as "lesser rank."

20. Ibid., pp. 130–31.

21. Pope Paul VI, *Laying Down Certain Norms*, p. 6.

22. Ibid., p. 9.

23. Title 3, Canons 21–25, *Constitutions & Canons for the Government of the Protestant Episcopal Church in the United States of America Otherwise Known as The Episcopal Church Adopted in General Conventions 1789–1979 Together with the Rules of Order* (New York: Seabury Professional Services, 1979), pp. 92–100. Canon 21, for example, is entitled "Of Ministers and Their Duties," the reference being to the three clerical orders.

24. *The Book of Common Prayer and Administration of the Sacraments and Other Rites and Ceremonies of the Church* (New York: Church Hymnal Corp. and Seabury Press, 1979), p. 390.

25. *Book of Common Prayer*, p. 855.

26. The Lambeth Conference 1958, *The Encyclical Letter from the Bishops together with the Resolutions and Reports* (London: S.P.C.K. and Greenwich, Ct.: Seabury Press, 1958), p. 50, chap. 1.

27. Ibid., p. 106, chap. 2.

28. *A Self-Supporting Ministry and the Mission of the Church*, by A Group of Sixty Bishops, Other Clergy and Lay People of the Episcopal Church (New York: The Division of Christian Ministries of the National Council of the Episcopal Church, and the Overseas Missionary Society, 1964), p. 8.

29. *The Book of Common Prayer and Administration of the Sacraments and Other Rites and Ceremonies of the Church according to the use of the Protestant Episcopal Church in the United States of America* (New York: Church Pension Fund, 1945), p. 535 (commonly called the 1928 *Book of Common Prayer*).

30. Essentially this is the position taken by J. Robert Wright in a report prepared for the Ministries' Commission and the Bishop of New York regarding the "permanent diaconate," where he argues for proliferation of a nonstipendiary priesthood as against a permanent diaconate, as though they are mutually exclusive. See J. Robert Wright, "Ministry in New York: The Non-Stipendiary Priesthood and the Permanent Diaconate," in *The St. Luke's Journal of Theology* 19 (December 1975) (Sewanee, Tn.: School of Theology), pp. 40–41. However, in an

address entitled "The Distinctive Diaconate in Historical Perspective," delivered at the National Conference on the Diaconate at Notre Dame University in June 1979, Wright concludes with the implication that the diaconate should be restored as a distinctive order (available from National Center for the Diaconate, Boston).

31. See Canon 34, Sec. 10 (b) (1), p. 83 and Canon 29, Sec. 2, pp. 68–69, *Constitutions and Canons (1958)*.

32. Ibid., Canon 34, Sec. 10, p. 83.

33. Canon 34, Sec. 10 (c), p. 77, *Constitution and Canons (1964)*. The General Convention deleted the prohibition and explicitly authorized this function for a congregation "unable to receive the services of a resident Priest."

34. Marion J. Hatchett, "The New Book: A Continuation of or a Departure from the Tradition?" in *Open*, The Newsletter of Associated Parishes, June 1977: 7.

35. H. Boone Porter, Jr., *Canons on New Forms of Ministry 1973* (Kansas City: Roanridge, n.d.), p. 1.

36. *The Church, The Diaconate, The Future, The Report of the Diaconate*, submitted by the Council for the Development of Ministry to the House of Bishops, The General Convention, September 1979, Denver, Co.

37. Ibid., 2.3.

38. Ibid., 2.5.

39. *Open*, June 1977; 1. The *Proposed Book of Common Prayer* became the official book in 1979.

40. George Khodr, "The Diaconate in the Orthodox Church," In *The Ministry of Deacons* (Geneva: World Council of Churches, 1965), p. 40.

41. Timothy Ware, *The Orthodox Church* (Baltimore: Penguin Books, 1964), p. 297.

42. George Florovsky, "The Problem of Diaconate in the Orthodox Church," in *The Diaconate Now*, ed. Richard T. Nolan (Washington: Corpus Books, 1968), pp. 85, 95.

43. Khodr, p. 41.

44. Ibid.

45. Ibid., p. 42.

46. Ware, p. 297. Florovsky, p. 95.

47. Khodr, p. 43.

48. Ibid., pp. 42–43.

49. Robert S. Paul, "The Deacon in Protestantism," in *The Diaconate Now*, p. 40.

50. Ibid., p. 41.

51. Ibid., p. 45.

52. "Report on the Ministry of Deacons," Lutheran Church in America, mimeographed, n.d.

53. Herbert Krimm, "The Diaconate in the Lutheran Church," in *The Ministry of Deacons*, p. 54.

54. Ibid.

55. Ibid., p. 55.

56. Claude Bridel, "Note on the Diaconal Ministry in the Reformed Churches," in *The Ministry of Deacons*, pp. 58–59.

57. Ibid., p. 61.

58. Robert W. Henderson, "Notes on the Diaconate in American Presbyterianism," in *The Ministry of Deacons*, p. 65.

59. Ibid.
60. Ibid., pp. 65–66.
61. Ibid., p. 66.
62. Ibid., p. 67.
63. Ibid.
64. George R. Beasley-Murray, "The Diaconate in Baptist Churches," in *The Ministry of Deacons*, p. 76.
65. Ibid.
66. Ibid., pp. 76–78.
67. John M. McBain, "What on Earth are Deacons For?" in *The Deacon* 7, no. 3 (April, May, June, 1977) (Nashville: Sunday School Board of the Southern Baptist Convention), p. 37.
68. Beasley-Murray, p. 77.
69. Howard Foshee, *The Ministry of Deacons* (Nashville: Convention Press, 1968, rev. 1974), pp. 32–35.
70. See *The Deacons in a Changing Church* by Donald F. Thomas (Valley Forge, Pa.: Judson Press, 1969) for a discussion of deacons in the churches of the American Baptist Convention and Foshee, in reference to the Southern Baptist churches. The Southern Baptists also publish *The Deacon* magazine, as has been mentioned, and make a number of other materials available. Address given under John M. McBain in Bibliography.
71. Kenneth L. Teegarden, *We Call Ourselves Disciples* (St. Louis: Bethany Press, 1975), pp. 74–76.
72. *Elders'-Deacons' Manual*, compiled by P. A. Willis (Cincinnati: Christian Restoration Association, 1968), p. 27.
73. Ibid., p. 29.
74. *The Book of Discipline of the United Methodist Church* (Nashville: Abingdon Press, 1980), par. 302, p. 169.
75. Ibid., par. 302–303, pp. 169–70.
76. Ibid., par. 307, p. 174.

CHAPTER 10

The Character and Place of the Diaconate

Clericalism

One of the major problems underlying the philosophy of the restored diaconate in the Anglican and Roman Catholic Churches at the present time is "clericalism." In both communions the diaconate is an integral part of holy orders, and holy orders in the traditional thought of both makes one distinct from the laity. This distinction is apparent at various points in the guidelines laid down by the U. S. Bishops' Committee of the Roman Catholic Church for the restoration of the diaconate. In the opening chapter the deacon is identified in terms of several relationships, but the most notable is that "of the threefold scope of service that he shares with bishops and priests."[1] Later in speaking specifically of the difference between clergy and laity, the guidelines draw a sharp and clear line: "From the point of view of sacred orders, the difference is between bishops and priests on the one hand and lay people—including religious—on the other."[2] Though the following sentence is encouraging and speaks of deacons constituting a bridge between clergy and laity, reminding both that our common identity is more important than our differences, the underlying clericalism remains.

This idea of a distinction not essentially of function but of lifestyle and perhaps infused character is foreign to the primitive Church and the consensus of the pre-Nicene age. Donald Tytler states that in the medieval view there were two kinds of Christians:

> The first is the clergy who live the authentic Christian life of entire devotion to God, manifested by their concentration on acts of worship and of theological reflection and also by the smallness of their income, which enables them to abstain from worldly things; the second is the laity, who practice a second-best type of Christianity, marred by com-

> promise with the world, in which they are thought to live in some way quite different from the clergy.[3]

Certainly this view is widely held today. Richard Rashke reports that 80% of American Roman Catholic priests believe there is an ontological difference between clergy and laity.[4] Though the idea of any ontological difference runs counter to the whole tenor of Vatican II and the principles of renewal held in the historic Western churches today, it would nevertheless all too often seem to underlie and subvert our thinking in subtle ways.

A Single Lifestyle

As we noted previously, the implications of such a delineation between clergy and laity are dualistic. Celibacy, which in itself and voluntarily chosen as a special calling can be meritorious, in the medieval period came to be a prime symbol of the fundamental difference in lifestyle between the clergy and the laity. Held up as the Christian ideal, it denied by implication the essential unity and goodness of all creation so absolutely affirmed in Christ by his incarnation and in his incarnate life.

We are reminded of the inherent goodness and value of marriage as well as the strong dualistic tendency in the Church by Karl Rahner in his discussion of celibacy in relation to the restored diaconate:

> It must always be borne in mind in this connection that in a true theology of marriage, marriage must really and truly not be regarded as a mere concession to human weakness (a conception attempted over and over again by an almost manichaean intellectual undercurrent in the Church) but must be seen to have an absolutely positive and essential function, not only in the private Christian life of certain individuals but also in the Church.[5]

Marriage, he sees, fills an "absolutely necessary function in the Church and for the Church" by being the "representation and living example of the mystery of Christ's union with the Church."[6]

While the abolition of compulsory celibacy in the Roman Catholic Church has been advocated by many as a matter of practicality in order to supply the number of priests needed regardless of other considerations (and may come about out of this necessity), it is far more important in its implications regarding the Christian life and ministry. Such a step would go a long way to enable Christians, both clerical and lay, to see that the fully committed Christian lifestyle is the same for all and that all are called to particular functions in the Church's ministry. Clerical celibacy has never been and is not now a matter of doctrine but of discipline in the Roman Church.

Bishop John A. T. Robinson is right when he suggests that the kind of distinction which creates two kinds of Christians should be abandoned altogether:

> I would put the question in all seriousness, whether, with the final disintegration of medieval Christendom, the distinction between *clergy and laity*, in contrast with the proper distinction between the various orders of the Body, should have any further validity.[7]

The Bishop thinks that abolishing this line of distinction between the clergy and the laity is primary in the restoration of the ministry to all Christians.[8] And in this connection he rightly objects to "the ministry" being used as a term in reference to the clergy, as it often is today.

In writing about the diaconate as a lifelong vocation Rahner maintains that the Church has shown by its practice that it does not see "any very close and necessary connection" between the diaconate and celibacy, since it does ordain men who are married. He strongly argues that celibacy should not be required for the restored diaconate:

> Marriage has a greater inner affinity with the office of deacon than has celibacy, since the deacon in his specific, official function is quite clearly the link between the clergy and the altar, on the one hand, and the world with its Christian task, on the other.[9]

Professionalism in the Various Ministries

To do away with clericalism and restore the original kinds of distinction between the various ministries of the Church is not, however, to deny the need for professionalism in the ranks of the Church's leadership. In the modern world of highly trained professionals and specialists in every field the Church more than ever needs those of high caliber and superior training as its leaders. Its requirements should attempt to insure such professional quality, and these characteristics should be kept in mind in the selection of leaders. Essentially, this is the concern shown in the early Church in legislation and other pronouncements commending those who had proven their ability and commitment to the Church by serving in other offices prior to being made bishops.

Subject to the Parish under the Leadership of the Priest (Pastor)

The place of the deacon in the parish church today is of primary importance both for its restoration and effective functioning. Rectors and pastors of parishes have sometimes felt threatened by proposals for the renewal of the diaconate. It is certainly true that those who have worked hard both to become and to serve as priests and pastors deserve reassurance that such a ministry will support rather than supplant them.[10] The principles needed for such assurance are to be found in the position of the deacon in the pre-Nicene Church.

The deacon in that period served the Church and was subject to its authority. This authority was expressed through the presbyteral council presided over by a bishop, though as time passed the bishop increasingly acquired the ruling authority of the presbyteral council in exchange for the presbyters acquiring the bishop's liturgical functions. The key factor here in this connection is that there was this exchange of function and that it occurred in the local church. Much confusion has emanated from failure to recognize that the priest or pastor of a parish today is far more comparable to the bishop of the early period than is the bishop himself. Bishops were pastors of the local churches, and dioceses had not yet emerged.

The idea, then, that deacons should serve under the bishop because they were originally the bishop's assistants is a misreading of history. Originally they were, as has been shown, servants of the Church working with the bishop, the presbyters, and others, all of whom were *laos*, laity. For a long time they remained essentially servants of the Church. They came to work largely under the presbyter when he became president of the local church, though some were indeed assistants to the bishop as he emerged as head of a diocese. But the primary ministry of the Church has always been and will always be on the level of the local congregation.

Increasingly today the leadership and governing functions of the local church are being broadened to include representatives of the laity as well as the clergy. In the Episcopal Church primary responsibility has long been exercised by the parish vestry in the "temporalities," the parish rector being its president. Today in some Episcopal and many Roman Catholic congregations parish councils have been given broad responsibilities and have proven of great value. In these parishes the priest does not surrender the role of parish leader but exercises it in a collaborative style, involving the body of the Church in problems and decisions, reflecting indeed the governing presbyteral council of the first centuries with the bishop at its head. Of great importance, this type of structure provides the broad leadership base that in many ways will insure the harmonious working together of all ministries.

Theologically, if the laity as well as the clergy are the Church, they should share in responsibility with the leaders of a parish for decisions relating to the spiritual as well as the material concerns of the Church. Pragmatically, in a society involved in an authority crisis, such as ours, shared responsibility is more acceptable and more productive. In parishes using this type of structure today the clergy usually find broader support for their ministries and more effectiveness in their leadership. Within the structure of such parishes deacons would normally play a vital role. Clearly they would not only be participants in but would be subject to its governing council. They would serve to support and strengthen the pastors or rectors both by gaining a new empathy with them in their work and by extending their ministries far beyond what they themselves can do.

However, until the Church generally recovers a structure which places governing authority on the local level in a council, the deacon whose ministry is exercised in the context of a parish must be made directly subject to the parish priest. As we have previously noted, failure to have this relationship clearly defined after the transition of the fourth century was an important contributing factor in the problems relating to the diaconate and its decline, and in modern times has hindered its restoration. And even when authority is shared, as with the presbyteral councils of the pre-Nicene age, it needs be remembered that the president of the congregation is its primary leader and structures are needed which foster support for the president's leadership by all members of the congregation. Other structures tend to be counterproductive.

Major Significance of Numbers in Parishes

It needs further to be pointed out that the restoration of the diaconate as a full and equal order envisions a number of deacons in the average parish. Even relatively small churches would normally have two or three deacons, and the larger the church the more deacons there would be. We often forget that Christian congregations tended to be very small until the fourth century. The Church at Ephesus, c. 60, probably numbered about fifty people.[11] And the situation did not change very much as the Church moved into the second century. The house-church of Doura-Europa in the first half of the third century could hold few more than sixty people in its largest room, which measured 40 feet by 16 feet, and such small numvers are confirmed elsewhere.[12] Yet the plural "deacons" is ordinarily used in reference to the churches.[13]

It is important in restoring the diaconate that we avoid the implication that truly committed discipleship involves ordination. Those ordained to the diaconate should be *representative* of the various Christian ministries of service. There should be equally committed lay people who are not ordained. One major factor in determining how many are to be ordained in a congregation is the need for liturgical functions which historically belong to the diaconate.

A group of deacons in a church would give the diaconate a considerably different character than would only one. The office would not then be identified with the personality of one particular individual. Any personality difference between a priest or pastor and a deacon would be of much less significance. But perhaps of more importance, such a body of deacons would be symbolic of the extensiveness of the Christian ministry of service as they functioned liturgically, pastorally, and charitably. The functioning of such deacons might do more than anything else to "declericalize" the Church's ministry, to bring Christians to believe that ministry belongs to every baptized member of the Church.

Diocesan Deacons

Though we have been considering deacons on the parish level, this does not, of course, rule out the possibility of "diocesan" deacons, subject directly to the bishop. These too are envisioned. Various kinds of ministry appropriate to the deacon are not necessarily related to the local parish and appropriately would be put directly under the bishop's oversight. These would include not only some of the more numerous nonstipendiary deacons but also some of those serving as full-time paid employees of the Church in such capacities as diocesan administrators, stewardship facilitators, and institutional workers.

Full Participation in Governing Structures

The status of deacons in a restored diaconate would be such as to allow them to participate fully in the same way as others in the governing structures of the Church. As members of a distinct order, they should be represented on parish councils and vestries and in diocesan conventions, councils, and other regional bodies. The principle of elected representation would apply here, the deacons of each parish electing from among their number those who are to represent them in each of these bodies. "Diocesan" deacons, where such exist, would elect from their own number.

The number of diaconal delegates to be selected for these various bodies would be determined by the appropriate legislative body. Provision should also be made for representation in synodical or national councils or conventions. In churches such as the Episcopal Church which provide for votes by orders on major issues at their diocesan conventions and synodical and national meetings, it would be appropriate for diaconal delegates to vote as a separate order. In this way they could pose no threat of diminishing the influence of the priesthood in the decision-making process. But more significantly, deacons living in society with the lifestyle of laity but at the same time being clergy would be in a position to make a unique contribution to these various legislative and policy-making bodies.

A Formal Agreement with Each Deacon

The guidelines of the Roman Catholic Bishops' Committee on the Permanent Diaconate wisely suggest the drawing up of a formal agreement for the ministry of each deacon.[14] Factors suggested in the formulation of such agreements are

1. The needs of the diocese
2. Capacities of the deacon
3. Consent of the deacon and his family
4. Consultation with the pastor, agency head, and/or involved structures such as a parish council

This type of an agreement might well serve, as the guidelines suggest, to avoid problems relating to authority:

> Such clear agreements, taking full account of limits, should help the bishop and the deacon—also the priests and lay people with whom the deacon will work—to recognize authority as service rather than power or domination. . . . With clear agreements, dialogue and mutual respect, inevitable authority conflicts should be minimal.[15]

In circumstances where the deacon's ministry is to be directly under the bishop, such agreements would, of course, be made between the bishop and the deacon. But in light of what has been said, it would seem that in the case of "parish" deacons, both from the theoretical and practical viewpoints, the agreement should be made between *the parish* and the deacon, signed by the pastor or rector and the diaconal candidate.

Experience will undoubtedly provide better insight into the specific content of such agreements. However, inclusion of the following points would seem advisable both to inform the deacon and the parish regarding the particular ministry involved and to insure that authority conflicts be kept minimal:

1. A clear statement that the parish church is a body with many members, each sent by Christ with special gifts to minister first to one another and then to others.

2. All ministries of the parish are exercised under the leadership of and coordinated by the pastor or rector.

3. The fundamental ministry of the deacon is to hold before the Church the character of the whole ministry of the Church as that of service and of its ministers as servants.

4. Part of any diaconal ministry is working in harmony with others in the parish church, especially its pastor or rector and other leaders, lending support, and seeking always to *build up* the Body of Christ.

5. The special area(s) or type(s) of ministry to be exercised by the deacon should be set forth.
6. A statement directing that problems arising which affect the welfare of the parish are to be brought to the pastor or rector and that the pastor's counsel and advice is to be followed.
7. The deacons will participate in any ongoing program for the diaconate that is applicable in which participation might reasonably be expected.
8. Reports are to be made at stated intervals to the pastor or someone designated by the pastor on the special ministry of the deacon.
9. The agreement automatically terminates when a deacon moves to another community and automatically expires every three years. It may be terminated at any time either by the deacon or the pastor or rector, provided that written notice be given to the other party first of the intention to terminate the agreement and then in no less than ten days a second notice that the agreement is terminated. Upon termination or expiration it must be formally renewed by both the parish and the deacon in order for the deacon to continue to minister as a deacon in that parish.

The ninth point above relating to termination of the agreement may seem to imply that the deacon, though ordained, is treated like a lay person licensed for a time for a particular ministry. However, in parish life the practice of what is outlined above would generally work otherwise. The dignity and permanence of ordination would act as a counterbalance to the temporary nature of the agreement. In most cases renewal of the agreement would be a matter of course and seem only a mere formality.

However, at this juncture in the restoration of the diaconate in its integrity and wholeness it would seem well advised to insure that the relationship between parish priests or pastors and deacons is well defined. Historically the lack of definition was a major reason for the decline of the office. Most would agree that there would normally be no problem in a parish so long as the pastor or rector in charge when the deacons are ordained remains. A problem could arise under a new parish head were a deacon, especially one who had been there many years, to forget the nature of the diaconate and become like what some have termed in the past a "lay pope." It is important that bishops, parish priests or pastors, and the Church generally have adequate assurance that parochial deacons will not be allowed to become a burden but will be the enormous asset they should and normally will be. At this juncture if we err, we should err on the side of too much rather than too little assurance.

It is envisioned that deacons operating within such a structure as outlined here would in all but a rare instance strengthen the work and ministry of the full-time priests and pastors. Even a new pastor or rector moving into a parish would have no reason to be threatened by the deacons already serving within that congregation. Their responsibility to support the parish's primary leader would be clearly agreed to by them in their agreement with the parish, and their tenure would ultimately rest upon the consent of the pastor or rector. It is only when such tenure is at the discretion of the bishop or other regional officer that clerical heads of parishes, especially those assuming that role in places with established deacons, might reasonably feel threatened by deacons who might forget that their ministry is one of *diakonia*.

Deacons Moving to Another Place

It is apparent from conciliar legislation of the early Church cited previously that the movement of clergy from one place to another has always been a problem in the Church, so much so that it was forbidden by the canons of more than one council. This problem has again come to the fore in connection with the kind of nonstipendiary (unpaid) office created in the restored diaconate, as was mentioned in the preceding chapter in connection with the Episcopal Church's experience. In our highly mobile society, deacons, earning their livelihood from non-Church sources, would certainly move to other communities and parishes with some frequency.

It is true that deacons transferring to another location may not be welcomed in some instances by the parish priests or pastors of their new churches. It is too much to expect that clergy, who have been trained to think of the Church's ministry largely in terms of their own and who know little about the nature of the historic diaconate, would know what to do with a deacon suddenly in the midst of the parish. In a time of transition this kind of problem is bound to arise.

In this situation the deacon should remember, first of all, that ordination did not confer an absolute right for the continuation of diaconal ministry even in the place of ordination. To think in such terms is in a profound sense a contradiction of the nature of the diaconate. Holding the office of deacon and being licensed to exercise that office in a given situation are not the same thing. This distinction is true for priests and bishops as well. The deacon rightly would want to serve in a diaconal ministry. But moving into a situation in which this diaconal ministry is not welcome, the deacon should see the opportunity for ministry by showing willingness to serve in some other needed way without insisting upon the kind of ministry formerly exercised either in liturgical or other terms. By the deacon demonstrating that diaconal ministry is truly *diakonia,* the priest or pastor may well come to want the full expression of the diaconate.

The fundamental difficulty here lies in what the Church is conceived to be. When the Church is conceived in organic as against hierarchic terms and ministry is seen as belonging equally to all members of the Church, the problem of deacons moving to other places is seen to be essentially the same as that of lay persons. Most parishes and their clergy are delighted to have committed lay people transferring into their midst. These lay people may have ministries and exercise them no less than deacons in the pastoral, charitable, and often the liturgical areas of the Church's life. There may be no place in the new parish for the particular ministry which the lay person has done in the former church, either liturgically or otherwise, though this is probably not often the case. But when it is, committed lay people habitually find new ways to serve. With the broad spectrum of ministries in the restored diaconate, certainly a deacon could as easily adjust.

Should not the problem be the opposite? Should not the clergy be concerned if there are no deacons to do the diaconal functions? Clergy who have lived for any length of time in most parishes today know that the diaconal functions of a pastoral, charitable, or liturgical nature, but especially the former two, are not adequately being done. The attempts in the various churches to compensate for the lack of real deacons by delegating their functions, especially liturgical, to lay people is less than satisfactory, though better than having them all concentrated in the parish priest or pastor.

It is true, as has been previously stated, that ordination confers special grace and the authorization of the Church and is desirable for these reasons. But there is in addition the matter of vocation. Vocation brings with it a different and enhanced sense of responsibility for the ministry and work involved, far more than do such things as a license to be a chalice administrator or lay reader or enrollment as a lector. Delegating such tasks tends to make them jobs to be done and leaves them unconnected to the pastoral and charitable concerns of the Christian community. On the other hand, a vocation to the diaconate brings the pastoral and/or charitable and liturgical functions of this ministry together and adds a sense of God's calling for a lifelong and many-sided work.

Ordination to a lifelong vocation in the diaconate does not exclude the possibility, as is pointed out in the report on "The Restoration of the Office of Deacon as a Lifetime State," that the deacon may at some later time be called to serve outside the office of deacon for good reason. The report specifically lists a change in secular employment as one of the reasons envisioned by the committee. Others enumerated in the report are limitation of physical health, preservation of psychic health, and a change in family situation.[16] Certainly there is no reason why a deacon, or a priest for that matter, cannot live and work effectively as a Christian in a parish without exercising the function conveyed through ordination. In a natural family functions change as the family situation changes. The role of parents changes radically as children grow from childhood to adulthood. As we saw earlier, the role of the presbyter changed radically between the middle of the third century and the end of the fourth century. A deacon's role may also be very different from one parish to another, even to the point that at times diaconal functions will no longer be exercised.

The mobility need not, then, create unwanted problems in a new location. It creates new opportunities. However, some safeguards can facilitate the transition. Provision should be made to require a year's residence in another parish, except for urgent necessity, before a written agreement may be entered into by the parish and the deacon. Meanwhile service as a deacon would not be envisioned in that parish, except perhaps for urgent cause and then only upon written request of the parish and its priest or pastor to the appropriate ecclesiastical authority. Such a requirement should go a long way to allow the Holy Spirit time to work in the situation and to insure both that the deacon wishes to minister as such in this new congregation and that the parish will find the ministry being offered an effective instrument to enhance its total ministry.

Dress, Title, Liturgical Vestments

It would be expected that deacons in a restored diaconate continue ordinarily to dress as they had before and avoid the use of clerical titles, though under special circumstances, such as a prison ministry, other procedures might be appropriate. The term "The Reverend," which many today believe outmoded for any of the clergy and does imply a false distinction between the clergy and the laity, is not appropriate for the restored diaconate and should not be permitted.

It is interesting to note that in 428, when the clergy at Rome dressed in the manner of the laymen at that time, Pope Celestine wrote to the bishops of the province condemning the use of special dress for the clergy.[17] There is certainly precedent for clergy wearing the attire of others, and deacons should not be set apart from others in their daily lives by this or other external means. An important part of their role is to symbolize the unity of the "sacred" and the "secular."

It is important, however, that the deacons wear customary vestments for their liturgical functions. Such attire serves to bring together in the office and person of the deacon the "sacred" and the "secular." Deacons who live as lay people, earning their living in the business world and bearing all customary social and family responsibilities, are at the same time those who, like priests, are ordained for the service of the altar. Symbolically the "secular" is caught up in the "sacred" and made holy.

The primary vestments of the deacon are the dalmatic and stole. The stole was originally the ancient handkerchief or neckcloth and seems to have become a distinctive mark of the clergy in the fourth century.[18] It has been worn by the deacon over the left shoulder since the seventh century, as directed by the Council of Toledo, c. 633. The council explains, "The right side of the body he must have free, in order that he may without hindrance, do his service."[19] Canon 28 of this council refers to the stole and alb as the special marks of the deacon in contrast to the stole and chasuble of the priest.[20]

The deacon's most distinctive vestment, however, is the dalmatic, which has a long and distinguished history in the Church. It was worn by the pope and the deacons of Rome in the fourth century, but then apparently only as customary daily dress along with laymen.[21] During the sixth century it seems to have been worn by bishops and deacons as a distinguishing mark of their attire.[22] By the ninth century the dalmatic was worn universally in the West by deacons.[23]

Though the dalmatic has never passed out of use in the West, its importance declined over the centuries as the diaconate became largely a transitional stage on the way to priesthood. It is the proper liturgical vestment for the deacon corresponding to the chasuble for the priest and, as such, should be restored as a major vestment of the Church. Its use symbolically asserts the importance of the office and its work in and to the Church.

NOTES

1. Bishops' Committee on the Permanent Diaconate, *Permanent Deacons in the United States: Guidelines on their Formation and Ministry* (Washington: United States Catholic Conference, 1971), p. 4, par. 7.
2. Ibid., p. 48, par. 149.
3. Donald Tytler, "Each in His Own Order," in *New Ways with the Ministry*, ed. John Morris (London: Faith Press, 1960), p. 23.
4. Richard L. Rashke, *The Deacon in Search of Identity* (New York: Paulist Press, 1975), p. 14.
5. Karl Rahner, in. vol. 5: *Later Writings*, trans. Karl H. Kruger, in *Theological Investigations* (Baltimore: Helicon Press, 1966), 5:294.
6. Ibid.
7. John A. T. Robinson, "Taking the Lid Off the Church's Ministry," in *New Ways with the Ministry*, ed. John Morris (London: Faith Press, 1960) p. 14.
8. Ibid., p. 17.

9. Rahner, *Theological Investigations*, 5:293.

10. H. Boone Porter, Jr., "Modern Experience in Practice," in *New Forms of Ministry*, ed. David M. Patton (London: Edinburgh House Press, 1965), p. 95.

11. Jean-Paul Audet, *Structures in Christian Priesthood: A study of home, marriage and celibacy in the pastoral service of the church*, trans. Rosemary Sheed (New York: Macmillan and Co., 1967), p. 96.

12. Ibid., pp. 97–98.

13. Some conciliar legislation, as that of Nicaea, Canon 15 (in vol. 14: *The Seven Ecumenical Councils*, ed. Henry R. Percival, in *Nicene and Post-Nicene Fathers of the Christian Church*, Second Series, ed. Philip Schaff and Henry Wace, 14 vol. [Grand Rapids, Mi.: William B. Eerdmans Publishing Co., 1956], 14:86), provided that "the deacons ought to be seven in number . . . even if the city be great." However, other documents state that the number should be in accord with the size of the church (See *The Constitution of the Holy Apostles* 3.19, in vol. 7: *Lactantius, Venantius, Asterius, Victorinus, Dionysius, Apostolic Teaching and Constitutions, Homily, and Liturgies*, in *The Ante-Nicene Fathers: Translations of the Writings of the Fathers down to* A.D. *325*, ed. Alexander Roberts and James Donaldson, Amer. reprint ed. A. Cleveland Coxe [Grand Rapids, Mi.: William B. Eerdmans Publishing Co., 1951], 7:432).

14. Bishops' Committee, *Permanent Deacons*, p. 45, par. 138–39.

15. Ibid.

16. "A Report on the Restoration of the Office of Deacon as a Lifetime State," a Committee of the Catholic Theological Society of America, chair. Edward Echlin, made at the request of the Bishops' Committee on the Permanent Diaconate (Roman Catholic), published in *The American Ecclesiastical Review* (March 1971) 164:3, par. 25, p. 198.

17. Percy Dearmer, *The Ornaments of the Ministers* (London: A. R. Mobray & Co. [new ed.], 1920) p. 26. Cf. L. Duchesne, *Christian Worship, Its Origin and Evolution: A Study of the Latin Liturgy Up to the Time of Charlemagne* (London: S.P.C.K. [5th ed.],1923), p. 381

18. A brief history of the diaconal vestments is given in the Appendix.

19. Council of Toledo, Canon 40, in Charles Joseph Hefele, vol. 4: *A History of the Councils of the Church, from the Original Documents,* A.D. *451 to* A.D. *680*, trans. William R. Clark, in *A History of the Councils of the Church* (Edinburgh: T. & T. Clark, 1895), 4:454.

20. Council of Toledo, Canon 40, Ibid., 4:453.

21. Dearmer, p. 24.

22. Ibid., p. 28. Cf. Cyril E. Pocknee, *Liturgical Vesture: Its Origin and Development* (London: A. R. Mowbray & Co., 1960), p. 37.

23. Walter Phillips, "Dalmatic," in vol. 6: *A New Survey of Universal Knowledge*, in *Encyclopedia Britannica*, Encyclopedia Britannica, Inc. (Chicago: William Benton, 1961), 6:994. Cf. Gilbert Cope, "Vestments," in *A Dictionary of Liturgy and Worship*, ed. J. G. Davies (New York: Macmillan Co., 1972), p. 376.

CHAPTER 11

Some Considerations Regarding Qualifications

Age

The first and simplest qualification of a deacon has to do with age. The legislation of the ancient councils is still sound. The Council of Carthage, 397, set the minimum age for ordination to the diaconate at 25 years.[1] Later councils such as Agde (506), Orleans (c. 537), and Trullo (692) affirmed this action.[2] This age would seem to allow time for individuals to gain sufficient maturity and Christian commitment to make responsible decisions in so weighty a matter and yet at the same time to be young enough for their patterns of living to be shaped more readily in this ministry. Much is to be said for maintaining this as the minimum age.

Pope Paul VI in his *General Norms for Restoring the Diaconate in the Latin Church* set the minimum age at 25 years,[3] but the guidelines of the Bishop's Committee of the Roman Catholic Church state that it is 35 years in the United States with bishops able to dispense for one year.[4] Recent legislation in the American Episcopal Church leaves the age up to the bishop, the Commission on Ministry, and the Standing Committee of the diocese but not less than 21 years.[5] One would hope the wisdom of the ancient councils will prevail in America and elsewhere.

Sexuality

It is beyond the scope of this study to present the arguments for and against the ordination of women to the clerical ministries of the Church. And such would seem unnecessary.

As has previously been observed in another connection, a study of the history and development of the Church's ordained ministry shows clearly that the Church has the authority to ordain women. The question then becomes one of whether or not such a course is that directed by the Holy

Spirit to meet the needs of the Church and its mission in the contemporary world. The fact that deaconesses were not female deacons in the early Church is not of great significance and would seem to have been largely due to cultural considerations.

In the case of the diaconate there would seem to be no compelling reason to make maleness a qualification for the diaconate, either from the point of view of function or symbol; and nothing in this study is intended to imply that the diaconate today should be open only to males. When masculine gender is used, it is used in the generic sense.

In recent years the Episcopal Church authorized the ordination of women to its diaconate. In 1971 the Catholic Theological Society of America in a study commissioned by the U.S. Bishops' Committee on the Permanent Diaconate recommended the ordination of women to the diaconate of that Church.[6] The report of a Task Force of the Catholic Theological Society of America published in 1978 concluded that the negative arguments do not "present any serious grounds to justify the exclusion of women from ordination to pastoral office in the Catholic Church."[7] The Bishops' Committee's own report states that among their candidates for the diaconate and the directors of diaconal programs "there is a growing conviction that women would strengthen the diaconal ministry immeasurably."[8]

Other Considerations

The qualifications for the diaconate listed in 1 Timothy 3, as we saw earlier, do not appear to be of Christian origin but rather were in general use in antiquity and were applied to this office in the Church. The principle here is applicable today. Individuals serving the Church in the diaconate are to be those of high standards and good reputation. They are to be reliable and respected members of the communities in which they live.

Stable marriages and sound family life are of major importance for married candidates. Married candidates need, in addition, the approval and support of their spouses for this ministry.

Of prime importance, there needs to be depth of commitment to Christ as is to be seen in style and manner of life and which has been tested by several years of living and serving within the Christian community. A desire for the *diakonia* particularly of charity should be in evidence. And there should be some sense of being called for this ministry by the Holy Spirit.

Another important requisite is acceptance by the Christian community. The congregation itself could play a major role in the selection of deacons as they did in the early Church.[9] Parish councils or other responsible groups might well take the initiative in urging qualified lay persons to seek ordination. In some small congregations there might be a consensus of the congregation generally.

There are certainly some compelling theological reasons to recommend the procedure of the Christian community electing qualified laity for the office. Of course, this procedure assumes that the community electing is informed about the nature of the diaconate and still small enough for the people generally to know each other. Certainly the Holy Spirit could work as well through this process as through any other—perhaps at times even better. A person so elected would always be free after reflection and prayer to accept or reject such an election. Further, the Church's screening process would be operative to forestall a misguided selection, should this occur.

A number of Roman Catholic programs have found an interview process helpful in the screening and development of diaconal candidates. Selection Research, Inc. (SRI) of Lincoln, Nebraska, developed the interview at the request of the Executive Committee of the national Association of Permanent Diaconate Directors in 1979. The interview is based on a model developed by analyzing ordained deacons who were regarded as best exemplifying the office. It centers around nine personality traits previously identified as important for deacons, such as "relator," "spirituality," "purpose," "family," "helping," and "teaming."[10] Interviewers are trained by Selection Research's Deacon Perceiver Academy.[11]

The priest-director of the Omaha Permanent Diaconate Program since its inception, Patrick McCaslin, reports that the interviews give him the tools he has needed to facilitate the screening of diaconal candidates. He says that by identifying the strengths of candidates, even those who do not belong in the program, they feel affirmed.[12] He recommends the screening process highly.

It is certainly appropriate that the Church use such a tool, essentially borrowed from the corporate and professional world. However, the Church must do so with the realization that such standardized tests have definite limitations. There is increasing evidence that these tests fall short of being the reliable indicators of future excellence they have been widely thought to be. Bowdoin College in Maine has abandoned use of the Scholastic Aptitude Test (SAT) for college entrance due to what it believes to be deficiencies, notably in the test's inability to measure the student's level of development, personality traits, or growth pattern in high school.[13] An article in the *New York Times Magazine* regarding tests for screening pre-medical students notes that they do predict reasonably well student grades in the first two years of medical school, when the courses are science-oriented. However, the article reports, "they have zero—yes zero—correlation with how well students do in the third and fourth years," when the students are involved with patients in clinical situations.[14]

The human personality is so intricate and complex that it is difficult to develop standardized tests that are a true measure of the potential of the individuals. A built-in limitation stems from the model used. In the case of the diaconate, the model in the SRI interview is that of men who tend to excel at accommodation and work as team members but are not strong leaders. Individuals of the type selected through this interview process are needed in the diaconate. However, the history of the diaconate suggests that a broader model is needed to allow room for deacons who will be able leaders. Athanasius and Gregory the Great come immediately to mind. The Church today needs deacons with leadership potential for various sorts of ministries. Further, it must always be remembered that Christians look to the guidance of the Spirit through prayer *along with* intelligent methods and approaches to be directed in its decisions, including the selection of its clergy.

Extensive Educational Requirements a Barrier

It is important to remember that the qualifications for a permanent diaconate are quite different from those for the priesthood. One of the major differences stems from the fact that preaching is not inherent in the office of the deacon as it is in that of the priest. It is preaching that requires extensive education, both general and theological. Certain deacons may have this training and could certainly be licensed to preach. But to impose the burden of this kind of education on the diaconate generally is not only *unnecessary* but a *serious barrier* to the development of a vital and effective diaconal ministry.

Extensive educational requirements will exclude both those who may be intelligent and capable, devout and committed, but lack the general educational background needed, and also those who have the broad educational requirements and other qualifications but whose other legitimate responsibilities in such areas as their work and family life prevent them from committing the time required for additional training in the theological disciplines.

Deacons should be carefully chosen and well trained, but the training should be for the particular functions of their ministries. There are many basically qualified persons today in our congregations who could serve the Church well in the diaconate with only a minimum of special training, some indeed already highly trained and skilled, much more so in fact than most of the clergy, in the *diakonia* of their special ministries.

The aim of the Church in the restoration of the diaconate is to make *deacons,* not "mini-priests" or "mini-pastors."

NOTES

1. Council of Carthage, Canon 4, in Edward Landon, *A Manual of Councils of the Holy Catholic Church,* vol. 1 (London: Griffith Farrar & Co., n.d.), 1:121.

2. Council of Agde, Canon 16, in Charles Joseph Hefele, vol. 4: *A History of the Councils of the Church, from the Original Documents,* A.D. *451 to* A.D. *680,* trans. William R. Clark, in *A History of the Councils of the Church* (Edinburgh: T. & T. Clark, 1895), 4:79. Council of Orleans, Canon 6, ibid., 4:205. Council of Trullo, Canon 14, in vol. 14: *The Seven Ecumenical Councils,* ed. Henry R. Percival, in *Nicene and Post-Nicene Fathers of the Christian Church,* Second Series, ed. Philip Schaff and Henry Wace, 14 vol. (Grand Rapids, Mi.: William B. Eerdmans Publishing Co., 1956), 14:372.

3. Pope Paul VI, *General Norms for Restoring the Permanent Diaconate in the Latin Church (Motu Proprio),* United States Catholic Conference, Washington, D.C., 18 June 1967, p. 3 (hereafter cited *Permanent Diaconate*).

4. Bishop's Committee on the Permanent Diaconate, *Permanent Deacons in the United States: Guidelines on their Formation and Ministry* (Washington: United States Catholic Conference, 1971), p. 44, par. 135.

5. Title III, Canon 10, Sec. 10 (a) (1), *Constitutions & Canons for the Government of the Protestant Episcopal Church in the United States of America Otherwise Known as The Episcopal Church Adopted in General Conventions 1789–1973 Together with the Rules of Order* (New York: Seabury Professional Services, 1973), p. 63.

6. Richard L. Rashke, *The Deacon in Search of Identity* (New York: Paulist Press, 1975), pp. 50–51.

7. *Research Report, Women in Church and Society,* ed. Sara Butler (Bronx, N.Y.: The Catholic Theological Society of America, 1978), p. 47.

8. Bishops' Committee, *Permanent Deacons,* p. 54, par. 168.

9. H. Boone Porter, Jr., "Modern Experience in Practice," in *New Forms of Ministry,* ed. David M. Patton (London: Edinburgh House Press, 1965), p. 96.

10. Information sheet describing the services of the Deacon Perceiver Academy of SRI.

11. Information is available from SRI Perceiver Academies, Jo Ann Miller, O. S. F., 2546 South 48th St. (Box 6438), Lincoln, Nb. 68506.

12. Personal communication to the author.

13. Benjamin Fine, *The Stranglehold of the I. Q.* (Garden City, N.Y.: Doubleday, 1975), p. 167.

14. E. B. Fiske, "Finding Fault with the Testers," in *New York Times Magazine,* 18 November 1979: 152.

CHAPTER 12

The Functions and Training of the Deacon

Functions of the New Diaconate

As we have already seen, the first and truly great function of the deacon is to be the symbol par excellence of the Church's ministry. Deacons are the embodiment of the servant ministry Christ has sent us all to share. Their particular functions are therefore important, because they are the things which give meaning and content to what the deacon is.

Our study of the diaconate reveals that the three primary areas in which deacons of the early Church exercised their ministry were liturgical, pastoral, and charitable or societal. These three areas, also enumerated by Paul VI in his apostolic letter, *Laying Down Certain Norms Regarding the Sacred Order of the Diaconate*, provide a more useful form of classification than those customarily used.[1] It is desirable to delineate pastoral and charitable/societal functions, though they are both "service" (*diakonia*), if for no other reason than to emphasize the deacon's ministry outside the confines of the Church.

The use of a separate category for the deacon's ministry of the word apparently stems from the widespread but erroneous belief that preaching is an inherent function of the diaconate. The deacon does, of course, have a ministry of the word, especially in reading the Gospel lesson at the Eucharist, but this is primarily liturgical. The verbal witness deacons make to Christ in their special pastoral and charitable ministries, whether or not this involves some form of catechesis, is also a genuine and important ministry of the word. But preaching, as we have seen, belongs essentially to the episcopate and presbyterate historically.

A review of the pastoral and charitable functions of the diaconate quickly indicates that full-time salaried deacons are not only possible but highly desirable in some situations. Large parishes and dioceses have many needs which could best be provided by deacons working as full-time employees, trained and skilled in their specialized ministries. As the diaconate grows and as resources become available, these ministries will undoubtedly become more numerous.

The deacons of the early Church and now are the ones above all others who bring together the worship (*leiturgia*) and the service (*diakonia*) of the Church. It is, therefore, important that the functions of liturgy and service, both pastoral and charitable, be given balance. In that way their essential relationship is made visible. The truth that "apart from Jesus the Servant there is no church ministry" becomes apparent.[2]

LITURGICAL FUNCTIONS

The following may be listed as among the proper liturgical functions of the deacon. Pastoral and/or charitable functions are put in parentheses to relate them to the liturgical function:

1. To carry the paschal candle, chant the Exsultet, and assist at baptism and the Eucharist at the Easter Vigil.
   (Ministry as servants of the Church.)
2. To assist in the administration of baptism and in some instances to officiate at baptism.
   (Ministry in precatechumenate, catechumenate, and postbaptismal catechesis.)
   (The Roman Church permits deacons solemnly to baptize *infants* with all rites and ceremonies of the office. The Episcopal Church authorizes deacons to officiate at baptism only when a priest is not available and with the bishop's authorization. It is appropriate for deacons to do the actual immersion or pouring for those they have prepared when a bishop or priest is presiding.)
3. To announce the stages of the Eucharistic Liturgy.
   (Ministry of representing the Church in helping God's people.)
4. To read the Gospel at the Eucharist.
   (Ministry of the word in counseling, teaching, and bearing witness in the world.)
5. To bid the prayers of the people.
   (Ministry to all with problems and other special needs.)
6. To prepare the people's oblations at the Eucharist.
   (Participate in offering up to God the needs, concerns, and lives of all God's people as well as the material creation.)
7. To administer the Bread and the Wine of the Eucharist.
   (Ministry to provide food, clothes, and other physical needs to the poor.)
8. To perform the ablutions at the Eucharist.
   (Ministry of servanthood.)

9. To take the Eucharistic Bread and Wine to the absent.
   (Ministry to the sick and disabled.)

10. To assist at marriages and to solemnize marriages in the absence of an ordinary minister (bishop or priest) of marriage.
    (Administering premarital instruction.)
    (Both Roman and Episcopal Churches require authorization of civil law for solemnizing marriages. The Roman deacon must be specifically delegated here by the bishop or pastor. Episcopal deacons may so function only when no bishop or priest is available and may not use the nuptial blessing.)

11. To administer Holy Unction to the sick.
    (Ministry to the sick.)
    (In the Roman Catholic Church today deacons may not anoint. In the Episcopal Church they may do so in case of necessity but using oil blessed by a bishop or priest.)

12. To preside at non-Eucharistic prayer services, such as Morning and Evening Prayer and nonsacramental penitential rites.
    (Ministry of prayer.)

13. To conduct services in homes for the aged and disabled.
    (Ministry of visiting the aged and shut-ins.)

14. To read services in congregations without a priest or pastor.
    (Ministry of pastoral concern.)

15. To lead the Church's music.
    (Ministry to the pastoral as well as liturgical needs especially of choristers.)

16. To officiate at burial rites, except the Eucharist.
    (Ministry to the dying.)

17. To deliver homilies when officiating at a baptism, marriage, burial, or other liturgical services in place of a priest or pastor.
    (The Roman Church authorizes deacons presiding at such services to preach. On occasions where the deacon is not presiding, he must have the authorization of the bishop. A deacon not trained for preaching could use a sermon prepared by one who is. Numerous homiletical services are currently available.)
    (Ministry of pastoral concerns for special needs.)

Deacons should be prominently in evidence as normal and *necessary* ministers in the Church's worship, especially at the Sunday Eucharist. Only in this way can they give visible expression to their dual role, which serves to give unity to their total ministry and that of the Church.

PASTORAL FUNCTIONS

The pastoral and charitable functions of the diaconate are usually considered together, and certainly no absolute distinction exists. There is a sense in which what is pastoral is charitable and vice versa. However, in the Church we have over the centuries become far too accustomed to think of ministry primarily in terms of the Church's ministering to its own people. Much of this attitude stems from the time when the Church and State were two names for the same society in which everyone belonged to both. But today, when this is very far from the truth, we urgently need to reform our habitual way of thinking. Therefore, in order to give greater emphasis to ways in which the Church's ministry can and should reach out into the world, a division is made here between its pastoral and charitable functions, the former having more to do with the Church's care for the welfare and nurture of its own people and the latter more with its concern for those in the world outside.

The proper pastoral functions of the deacon are broad and varied. The following are functions which ordinarily are primarily focused upon ministry to the Church's own people and illustrate the kinds of things they might encompass:

1. To visit the sick and the shut-ins.
2. To care for and about the parish's poor.
3. To coordinate a program for visiting and integrating newcomers.
4. To visit prospects for entering the Church.
5. To instruct adults in the precatechumenate, catechumenate, and postbaptismal catechesis.
6. To teach the children of the Church.
7. To lead small study/prayer/sharing groups.
8. To organize and head groups and activities to serve special needs within the Christian community.
9. To train acolytes or altar servers.
10. To work with student groups.
11. To instruct parents and godparents for baptisms.
12. To lead parish discussion groups.
13. To organize and coordinate retreats, workshops, and similar activities.
14. To coordinate ushers or "parish hosts."
15. To develop youth programs and activities.
16. To counsel those with problems.
17. To coordinate and train lectors.
18. To assume responsibility for some aspect of parish or diocesan administration.

CHARITABLE/SOCIETAL FUNCTIONS

In a highly sophisticated, complex industrial society such as ours, Christian ministry can be and increasingly is exercised in numerous and sometimes imaginative ways. However, categorizing and listing such functions, as we have in the liturgical and pastoral areas, does not seem to do justice to *diakonia* with the special character we are classifying as charitable or charitable/societal. Such a list might include the following, again simply as illustrative:

1. To help and befriend the powerless who are in need: prisoners, the poor, the rejected.
2. To counsel the troubled.
3. To work in referral programs to help those in crisis situations.
4. To lead or work in community action groups to effect social change.
5. To organize and promote community activities or programs to meet special needs: drug and alcohol dependencies, unwed parents, etc.
6. To work with juveniles and adults in hospitals, prisons, orphanages, half-way houses, and other institutions.
7. To serve youth in various educational and recreational programs.
8. To care for the needs of the elderly and disabled.
9. To visit the lonely and neglected, especially those in institutions.
10. To work with the handicapped.
11. To provide employment help to those leaving institutions, such as prisons, half-way houses, drug and alcohol treatment centers.

These activities all serve to illustrate the kinds of charitable/societal functions which are proper to the diaconate. However, the possibilities for these functions seem far more numerous, challenging, and creative than this list seems to imply.

The modern diaconate should serve to enable and encourage those in varied occupations and life situations to develop special ministries of service, though these do not lend themselves to precise categories. Some of these ministries would be natural outgrowths of occupational vocations. A nurse or a lawyer might give part of his or her time to service in a free clinic on a regular and continuing basis. Such service, enlightened and informed by the Spirit, is a *diakonia* of love and rises above the level of mere social service.

A teacher might offer special classes or personal instruction to children with learning problems. A salesperson could offer time and expertise to teach volunteers how to "sell" charitable organizations to prospective supporters to raise needed financial support. A carpenter, an electrician, and a "handy man" might use their particular knowledge and skills by setting aside a part of their time to help the elderly, and especially the elderly poor, maintain their homes or, perhaps, to work with the younger poor to upgrade theirs. A psychologist might offer counsel or lead a support group for men and women who befriend children of single-parent homes. Another might conduct classes in child rearing for young couples.

Others may develop ministries in other ways. A housewife who has recovered from breast cancer could have a real ministry in teaching groups of women the procedures urged for early detection and in giving support to those who, like herself, contract the disease. One who has conquered an alcohol problem in his or her own life can help others similarly afflicted, as has been repeatedly demonstrated by members of Alcoholics Anonymous. Recovered drug abusers can be equally effective. A father or mother whose children have left home might offer much to boys or girls from single-parent homes over the years as a "big brother" or "big sister" to them or to more troubled youth in other programs of this nature.

Many have hobbies or knowledge and/or special talents which may be utilized in the service of others. Using one's talents to teach crafts and hobbies in such places as regional mental health centers or senior citizen centers can constitute an important and vital ministry. Offering one's services in continuing work with youth in sponsoring a basketball team or coaching wrestling or judo at a Y. M. C. A. or community center can be equally the work of Christ.

The kinds of service which might properly be seen to be appropriate functions for the charitable ministry of the deacon seem almost endless, so many and varied are the needs of people in modern society. However, it is not simply in the doing of these things that we find Christian ministry. The work becomes a true ministry when it is motivated by the desire to serve in the name of Christ and is done with caring love. There comes to it a perseverance which often is not otherwise present. Though the person involved in such work tends to find it rewarding and fulfilling, he or she is motivated more by the needs of others. Christian *diakonia* tends to have a distinctive character, flowing as it does from a life committed to Christ, empowered by his Holy Spirit, informed by his word, made loving through prayer, and made humble through Christ-like service.

Ordination to the diaconate of some who render such services in the name of Christ, or seek to do so, would serve a number of important purposes. First, it would broaden the concept of Christian ministry both in the eyes of Christians and of the world. The symbol of *diakonia* would be embodied and made real in areas which are meaningful to modern men and women. The Church would be visibly reaching out into the world and be seen to care about the needs of all humanity. Further, the distinctive Christian workstyle and lifestyle of these deacons would provide a model and a witness to inform others of what it can mean to live and work as a Christian in their world.

Symbolically also each of these deacons would by virtue of the diaconal office assert the unity of the "sacred" and the "secular," of all of life, another witness much needed in the midst of our fragmented world. And last, but of great importance, such ministries would be "strengthened by sacramental grace," as Pope Paul VI has affirmed.[3] Their quality would be enriched and their vitality enhanced.

It is readily apparent that a corps of deacons in a parish could not only relieve the overwhelming burden borne by the clergy today but would multiply the effective ministry of the Church both among its own people and in the community around it manyfold. Diaconal training programs should center upon such liturgical, pastoral, and charitable/societal functions. Training centered on these functions would give them the "radical ministerial focus," by which is meant a focus upon "service in the community," that they can and should have.[4]

Training for the Restored Diaconate

The character of the diaconate as a full and equal order being proposed here requires a radically different philosophy of training than that which underlies the training program for the "transitional deacons" who are on their way to the priesthood or those for the lifelong diaconate of contemporary Roman Catholicism and Anglicanism which are essentially based on the seminary model. The fundamental problem with these programs for the restored diaconate is that the underlying philosophy seems more aimed at creating religious professionals within the Church than preparing people to minister. If indeed all are ministers in the Church, as the early Church so clearly understood, then what justification is there for insisting that every order of the clerical ministry regardless of its function be theologically trained beyond what is reasonable and desirable for the committed lay person?

When the ministry is conceived of functionally with all members having a ministry, it is apparent that professional theological training and qualifications are neither required nor desirable for most. This principle is recognized in the report of a group of 60 bishops, other clergy, and lay people of the Episcopal Church who met in 1964 to consider the requisites of a "self-supporting ministry." The group asserts that seminary training for most of those entering this type of ministry is not necessary and probably not desirable.[5] The guidelines of the Roman Catholic U. S. Bishops' Committee regarding theological training or formation, as they term it, also state that the goal of their study program is "to prepare ministers of the gospel rather than professional theologians."[6] However, the next section outlines areas of study which would seem to be drawn from a seminary model, though in succeeding sections this is perhaps to some extent ameliorated.[7]

The character of the diaconal ministry is *service*. Careful consideration of this representative ministry of *diakonia* makes it apparent that professional training in the theological disciplines is not designed for most forms of this ministry and reveals the most serious error in most of the training programs in both the Episcopal and Roman Catholic Churches to be that they have used a "mini-seminary" model. This is not more than could be expected today, since the image of the deacon has been the "transitional deacon" for many centuries. Even the clergy for the most part at the present time have very little conception of the diaconate as a lifelong vocation. In the minds of most there is a real but unconscious image of the deacon as a "mini-priest" or "mini-pastor."

This error is tacitly acknowledged in a letter to the author, written in 1977, from the Roman Catholic director of the Permanent Diaconate Program of the Archdiocese of Omaha and President then of the Association of Permanent Diaconate Directors, a priest, Patrick McCaslin. He wrote regarding the weakness of their program:

> We have gone from a seminary model of education, with a teacher talking at them, to our present methodology which utilizes facilitators directing and guiding but with the men and women doing all the reading, reflecting and responding in small groups of eight.[8]

Such a change is a major step in the right direction. However, one may question whether this revised method will meet the requirements set forth in the *Guidelines* of the Bishops' Committee on the Permanent Diaconate alluded to above.

A personal visit to one such group in early 1979 did reveal that at least in this archdiocese the seminary model has given way to the small study/sharing group model. The group and the meeting observed are apparently typical of the program. The group consisted of five men, one already a deacon who had been ordained in an earlier program several years before, and their wives. They met in the home of a parish priest, who acted as group facilitator. One couple was responsible for the opening prayers or prayer time. Most of the evening was devoted to discussion-type study based on two chapters of a book currently in use in a religion course in one of the diocesan high schools. A series of study questions in mimeographed form, originally prepared for the high school class, formed the basis for discussion, which had considerable depth and revealed profound understanding of and concern for the gospel.

The diaconal candidates were learning to think theologically. In many, perhaps most, ways, it was typical of many small group meetings of committed lay people concerned with Christian growth which occur in parishes throughout the United States today. The study course, in this instance on Christian ethics, was presented in nontechnical terms. It provided the input needed to prevent the group from being what has become all too common in American Christianity of recent years, a sharing group of what has been termed "pooled ignorance." The Omaha program has continued to use comparable study courses.

Though the approval and support of a spouse is essential for married diaconal candidates, the spouse's participation in the training or formation program should be entirely voluntary. The spouse may not be called to the diaconate and may have other interests and obligations to pursue, while at the same time able to be supportive and enthusiastic of the diaconal ministry.

The School of Theology of the University of the South, an Episcopal institution, has developed a somewhat unique training program designed for ecumenical use in training for lay ministry called "Education for Ministry."[9] Several Episcopal dioceses have recommended the program for diaconal candidates. Though it presents the "core curriculum" of a seminary, the program is not that of a seminary model. In four years the traditional disciplines of a theological seminary are interwoven within the framework of following the story of the people of God. The content is imparted through individual weekly study and reading. The weekly group meetings are concerned with theological reflection on incidents from the lives of participants. Problem solving is not permitted. Content is of a high caliber and is ecumenically oriented. The program has now spread to several continents. Such training as that of the Archdiocese of Omaha and "Education for Ministry" seem far more appropriate for the functions of the diaconate than the "mini-seminary" model provides.

It should be recognized that though most deacons would not be full-time paid employees of the Church, a restored diaconate would include deacons professionally trained to serve the Church as full-time salaried workers. In some areas, such as Christian education, these deacons would be seminary trained. In others, e.g. parish administration, stewardship promotion, secretarial work, evangelism promotion, Church music, or Christian counseling (family, penal, etc.), their training might consist of a specially designed program combining appropriate seminary and college work. Seminaries should develop and offer suitable programs to provide for these needs.

The canonical requirements of the Episcopal diaconate, revised in 1973, have moved in the direction of diaconal training on a nonseminary model for those aspiring to the restored diaconate, though apparently with some hesitation, as is seen by the use of the phrase "in special cases, under urgent circumstances" to designate those for whom training and examinations may be lessened.[10] Porter, in his commentary on these canons, seems to go beyond the intent of the canon as it stands, though probably not beyond that of some of its authors, when he writes that the pertinent section

> plainly envisions a quite different approach. Now the needs of particular individuals and particular situations are the basis for decisions as to the extent of such theological study. . . . In other words, theological scholarship is not a necessary prerequisite for ordination.[11]

His interpretation is prophetic, one hopes.

The canon itself lists the various topics for study and does so in terms which seem appropriate for committed lay people generally. The bishop is, in addition, to "appoint such other training or practical experience as is suitable to the Candidate's occupation, his role in the community, and his ecclesiastical ministry."[12] Further, the examination required is not the canonical examination required for "transitional deacons" but a simpler one to be conducted by diocesan commissions on ministry.[13]

It should be noted at this point that a diaconate which is no longer transitional would eliminate one of the most serious problems associated with the Episcopal Church's "perpetual diaconate" of the post-World War II era. The training for this program was basically a scaled-down version of that for priests and not for the ministry of service of a true diaconate.[14] Functions often were largely liturgical. The office itself was usually seen as definitely inferior to that of the priest. All of this suggested that the diaconate should be viewed as a transitional office. The result was that more often than not the deacons would then seek the priesthood, though their training for it was usually inadequate, sometimes woefully so. But a diaconate which no longer accommodates those called to priesthood would have different qualifications and requirements. Not only would there be no inherent suggestion of the priesthood, but a deacon who did afterwards feel called to a priestly ministry would clearly and canonically be required to undergo training for that ministry, training which would certainly usually mean the seminary itself or, at least, that based on its model.

All Christians need theological training. But it is difficult to justify the need for deacons to have extensive training beyond that which committed laity should have unless such training is directly related to a special ministry a particular deacon is to perform. Surely, if a deacon is to lead a Bible study group, he or she would benefit by special training in that area, as would any other. But the principle involved here is to train deacons for their *diakonia*, not to make them a kind of "paraprofessional" similar to the "paramedics" in the medical profession.

Training programs that tend to make the deacon a kind of "paraprofessional" or "mini-priest" are actually disparaging to the order. They involve an implied assumption that the priesthood is the higher order and forms the essential model for the diaconate, though this has not often been recognized. So long as this is the case, the diaconate will not be the full and equal order that will hold the image of the servant-Christ before the Church and the world as the model for all ministry.

Were preaching an inherent function of the diaconate, as it has often been thought to be, then comprehensive theological education would certainly be important in the training of diaconal candidates. Undoubtedly, part of the impetus for this type of preparation has been due to this assumption. However, as we have conclusively shown, preaching was never a function belonging to the diaconate in the early Church. To make it so now would seem neither helpful nor desirable but in fact would seem counterproductive. Of course, there will probably be deacons along with lay people who are eminently qualified and possess a charisma of the Spirit for preaching. These should by all means be specially licensed by the Church.

The Roman Catholic Church in the United States currently authorizes deacons to preach on occasions when they officiate or preside at a sacramental or liturgical rite. But it is to be remembered that they preach then because they preside, not because they are deacons. Presiding is by virtue of the order a presbyteral or episcopal function. The Bishops' Committee on the Liturgy's Study Test VI, *The Deacon, Minister of Word and Sacrament*, lists as occasions on which the deacon may preach when presiding; baptism of infants and some of the adult rites of Christian initiation, matrimony, benediction of the blessed Sacrament, a wake or Christian burial service apart from the Eucharist or in a cemetery, Morning or Evening Prayer or other rites of the liturgy of the hours, and the visitation of the sick.[15] When the deacon presides at such services, preaching is often desirable, but provision could better be made by providing the deacon with a homily prepared for the purpose by one properly trained in theology and homiletics. Deacons could, of course, make adaptations for the particular occasion and would not have to follow the text slavishly. But would it not be generally better for the deacon, the congregation, and the Church to meet this need in this way?

Liturgical preaching by the deacon on occasions such as the Eucharist require the bishop's authorization or approval by "diocesan norms" in the Roman Church.[16] The specific requirement of the Episcopal Church for a deacon to be licensed to preach by the bishop has been removed from the *Book of Common Prayer*. However, the requirement of a license by appropriate church authority would more clearly delineate the proper functions of the office. The character of the diaconate is servanthood, not the role of leadership expressed through presiding and its accompanying activities. At the same time a license would allow for those trained homiletically and possessed with the charisma of preaching to contribute to the life of the Church in this way. Further, it would definitely remove the obligation of preaching from those who might be extremely gifted deacons in functions more characteristic of the office.

Wilhelm Schamoni writes in relation to the problem of diaconal training that a "genuinely spiritual man," who has demonstrated by the "way he brings up his children and presides in his home that he could just as well preside in the House of God," does not necessarily need to acquire special knowledge or undergo any special training and could be ordained without lengthy preparation.[17] Boone Porter emphasizes the same point when he observes, "indeed it is the depth of personal commitment to Jesus Christ, compassion, love of the scriptures, and the ability to communicate the faith to others, that are primary needs for a deacon."[18]

It is also true and important that those earning their own living with family and social responsibilities would not have sufficient time for extensive diaconal training. The problem here is, as Richard Rashke affirms, too much training will keep qualified individuals away while too little will give the program a bad reputation.[19] But would not the kind of training which most would consider reasonable and desirable for committed laity be adequate? Training which is beyond what committed laity should have and is not related to their function will inevitably exclude many who are qualified and who would enhance and enrich the Church by using their special gifts and abilities in the specific ministry of the deacon.

In writing of the restored diaconate Karl Rahner advocates this type of religious training. He recognizes that there need to be differences in different areas and situations. The religious training of what he terms the "absolute" deacon (not transitional) should "correspond to what is customary and possible in the case of an educated Christian layman in a particular region."[20] He also speaks of the need for professional training for the particular work they will do, as a welfare or social worker, a catechist, or an ecclesiastical administrator.[21]

Cardinal Suenens of Belgium, who enjoys the respect of Christians of all communions throughout the world, has recommended that those who are already doing diaconal services should be ordained.[22] The "Decree on the Missionary Activity of the Church" of Vatican II affirms the belief of Cardinal Suenens and recommends the ordination of those so serving the Church. The council fathers urge the restoration of the diaconate where episcopal conferences approve this and go on to say

> For there are men who are actually carrying out the functions of the deacon's office, either by preaching the Word of God as catechists, or by presiding over scattered Christian communities in the name of the pastor and the bishop, or by practicing charity in social or relief work. It will be helpful to strengthen them by that imposition of hands which has come down from the apostles, and to bind them more closely to the altar. Thus they can carry out their ministry more effectively because of the sacramental grace of the diaconate.[23]

In the Episcopal Church one of its leading scholars, Massey Shepherd, has similarly suggested that there are lay readers doing such diaconal service who should be ordained.[24] Additional training would hardly seem appropriate for these.

A training program should include the following:

1. A study of the diaconate itself.
2. An examination of the meaning of personal commitment.
   The biblical view of the Christian as one totally committed to God, offering all one is and has to God, should be examined and applied in depth.
3. Emphasis on spiritual development.
   Instruction should include discussion of prayer and the spiritual life. Each candidate should be committed to using the means of spiritual growth. Special attention should be given to the Sunday Eucharist, daily prayer, regular personal use of the Scriptures, and participation in the total life of the Christian community.
4. A review of the Church's basic teaching.
   Primary areas of instruction in this adult-level review would be the Holy Scriptures; Christian doctrine particularly relating to the Creeds, the Sacraments, and the nature of the Church and its ministry; prayer and Christian worship; the history of the Church; and Christian conduct or ethics.
5. A comprehensive knowledge of the Bible.
   Though this is included under item four, it is of sufficient importance to list separately. Deacons as adult members of the Church generally should have an extensive knowledge of its Bible and know how to use it responsibly. Training in this area should include how to think theologically about any problems presented to them, whether in the Church or in the world.

6. Specific training in the particular ministry or ministries anticipated for the respective diaconal candidate, when appropriate. This may be practical or theoretical or both.
7. Participation in a "support group" within the parish structure, if possible. The primary emphasis here should be on the Christian community. Any tendency towards an "elitism" or "exclusivism" which could occur if such a group is composed of deacons from a single parish should be avoided.[25]
8. Participation in a continuing support program for deacons. This program would include meetings of deacons on a regular basis, as need indicates, in both parishes and regional or diocesan areas.

The time needed for the specific training of the diaconal candidate prior to ordination could well be less than the two years called for in the U. S. Roman Catholic program or even the year and a half normally required in the Episcopal Church.[26] Candidates would normally already have demonstrated their Christian conviction and basic fitness for this ministry by their life in the Christian community. A year could, in many instances at least, give ample time both for adequate special instruction and for testing the vocation to this form of ministry.[27] However, at this juncture it would perhaps generally be better to require at least a year for training and testing prior to formal admission to candidacy, and then another several months before ordination, more to allow time for testing than for training.

Examination of those in the diaconal program would come primarily prior to their formal admission as candidates and would be more concerned with sincerity of commitment and purpose than content of knowledge. Following approval, it is fitting and proper that formal admission take place at a public service, which would best take place in the parish church when the congregation is gathered together, such as in the context of the Sunday Eucharist.

Training for this ministry, as indeed for all others, needs to be a continuing process so long as the deacon remains active in this ministry. In this connection it should be emphasized that one of the most important parts of this postordination training involves participation when possible in a support system involving other deacons, as has been previously suggested.

Undoubtedly experience in training programs will lead to deeper insight into the content and character of these programs and will help mold those of the future, as has already occurred in some of the Roman Catholic programs.[28] Meanwhile, the Church might do better to err on the side of emphasizing too little theological training rather than too much for this ministry. The training of devout and committed lay people, which puts training for *diakonia* at the heart of the program, will encourage a broad spectrum of candidates with many diverse gifts, often already developed, to seek the diaconate and will provide the Church with an abundance of "servant flags" to recall all the people of God to their servant ministries.

NOTES

1. Pope Paul VI, *Laying Down Certain Norms Regarding the Sacred Order of the Diaconate* (*Ministeria Quaedom*), issued *motu proprio*, 15 August 1972, printed in *The Deacon, Minister of Word and Sacrament*, Study Text VI, prepared by the Bishops' Committee on the Liturgy (Washington: United States Catholic Conference, 1979), p. 4.
2. Bishops' Committee on the Permanent Diaconate, *Permanent Deacons in the United States: Guidelines on Their Formation and Ministry* (Washington: United States Catholic Conference, 1971), p. 9, par. 18.
3. Pope Paul VI, *Approval of a New Rite for the Ordination of Deacons, Priests and Bishops*, Apostolic Constitution, 18 June 1968, United States Catholic Conference, Washington, D.C., p. 5.
4. Bishops' Committee, *Permanent Deacons*, p. 32, par. 98.
5. *A Self-Supporting Ministry and the Mission of the Church*, A Group of Sixty Bishops, Other Clergy and Lay People of the Episcopal Church (New York: The Division of Christian Ministries of the National Council of the Episcopal Church, and the Overseas Missionary Society, 1964), p. 5. Though this statement appears in a section of the report relating to "a Self-Supporting Priesthood," the report later states that this applies also to deacons.
6. Bishops' Committee, *Permanent Deacons*, p. 28, par. 82.
7. Ibid., pp. 28, 29, par. 84–88.
8. Letter dated 8 July 1977 to the author.
9. Address: Education for Ministry, Bairnwick, Sewanee, Tn. 37375.
10. Title III, Canon 5, Sec. 2 (a), *Constitutions & Canons for the Government of the Protestant Episcopal Church in the United States of America Otherwise Known as The Episcopal Church Adopted in General Conventions 1789–1976 Together with the Rules of Order* (St. Paul, Mn.: North Central Publishing Co., 1976), p. 63.
11. H. Boone Porter, Jr., *Canons on New Forms of Ministry* (Kansas City: Roanridge, n.d.), p. 7.
12. *Constitutions & Canons* (1976), Title III, Canon 5, Sec. 2 (a), p. 63.
13. Ibid.
14. Porter, *Canons on New Forms of Ministry*, p. 7.
15. *The Deacon, Minister of Word and Sacrament*, p. 46.
16. Ibid.
17. Wilhelm Schamoni, *Married Men as Ordained Deacons*, trans. Otto Eisner (London: Burns & Oates, 1955), p. 36.
18. Porter, *Canons on New Forms of Ministry*, p. 7.
19. Richard L. Rashke, *The Deacon in Search of Identity* (New York: Paulist Press, 1975), p. 69.
20. Karl Rahner, in vol. 5: *Later Writings*, trans. Karl H. Kruger, in *Theological Investigations* (Baltimore: Helicon Press, 1966), 5:312.

21. Ibid.

22. Edward Echlin, *The Deacon in the Church Past and Future* (Staten Island, N.Y.: Alba House, 1971), p. 117.

23. "Decree on the Missionary Activity of the Church" 2.3.16, in *The Documents of Vatican II, All Sixteen Official Texts Promulgated by the Ecumenical Council 1963–65*, ed. Walter M. Abbot (New York: Guild Press, 1966), p. 605.

24. Personal communication to the author.

25. Interestingly, the diaconal candidates visited by the author in their two-year preordination training program in the Archdiocese of Omaha began apparently as members of a nonchanging diaconal group but more recently have been shuffled at regular intervals.

26. Bishops' Committee, *Permanent Deacons*, p. 30, par. 90. *Constitutions & Canons (1979)*, Title III, Canon 10, Sec. 2. The Episcopal canon provides that "under special circumstances" the time may be shortened to six months.

27. Porter, *Canons on New Forms of Ministry*, p. 7.

28. Note the portion of a letter from the priest directing the Permanent Diaconate Program of the Archdiocese of Omaha quoted earlier in this chapter. "The Basic Philosophy of the Permanent Diaconate Program for the Archdiocese of Omaha" also points this out (Mimeographed, c. 1977, Archdiocese of Omaha),p. 5.

CHAPTER 13

The Wholeness of the Church

The renewal of the diaconate envisioned here involves no less than its restoration as a full and equal order. This does not, of course, mean a reconstruction of the office as it was in the early Church but rather its renewal in the modern world to serve the Church in terms of our own day and our particular needs. The deacon will again be the symbol par excellence of the servant-Christ and the whole mission of service given by him to us his people. The office of the deacon will then again be the measure by which all ministry is taken, it being the representative form of the whole.

The implications of the restoration of the integrity of the diaconate are so far-reaching and profound that we can only begin to see them. No less than the nature of the Church and its wholeness is involved.

The restoration of the diaconate as a full and equal order would go a long way towards recovery of a truly organic conception of the Church and its ministry. Probably no single step could do more to bring about expansion of lay ministry in the Church today than making deacons of those who will in the minds of most remain "lay people." Perhaps we shall begin to recover the original and total ministry of the apostolic and pre-Nicene Church in which all are "laity." Perhaps we shall find again the essential oneness of creation seen in Jesus' incarnation as the "sacred" and the "secular" are united in the deacon of today. Perhaps the Church shall again be a servant people who will astound the world and bring forth the accolade, "See how they love one another!"

Could it be that the form of ministry the Church chose so long ago to designate by the lowly term "servant" will be that form which will again make us and the Gospel we bear of our servant-Lord credible to the world?

Appendix

THE ARCHDEACON

The office of archdeacon appears in the latter part of the fourth century. The first reference to the office is that of Optatus, Bishop of Milevis, writing c. 365.[1] Jerome mentions archdeacons as an order[2] and says that every church has a single archdeacon.[3] After his time they are common in both the East and the West.[4] However, the direction of the Spanish Council of Merida in 666 that "every bishop shall have in his cathedral an archpresbyter, archdeacon, and primiclerus" suggests that the practice may not have been universal.[5] Originally the term was used to designate the "bishop's deacon" and not the chief deacon.[6] He was, for many centuries, in deacons' orders.

As the diaconate in general declined in the early middle ages, the position of the archdeacon increased in importance. Though the letters of Pope Leo, 453, in which he objects to Bishop Anatolius of Constantinople removing his Archdeacon Aetius from office by making him a presbyter "under the pretense of promotion" may not be genuine, they serve to illustrate the importance of the office in the fifth century.[7] Archdeacons were assistants and sometimes representatives of the bishop particularly in the administrative and governmental affairs of the Church.[8] As the bishop's principal assistant, he had jurisdiction over other deacons and those in the minor orders in the West,[9] but never in the East.[10] In the East during a vacancy in a see the archdeacon appears to have been its guardian or co-guardian, but evidence for this function in the West is lacking.[11]

Often they administered the charitable distributions of the Church as is to be seen in the collection of canons compiled prior to the end of the sixth century under the name of the Fourth Council of Carthage. Its seventeenth canon directs that "the affairs of widows, orphans, and strangers shall not be transacted personally by the bishop, but through the arch-presbyter or archdeacon."[12] Such legislation as that of the Fourth Council of Toledo, 633, which defines the role of the archdeacon in the meetings of councils, indicates the importance and extent of his position.[13] In 774 Bishop Heddo of Strasburg divided his diocese into three archdeaconries, and from that time on in the West dioceses were divided into archdea-conries to relieve the bishop of administrative duties.[14]

However, by the ninth century priests began to hold the office, and in the twelfth century in the West the archdeacon was generally a priest[15] and had therefore passed out of the history of the diaconate. In the East the archdeacon has never been a priest. They may still be found with some bishops, but they do secretarial work, such as keeping registers and accounts and taking care of correspondence.[16]

DIACONAL VESTMENTS

It is to be noted that the Church did not invent vestments for its clergy. For a long time the clergy wore the same dress as others in the society in which they lived and worked. Pope Celestine wrote to the bish-ops of the province of Vienne and Narbonne, c. 428, condemning the use of special dress for the clergy. He stated, "We should be distinguished from the people by our learning not by our clothes."[17] A picture of Gregory the Great (d. 604) with his father, Gordianus, and his mother, Silvia, shows that as late as the end of the sixth century laymen continued to wear the dalmatic and chasuble over the alb,[18] which had for a long time been the dress of Roman society. The only difference between the dress of Gregory and that of his parents is that the pallium distinguishes the Pope.[19] However, in time the influence of the barbarian invaders, with their shorter garments, altered the classical dress of ancient Roman society, that dress gradually becoming vestments worn by the clergy.[20]

Christian vestments are then derived primarily from the customary dress of the people of the late Roman Empire. But before considering the specific vestments of the deacon, a brief statement by Gilbert Cope giving an overview of the subject, which is often complex and confusing, is help-ful to provide a frame of reference:

> The basic garments are: (1) an *indoor tunic;* (2) an *outdoor cloak.* The classical form of the tunic is the white *alb,* while the cloak exists as both the *chasuble* and the *cope.* Derivatives and variations of the tunic include the following garments: tunicle, dalmatic, rochet, surplice, and cotta. Obviously, in clement weather, indoor clothing may also be worn outside without an overgarment, just as, conversely, for cere-

monial reasons, outdoor robes may be worn indoors. It should be remembered that, though worn under a chasuble, or cope, the tunic is an outer-garment rather than an under-garment.[21]

The Alb

The alb originated from the *tunica alba* of antiquity, which existed in two forms: first, a knee-length garment sometimes without sleeves called in Greek *chiton* and, second, the longer *chiton poderes* or in Latin *tunica talaris* reaching to the feet with either narrow or wide sleeves.[22] This tunic was made of linen or wool and was frequently decorated with a dark russet or purple stripe on either side reaching from the shoulder to the hem or sometimes a single stripe down the middle in front and back, an ornamentation which disappeared as the dalmatic came to be worn over the tunic.[23]

Though some have thought that the *tunica alba* was originally an undergarment,[24] it is more likely that it was simply an indoor garment. It is uncertain when it came to be worn under the dalmatic, but it is definitely present as an undergarment in the sixth century mosaic of Archbishop Maximianus and two deacons in the Church of St. Vitale at Ravenna.[25] The narrow-sleeved alb is clearly visible protruding at the wrist from under the wide sleeves of the dalmatic on the figure of the Archbishop. Though it is not in evidence on the deacons, it is possible that the dalmatics of the deacons were worn "doubtless over albs," as Dearmer thinks,[26] particularly since the deacons were men of considerable prestige at that time. But in the event the alb was not yet customarily worn by the deacons at this time, it soon came to be.

The alb was worn by all clerical orders until the eleventh century. At that time a transition occurred in the West. The surplice began to develop, as we shall shortly discuss, for use both in choir and in non-Eucharistic worship.[27] It was also at this time that an ornamental border or orphrey came to be put around the border of the alb, which was soon reduced to two oblong pieces called apparels on the hem and one on each sleeve.[28]

The Girdle

In antiquity the tunic was normally gathered at the waist by a girdle of some sort for the sake of convenience.[29] The girdle then, as a matter of course, continued to be used with the tunic as that garment acquired the character of a vestment. However, in the Eastern Orthodox Churches the girdle is not worn by the deacon with the *sticharion,* as the version of the alb there is called, though bishops and priests do wear it in the form of a belt called a *zone.*[30] In the West it has in the past been a belt, sometimes called a cincture, of varied color and material,[31] but today, it is usually a long rope with knotted or tasseled ends.

The Amice

The amice, which has never been classed among the official vestments of the Eastern Orthodox Churches, was originally a neckerchief in use in the ancient world as an optional article of apparel to protect other clothing.[32] Mosaics of clergy from the sixth century do not show the amice. By the eighth century it had come into common use among the clergy in the West, though it seems still not to have been used invariably as late as the beginning of the ninth century.[33] Evidence for the decorated amice comes from the tenth century, this ornamentation taking the form of a strip of material called an apparel in the twelfth century.[34] These apparels were in the color of the stole and maniple, contrasting with that of the chasuble or dalmatic.[35]

Originally this rectangular linen garment was put on over the alb, a practice which still survives at Lyons and Milan, though elsewhere the custom of beginning with the amice, which arose in the tenth century due to longer hair styles, is prevalent.[36]

The Stole

The origin of the stole is uncertain. Some have thought that it was originally simply the ancient handkerchief or neckcloth, which was modified to become part of the ceremonial dress of the clergy.[37] However, more recently, it has been maintained that it derives from a scarf worn over the tunic and chasuble in ancient Rome by senators and consuls as an ensignia of their status.[38] This latter view would seem more probable and could indicate a common origin with the pallium worn by the bishops.[39]

The original name of the stole was the *orarium,* which appears to come from the Latin *oro,* meaning to pray, thus implying that it is the special ensign of those who lead public worship.[40] The term *orarion* is still used for the stole in the Eastern Orthodox Churches today.[41] In the West the change in terminology from *orarium* to stole seems to have commenced in the ninth century as a Franco-Germanic innovation but was not apparently used throughout the West as the preferred designation until the thirteenth century.[42]

The stole seems to have been worn as a distinctive mark of the clergy first in the fourth century. The Council of Laodicea, 343–381 states that the subdeacon has no right to wear the stole.[43] Since it is not mentioned in the previous canon respecting the place of deacons, clearly it is worn by them. However, it would appear that as time passed certain of the minor orders adopted the stole. Records of the ninth century reveal that subdeacons and acolytes as well as bishops, priests, and deacons were wearing the stole at that time.[44] But the diaconal stole apparently was not used at Rome until the ninth or tenth century, though it had been adopted universally elsewhere.[45]

The stole seems originally to have been white. Though in the West the material of the deacon's stole is uncertain, in the East it was of linen.[46] Isidore of Pelusium, d. c. 435, records that it was like the bishop's pallium except made of linen instead of wool.[47] In the middle ages in the West the diaconal stole came to be made from richer materials and was heavily embroidered in colors like those of the apparels and in contrast to the colors of the dalmatic. The long, narrow stole of the middle ages becomes the shorter, less graceful stole with wider ends at the close of the medieval period.[48]

The Council of Braga, 563, directs the deacons to wear the stole over the shoulder and outside the tunicle, so that they will not be confused with the subdeacons.[49] It seems probable that the deacons wore their stoles outside their dalmatics and hanging straight down from the left shoulder, as is still the custom in the Eastern Orthodox Churches today.[50] The Council of Toledo, 633, mentions the stole in connection with bishops, priests, and deacons only and specifies that it be worn by the deacon over the left shoulder, "because he *orat, id est praedicat.*" It continues to explain, "The right side of the body he must have free, in order that he may without hindrance, do his service."[51] This is of importance because here we see the primitive emphasis on *diakonia* asserted and symbolized in the deacon's stole. Canon 28 of this council refers to the stole and the alb as the special marks of the deacon in contrast to the stole and chasuble of the priest.[52] Later, when the stole was finally adopted at Rome, it was worn over the left shoulder by the deacon but *under* the "dalmatic or chasuble."[53] Though the chasuble is not usually considered to be a diaconal vestment, for many centuries it apparently was worn by acolytes and subdeacons as well as deacons, priests, and bishops.[54] Duchesne and Dearmer both report that it is still worn in Europe by deacons and subdeacons during penitential seasons.[55] Wearing the stole under the dalmatic may account, as Duchesne believes, for its coming to be caught together on the right side at the waist.[56]

The Dalmatic

The dalmatic seems to have originated as a garment of ordinary dress in the province of Dalmatia, being made from the fine wool for which the province was noted. It was a long white tunic, reaching almost to the ankles, and had wide sleeves.[57] At an early time it came to have a stripe on each side reaching from the shoulder to the hem in both front and back and two similar stripes around the wide sleeves near the border.

Such ornamentation is seen in the picture of a woman praying in the catacomb of Callisto in Rome dating from the middle of the third century.[58] The stripes seem generally to have been either linen or wool.[59] The dalmatic continued for a long time to fit this general description in many places, though by the seventh century other richer materials and colors were beginning to be used.[60]

It is not certain when the dalmatic came to be a distinctive clerical vestment.[61] Though it has been thought that Cyprian wore a dalmatic to his martyrdom,[62] the evidence would not seem to support this contention.[63] There is conclusive evidence that in the time of Pope Damasus, 368–384, bishops and deacons at Rome, and perhaps in that region, wore the dalmatic. But as Dearmer points out, "This early mention of the Christian use of the dalmatic can only refer to its general everyday use."[64] There is no indication that others at Rome had ceased to wear the dalmatic. It appears to have been during the sixth century that deacons and bishops wear the dalmatic as a distinguishing mark of their dress with the bishops adding the chasuble and pallium, though it was probably during the seventh century that the dalmatic finally becomes obsolete in general usage.[65]

The origin of the dalmatic as an ecclesiastical vestment is particularly associated with the Church at Rome. The evidence would seem to indicate that the dalmatic was not worn by deacons in Africa, Spain, and Gaul at least in the latter part of the fourth century, when we know it was at Rome.[66] Not only did it come to be worn by the pope and his deacons, but in time the Roman bishops came to award the use of the dalmatic as a special privilege to certain bishops and deacons of other places. The first recorded instance of this practice is thought to be that of Pope Symmachus, who granted this right to the deacons of Arles c. 500.[67] However, by the ninth century the dalmatic had come to be worn everywhere in the West.[68]

The Surplice

The surplice, as noted earlier, is derived from the alb. In the unheated churches of northern Europe in the middle ages a gown lined with furs was worn during the winter, making it difficult to wear the narrow-sleeved alb over it. As early as the eleventh century there is evidence for the *superpelliceum,* a word meaning a garment worn over the *pelliceum* or fur coat, which has been contracted into the English "surplice." It apparently became a liturgical vestment in the twelfth century and gradually displaced the alb as clerical attire in choir. In the fourteenth century it had come into wide usage. It was

> everywhere established as the essential choir-habit, the substitute for the alb in procession, in the ministrations of Sacraments and all rites outside the actual service of the altar: it was also the official (though not the only) vestment of the lower orders of the ministry.[69]

The early form of the surplice reached like the alb almost to the feet and had sleeves shaped much like the alb except somewhat broader and extending beyond the fingers. The sleeves soon became much fuller, as they have remained until the present time.[70] Though the length of the surplice seems to have varied somewhat prior to the sixteenth century, it remained quite long until the latter part of that century. It was at that time that it began to be abbreviated, except in England where its length and simplicity tended to remain unchanged. In the seventeenth century lace came into use as an embellishment.[71] In Anglicanism in the latter half of the nineteenth century surplices in some places began to be shortened both in the sleeves and the skirt,[72] though most of the clergy continued to wear knee-length or sometimes longer garments. Lace surplices have been a relative rarity in Anglicanism. A marked trend towards the restoration of the simpler and fuller surplice is evident in the liturgical churches of the West today.

NOTES

1. Optatus, *The Work of St. Optatus Bishop of Milevis Against the Donatists*, trans. O. R. Vassall-Phillips (London: Longmans, Green, and Co., 1917), p. 31. Though Vassall-Phillips dates Optatus's first edition c. 373 (p. xxii), Berthold Altaner (in *Patrology*, trans. Hilda C. Graef [New York: Herder & Herder, 1960], p. 435) prefers 365.
2. Jerome, *Epistle* 146 *To Evangelus*, in vol 6: *St. Jerome: Letters and Select Works*, trans. G. Martley, in *Nicene and Post-Nicene Fathers of the Christian Church*, Second Series, ed. Philip Schaff and Henry Wace, 14 vol. (Grand Rapids, Mi.: William B. Eerdmans Publishing Co., 1954), 6:288.
3. Jerome, *Epistle* 125 *To Rusticus* 15, Ibid., 6:249.
4. A. J. Maclean, "Ministry (Early Christian)," in *Encyclopedia of Religion and Ethics*, ed. James Hastings, 12 vol. (New York: Charles Scribner's Sons, 1916), 8:667.
5. Charles Joseph Hefele, vol. 4: *A History of the Councils of the Church, from the Original Documents,* A.D. *451 to* A.D. *680*, trans. William R. Clark, in *A History of the Councils of the Church* (Edinburgh: T. & T. Clark, 1895), 4:483. The primiclerus was the superintendent of those in minor orders including the subdeacons. In the fourth century the title of archpriest was given to the presbyter who presided in the bishop's place over parishes uniting for the principal Sunday Eucharist. In the fifth century the archpriest was the senior presbyter either in years or by appointment of a city who performed many of the bishop's

functions in his absence. His importance declined with the establishment of separate parishes.

6. Edward R. Hardy, "Deacons in History and Practice," in *The Diaconate Now,* ed. Richard T. Nolan (Washington: Corpus Books, 1968), p. 21. Cf. John Bligh, "Deacons in the Latin West since the Fourth Century," in *Theology* 58 (London:1955): 426.

7. Leo, *Epistles* 111–113, in vol. 12: *The Letters and Sermons of Leo the Great,* trans. Charles Lett Feltoe: *The Book of Pastoral Rule and Selected Epistles of Gregory the Great,* trans. James Barmby, in *Nicene and Post-Nicene Fathers,* Second Series (1956), 12:82. Cf. vol. 34: *St Leo the Great, Letters,* in *The Fathers of the Church,* trans. Francis X. Glimm, Joseph M. F. Marique, and Gerald G. Walsh (New York: Cima Publishing Co., 1947), 34:198. The translator notes that these letters are said to be spurious by Silva-Tarouca, *Nuovi Studi,* p. 183.

8. Emil Albert Friedberg, "Archdeacon and Archpriest," in *The Schaff-Herzog Encyclopedia of Religious Knowledge,* ed. Samuel M. Jackson (New York: Funk & Wagnalls, 1908), 1:260. Cf. Bligh: 426, and Bingham (Joseph Bingham, in vol. 1: *The Antiquities of the Christian Church, Books I–III,* in *The Works of Joseph Bingham,* ed. R. Bingham [London: Oxford University Press (new ed.), 1855]), 1:275–81.

9. Bingham, 1:275–76. Cf. Bligh: 426.

10. Edwin Hatch, "Archdeacon," in *Dictionary of Christian Antiquities*, ed. William Smith and Samuel Cheetham (Hartford: J. B. Burr Publ. Co., 1880), 1:138.

11. Ibid.

12. Charles Joseph Hefele, vol. 2: *A History of the Councils of the Church, from the Original Documents,* A.D. *326 to* A.D. *429,* in *A History of the Councils of the Church,* trans. Henry N. Oxenham (Edinburgh: T. & T. Clark, 1876), 2:409–12.

13. Charles Joseph Hefele, vol. 1: *A History of the Christian Councils, from the Original Documents to the Close of the Council of Nicaea,* A.D. *325,* in *A History of the Councils of the Church,* trans. William R. Clark (Edinburgh: T. & T. Clark [2nd ed., rev.], 1894), 1:65. It is to be noted that his function here is liturgical and administrative, not deliberative.

14. Hatch, 1:136.

15. Bingham, 1:280.

16. Leo Gillet, "Deacons in the Orthodox East," in *Theology* 58:417.

17. Percy Dearmer, *The Ornaments of the Minister* (London: A. R. Mowbray & Co. [new ed.], 1920), p. 26. Cf. L. Duchesne, *Christian Worship, Its Origin and Evolution: A Study of the Latin Liturgy Up to the Time of Charlemagne* (London: S.P.C.K. [5th ed.], 1923), p. 381.

18. Cyril E. Pocknee, *Liturgical Vesture: Its Origins and Development* (London: A. R. Mowbray & Co., 1960), Plate 2, opposite p. 21. The picture is believed to be contemporary. Cf. Dearmer, p. 29.

19. Pocknee, p. 14.

20. M. McCance, "Alb," in *New Catholic Encyclopedia* (New York: McGraw-Hill, 1967), 1:245.

21. Gilbert Cope, "Vestments," in *A Dictionary of Liturgy and Worship,* ed. J. G. Davies (New York: Macmillan Co., 1972), p. 365.

22. Ibid., p. 366. Cf. Pocknee, p. 25.

23. Dearmer, p. 41; Pocknee, p. 25; Cope, p. 366.

24. Dearmer, p. 21; Pocknee, p. 25. Dearmer inconsistently tells us that the

ornamentation disappears from the tunic, which he says was originally an undergarment, when the dalmatic came to be worn over it, p. 41.

25. Pocknee, Plate 1, opposite p. 20. See also Dearmer, Plate 8, p. 28. Dearmer states that this portrayal is typical of others.

26. Dearmer, p. 56. Pocknee,pp. 25, 26, seems to agree.

27. Cope, p. 367.

28. Dearmer, pp. 41–42. Cf. Cope, p. 367.

29. Cope, p. 368.

30. Cope, p. 368. Cf. Pocknee, p. 26.

31. Christa C. Mayer-Thurman, *Raiment for the Lord's Service: A Thousand Years of Western Vestments* (Chicago: The Art Institute of Chicago, 1975), p. 30. Cf. Cope, p. 368.

32. Cope, p. 367; Dearmer, p. 80; Pocknee, p. 18. The picture of a sculpture from the second century of the sailor, Blussus, shows him in tunic, amice, and chasuble. Dearmer, Plate 4, p. 15.

33. Cope, pp. 367–68.

34. Dearmer, p. 80.

35. Cope, p. 368.

36. Ibid.

37. Both Duchesne, pp. 390–91, and Dearmer, p. 62, maintain this origin for the stole.

38. Pocknee, pp. 21–22. Cf. Cope, p. 368.

39. Pocknee, p. 21. Cf. Duchesne, p. 391.

40. Pocknee, p. 23.

41. Cope, p. 368.

42. Pocknee, pp. 22–23.

43. *Council of Laodicea*, Canon 22, in vol. 14: *The Seven Ecumenical Councils*, ed. Henry R. Percival, in *Nicene and Post-Nicene Fathers*, Second Series (1956), 14:140.

44. Duschesne, p. 390.

45. Dearmer, p. 63, indicates its adoption at Rome in the ninth century. Duchesne says it was unknown for the deacon and the priest at Rome in the tenth century, p. 390.

46. Duchesne, p. 394.

47. Ibid., p. 391.

48. Pocknee, pp. 23–24.

49. Council of Braga, Disciplinary Canon 9, in Hefele, *History of the Councils*, 4:385.

50. Dearmer, p. 64. Cf. Pocknee, p. 23. Dearmer says that the Orthodox deacon sometimes brings one end round over his right shoulder.

51. Council of Toledo, Canon 40, in Hefele, *History of the Councils*, 4:454. Canon 41 of Toledo is the first synodical legislation ordering a tonsure in the form of a *corona,* which is to be worn by all clergy, "even lectors," as well as priests and deacons (Edward Landon, *A Manual of Councils of the Holy Catholic Church* [London: Griffith Farrar & Co., n.d.], 2:158). Heretofore, the clergy have worn long hair like the laity, only having shaved a little circle in the middle of the head (Canon 41, in Hefele, *History of the Councils,* 4:454).

52. Council of Toledo, in Hefele, *History of the Councils*, 4:453. The canon deals with the restoration of deposed clergy and directs that these vestments be presented before the altar in restoring the lost degree.

53. Duchesne, p. 392.

54. Ibid., pp. 380, 381. Dearmer, pp. 46, 47.
55. Duchesne, p. 381 fn. Dearmer, p. 47.
56. Duchesne, p. 392 fn.
57. Pocknee, p. 37.
58. A picture of this fresco is reproduced by Dearmer, Plate 13, p. 55.
59. Dearmer, pp. 13, 57; Pocknee, p. 37; Cope, p. 376.
60. Pocknee, p. 38.
61. Duchesne, p. 382 fn. He states that ascribing the introduction of the dalmatic to Pope Silvester (314–335), as Herbert Norris and others have done, even as late as 1949, is due to the legendary account of his life written in the fifth century. See Herbert Norris, *Church Vestments: Their Origin and Development* (London: J. M. Dent & Sons, 1949), p. 46.
62. Duchesne says that Cyprian wore "a linen tunic, a dalmatic, and an over-garment, answering to the *paenula,* or planeta" to his martyrdom c. 259 (p. 382).
63. Joseph Bingham is probably correct in asserting that this idea is due to a corruption in the text, since the dalmatic was not at that time a common garment among the Romans and there is no other mention of it among the clergy, 2:299.
64. Dearmer, p. 24.
65. Ibid., p. 28. Cf. Pocknee, p. 37. Duchesne maintains (p. 382) that this had happened by the end of the fifth century, when he says the dalmatic was no longer worn by others, but this is probably too early.
66. Dearmer, p. 24.
67. Ibid., p. 28. Cf. Pocknee, p. 37.
68. Walter Phillips, "Dalmatic," in vol. 6: *A New Survey of Universal Knowledge,* in *Encyclopedia Britannica,* Encyclopedia Britannica, Inc. (Chicago: William Benton, 1961), 6:994. Cf. Cope, p. 376.
69. Dearmer, p. 94.
70. Ibid. Also, see Plates 17 (p. 68), 19 (p. 73), and 20 (p. 74) showing fourteenth and fifteenth century examples of clerical dress including the surplice.
71. Ibid., pp. 94–95.
72. Pocknee, p. 42.

Selected Bibliography

Abbott-Smith, G. *A Manual Greek Lexicon of the New Testament.* Edinburgh: T. & T. Clark, 1937.

Albright, W. F., and Mann, C. S. *Matthew.* The Anchor Bible Series, vol. 26. Garden City, N. Y.: Doubleday & Co., 1971.

Altaner, Berthold. *Patrology.* Translated by Hilda C. Graef. New York: Herder & Herder, 1960.

Ambrose. *Duties of the Clergy.* See *Nicene and Post-Nicene Fathers,* Second Series, vol. 10.

Ambrose. *Saint Ambrose, Letters.* Translated by Mary M. Beyenka. *The Fathers of the Church.* Edited by Roy J. Defarrari. New York: Fathers of the Church, Inc., 1954.

Ambrosiaster. *Pseudo-Augustini. Quaestiones Veteris et Novi Testamenti CXXVII.* Translated by Alexander Souter. *Corpus Scriptorum Ecclesiasticorum Latinorum,* vol. 50. 1908. Reprint. New York: Johnson Reprint Corp., 1963.

The Ante-Nicene Fathers: Translations of the Writings of the Fathers down to A.D. 325. Edited by Alexander Roberts and James Donaldson. American Reprint of the Edition edited by A. Cleveland Coxe. Grand Rapids, Mi.: William B. Eerdmans Publishing Co.

Vol. 1. *The Apostolic Fathers with Justin Martyr and Irenaeus.* 1956.

Vol. 2. *Fathers of the Second Century: Hermas, Tatian, Athenagoras, Theophisbus, and Clement of Alexandria* (entire). 1956.

Vol. 3. *Latin Christianity: Its Founder, Tertullian.* 1957.

Vol. 4. *Tertullian, Part Fourth; Minucius Felix; Commodian; Origen, Parts First and Second.* 1956.

Vol. 5. *Fathers of the Third Century: Hippolytus, Cyprian, Caius, Novatian, Appendix.* 1951.

Vol. 7. *Lactantius, Venantius, Asterius, Victorinus, Dionysius, Apostolic Teaching and Constitutions, Homily, and Liturgies.* 1951.

Vol. 8. *Fathers of the Third and Fourth Centuries: The Twelve Patriarchs, Excerpts and Epistles, the Clementina, Apocrypha, Decretals, Memoirs of Edessa and Syriac.* 1951.

Vol. 9. *Documents, Remains of the First Ages; Biographical Synopsis; Index.* 1951.

Apocalypse (Vision) of Paul. The Ante-Nicene Fathers: Translations of The Writings of the Fathers down to A.D. *325.* Vol. 9, 5th Edition. Edited by Allan Menzies. New York: Charles Scribner's Sons, 1925.

Associated Parishes. *Newsletter.* Alexandria, Va.: June, 1977.
Audet, Jean-Paul. *Structures in Christian Priesthood: A Study of Home, Marriage, and Celibacy in the Pastoral Service of the Church.* Translated by Rosemary Sheed. New York: Macmillan, 1967.
Augustine. *The City of God.* Vol. 2. Translated by John Healy. Edited by R. V. G. Tasker. London: J. M. Dent & Sons, 1945.
Augustine. *St. Augustine's City of God.* Abridged and translated by J. W. C. Wand. London: Oxford University Press, 1963.
Augustine, *City of God. Nicene and Post-Nicene Fathers.* First Series, Vol. 2.
Augustine. *The City of God.* Translated by Henry Bettenson. Harmondsworth, Middlesex, England: Penguin Books, 1972.
Ayer, Joseph Cullen, Jr. *A Source Book for Ancient Church History from the Apostolic Age to the Close of the Conciliar Period.* New York: Charles Scribner's Sons, 1948.
Barrett, C. K. *A Commentary on the Epistle to the Corinthians.* Harper's New Testament Commentaries. Edited by Henry Chadwick. New York: Harper & Row, 1968.
Barrett, C. K. *A Commentary on the Epistle to the Romans.* New York: Harper & Brothers, 1957.
Barrett, C. K. *The Pastoral Epistles in the New English Bible.* London: Oxford University Press, 1963.
"The Basic Philosophy of the Permanent Diaconate Program for the Archdiocese of Omaha." Mimeographed. n.d.
Beare, F. W. *A Commentary on the Epistle to the Philippians.* New York: Harper & Brothers, 1959.
Beasley-Murray, George R. "The Diaconate in Baptist Churches." *The Ministry of Deacons.* Geneva: World Council of Churches, 1965.
Bible, The Holy. *The New Oxford Annotated Bible with the Apocrypha: Revised Standard Version Containing the Second Edition of the New Testament with an Expanded Edition of the Apocrypha.* Edited by Herbert G. May and Bruce M. Metzger. New York: Oxford University Press, 1977.
Bible, The Holy. *The Oxford Annotated Bible: Revised Standard Version Containing the Old and New Testaments.* Edited by Herbert G. May and Bruce M. Metzger. New York: Oxford University Press, 1962.
Bingham, Joseph. *The Antiquities of the Christian Church: The Works of Joseph Bingham.* Edited by R. Bingham (new edition). Oxford University Press, 1855.
Vol. 1: Books 1–3 of *The Antiquities.*
Vol. 3: Books 8–10 of *The Antiquities.*
Bishops' Committee on the Permanent Diaconate. *Permanent Deacons in the United States: Guidelines on Their Formulation and Ministry.* Washington, D.C.: U. S. Catholic Conference, 1971.
Blenkinsopp, Joseph. *Celibacy, Ministry, Church.* New York: Herder & Herder, 1968.
Bligh, John, S. J. "Deacons in the Latin West since the Fourth Century." *Theology* 58: 421–429. London: 1955.
Bonansea, Bernardino M. "Celibacy." *The Encyclopedia Americana.* International Edition, Vol. 6. New York: Americana Corporation, 1977.
Bonner, Gerald. *St. Augustine of Hippo, Life and Controversies.* Philadelphia: The Westminster Press, 1963.
The Book of Common Prayer and Administration of the Sacraments and Other

Rites and Ceremonies of the Church. New York: The Church Hymnal Corporation and The Seabury Press, 1979.

The Book of Common Prayer and Administration of the Sacraments and Other Rites and Ceremonies of the Church According to the Use of the Protestant Episcopal Church in the United States of America. New York: Church Pension Fund, 1945.

The Book of Discipline 1980 of the United Methodist Church. Nashville: Abingdon Press, 1980.

Bowden, John William. *The Life and Pontificate of Gregory the Seventh*. New York: J. R. Dunham, 1845.

Bradshaw, Paul F. *The Anglican Ordinal: Its History and Development from the Reformation to the Present Day*. Alcuin Club Collections, No. 53. London: S. P. C. K., 1971.

Bridel, Claude. "Note on the Diaconal Ministry in the Reformed Churches." *The Ministry of Deacons*. Geneva: World Council of Churches, 1965.

Brockman, Norbert. *Ordained to Service: A Theology of the Permanent Diaconate*. Hicksville, N.Y.: Exposition Press, 1976.

Bruce, F. F. *Commentary on the Book of the Acts*. The New International Commentary on the New Testament. Grand Rapids, Mi.: William B. Eerdmans, 1956.

Callebaut, André. "Saint Francois lévite." *Archivum Franciseanum Historicum* 20 (1927): 193–96.

The Catholic Encyclopedia: An International Work of Reference on the Constitution, Doctrine, Discipline, and History of the Catholic Church. Edited by Charles G. Herbermann et al., vol. 4. New York: The Encyclopedia Press, 1908.

Chrysostom, John. "De Beato Philogonia" 6, *Contra Anomoeos*. In *Patrologia sive Latinorum sive Graecorum*, vol. 48. Edited by J. P. Migne. Tournhout, Belgium: Brepols, n.d.

Chrysostom, John. *Homily* 14. *On Acts 5:34*. *Nicene and Post-Nicene Fathers*. First Series. Vol. 11.

The Church, The Diaconate, The Future. The Report of the Diaconate submitted by The Council for the Development of Ministry to the House of Bishops, The General Convention (Episcopal Church), Denver, Colorado. 1979.

Clement. "The Letter of the Church of Rome to the Church of Corinth, Commonly called Clement's First Letter"—Introduction. Translated by Cyril C. Richardson. *Early Christian Fathers*. Library of Christian Classics. Philadelphia: Westminster Press, 1953.

Cockin, F. A. "Ministers of the Priestly People." *Theology* 65 (January, 1962).

Constitution and Canons for the Government of the Protestant Episcopal Church in the United States of America. 1958. Also 1964 Edition.

Consultation on Church Union. *A Plan of Union for the Church of Christ Uniting*. Executive Committee of the Consultation on Church Union. COCU Distribution Center, P. O. Box 989, Philadelphia, Pa., 19105, 1970.

Cope, Gilbert. "Vestments." *A Dictionary of Liturgy and Worship*. Edited by J. G. Davis. New York: Macmillan Co.

Craig, Clarence F. "Introduction and Exegesis," "The First Epistle to the Corinthians." *The Interpreter's Bible*, vol. 10. New York; Abingdon-Cokesbury Press, 1953.

Cullman, Oscar. *Peter, Disciple—Apostle—Martyr*. Translated by Floyd V. Filson. Philadelphia: Westminster Press and London: S. C. M. Press, 1953.

Dale, Alfred W. W. *The Synod of Elvira and Christian Life in the Fourth Century.* London: Macmillan & Co., 1882.

De Ecclesia: The Constitution on the Church of Vatican Council II Proclaimed by Pope Paul VI, November 21, 1964. Edited by Edward H. Peters. Glen Rock, N. J.: Paulist Press, Deus Book, 1965.

The Deacon, Minister of Word and Sacrament. Study Text VI. Prepared by the Bishops' Committee on the Liturgy. Washington, D.C.: United States Catholic Conference, 1979.

Dearmer, Percy. *The Ornaments of the Ministers.* New ed. London: A. R. Mowbray & Co., 1920.

Delhaye, P. "History of Celibacy." *New Catholic Encyclopedia,* vol. 3. New York: McGraw-Hill, 1967.

Denzer, George A. "The Pastoral Letters." *The Jerome Biblical Commentary,* vol. 2. Englewood Cliffs, N.J., Prentice-Hall, Inc., 1968.

Diaconal Quarterly. Vol. 2, Winter, 1977. Vol. 7, 1, Winter, 1981. Bishops' Committee on the Permanent Diaconate. Washington, D. C.: 1312 Massachusetts Avenue, N. W.

Dibelius, Martin, and Conzelmann, Hans. *The Pastoral Epistles.* Translated by Philip Buttolph and Adela Yarbro. Edited by Helmut Koester. Philadelphia: Fortress Press, 1972.

A Dictionary of Christian Biography and Literature to the End of the Sixth Century A.D. *with an Account of the Principal Sects and Heresies.* Edited by Henry Wace and William C. Piercy. Boston: Little, Brown & Co., 1911.

The Didache: "The Teaching of the Twelve Apostles, Commonly called the Didache." Edited by Cyril C. Richardson. *Early Christian Fathers.* The Library of Christian Classics, vol. 1. Philadelphia: Westminster Press, 1953.

The Didache or Teaching of the Twelve Apostles. Translated by Francis X. Glimm. *The Fathers of the Church.* Vol. 1, *The Apostolic Fathers.* Translated by Francis X. Glimm, Joseph M. F. Marique, Gerald G. Walsh. New York: Cima Publishing Co., 1947.

Didascalia Apostolorum: The Syriac Version. Translated by R. Hugh Connolly. Oxford: Clarendon Press, 1929.

Dix, Dom Gregory. "The Ministry in the Early Church c. A.D. 90–410." In *The Apostolic Ministry: Essays on the History and the Doctrine of Episcopacy,* pp. 183–304. Edited by Kenneth E. Kirk. London: Hodden & Stoughton, 1946.

Dix, Dom Gregory. *The Shape of the Liturgy.* Westminster: Dacre Press, 1945.

Dix, Dom Gregory, ed. "Textual Materials." *The Treatise on the Apostolic Tradition of St. Hippolytus of Rome.* London: S. P. C. K., 1937.

The Documents of Vatican II, All Sixteen Official Texts Promulgated by the Ecumenical Council 1963–65. Edited by Walter M. Abbott. New York: Guild Press, 1966.

Dods, Marcus, trans. Augustine. *City of God. Nicene and Post-Nicene Fathers,* First Series, vol. 2.

Duchesne, L. *Christian Worship, Its Origin and Evolution: A Study of the Latin Liturgy Up to the Time of Charlemagne.* 5th Edition. London: S. P. C. K., 1923.

Duckett, Eleanor Shipley. *Alcuin, Friend of Charlemagne.* New York: Macmillan Co., 1951.

Easton, Burton Scott. *The Pastoral Epistles.* New York: Charles Scribner's Sons, 1947.

Echlin, Edward, S. J. *The Deacon in the Church Past and Future.* Staten Island, N. Y.: Alba House, Society of St. Paul, 1971.

Elders'-Deacons' Manual. Compiled by P. A. Willis. Cincinnati: Christian Restoration Association, 1968.

Ennodius. *Opuscula miscella* 9 and 10. "Benedictio Cerei." *Corpus Scriptorum Ecclesiasticorum,* vol. 6. *Magni Felicis Ennodii: opera omnia.* Recensuit et commentario, Guilelmus Hartel. Apud C. Geroldi Filium Bibliopolam Academiae. Vendobonae, 1882.

Eusebius. *The Church History of Eusebius.* See *Nicene and Post-Nicene Fathers,* Second Series, vol. 1.

Eusebius, *Life of Constantine.* See *Nicene and Post-Nicene Fathers,* Second Series, vol. 1.

Evans, Ernest. *Tertullian's Homily on Baptism: The Text edited with an Introduction, Translation and Commentary.* London: S. P. C. K., 1964.

Farrar, Frederic W. *Lives of the Fathers,* vol. 2. Edinburgh: Adam and Charles Black, 1884.

Filson, Floyd V. *A Commentary on the Gospel According to St. Matthew.* Harper's New Testament Commentaries. Edited by Henry Chadwick. New York: Harper & Brothers, 1960.

Filson, Floyd V. "Exegesis." "The Second Epistle to the Corinthians." *The Interpreter's Bible,* vol. 10. New York: Abingdon-Cokesbury, 1953.

Fine, Benjamin. *The Stranglehood of the I. Q.* Garden City, N. Y.: Doubleday, 1975.

Fisk, E. B. "Finding Fault with the Testers." *New York Times Magazine.* 18 November 1979.

Fitzmyer, Joseph A. "The Letter to the Philippians." *The Jerome Bible Commentary,* vol. 2. Englewood Cliffs, N.J.: Prentice-Hall, 1968.

Florovsky, George. "The Problem of Diaconate in the Orthodox Church." *The Diaconate Now.* Edited by Richard T. Nolan. Washington, D. C.: Corpus Books, 1968.

Ford, J. Massingberd. *A Trilogy on Wisdom and Celibacy.* The Cardinal O'Hara Series. Studies and Research in Christian Theology at Notre Dame. Notre Dame: University of Notre Dame Press, 1967.

Foshee, Howard B. *The Ministry of the Deacon.* Nashville: Convention Press, 1968, rev. 1974.

Fox, J. J., "Papacy." *The Encyclopedia Americana.* New York: Americana Corp., 1938.

Frere, Walter Howard. "Early Forms of Ordination." *Essays on the Early History of the Church and the Ministry by Various Writers,* 2nd ed. Edited by H. B. Swete. London: Macmillan & Co., 1921.

Friedberg, Emil Albert. "Archdeacon and Archpriest." *The Schaff-Herzog Encyclopedia of Religious Knowledge,* vol. 1. Edited by Samuel M. Jackson. New York: Funk & Wagnalls, 1908.

Fuller, Reginald H. "Church." *A Theological Word Book of the Bible.* Edited by Alan Richardson. New York: Macmillan, 1951.

Fuller, Reginald H. *Early Catholicism in the New Testament.* Lectures at the Graduate School of Theology, Sewanee, Tenn., 1970.

Fuller, Reginald H. *Preaching the New Lectionary: The Word of God for the Church Today.* Collegeville, Mn.: The Liturgical Press, 1974.

Gillet, Leo. "Deacons in the Orthodox East." *Theology* 58 (London: 1955): 415–421.

Goodspeed, Edgar J. *The Apostolic Fathers—An American Translation.* New York: Harper & Brothers, 1950.

Goodspeed, Edgar J. Revised and enlarged by Robert M. Grant. *A History of Early Christian Literature.* University of Chicago Press, 1966.

Gregory, Bishop of Tours. *History of the Franks.* Translated by Ernest Brehaut. New York: Columbia University Press, 1916.

Gregory, Bishop of Tours. *De Gloria Confessorum.* In *Patrologiae Latinorum,* vol. 71. Edited by J. P. Migne. Paris: 1879.

Gregory Nazianzen. "On St. Basil the Great." *Funeral Orations by St. Gregory Nazianzen and St. Ambrose.* Translated by Leo P. McCauley. In *Fathers of the Church,* vol. 22. New York: Fathers of the Church, Inc., 1953.

Gwatkin, Henry M. "Deacon." *A Dictionary of the Bible: Dealing with Its Language, Literature, and Contents,* vol. 1. Edited by James Hastings. New York: Charles Scribner's Sons, 1911.

Haddan, Arthur W. "Chorepiscopus." *A Dictionary of Christian Antiquities,* vol. 1. Edited by William Smith and Samuel Cheetham. Hartford: J. B. Burr, 1880.

Haenchen, Ernst. *The Acts of the Apostles, a Commentary.* Philadelphia: Westminster Press, 1971.

Hanson, A. T. "Shepherd, Teacher and Celebrant in the New Testament Conception of the Ministry." In *New Forms of Ministry,* pp. 16–35. Edited by David M. Paton. Research Pamphlets No. 12. World Council of Churches Commission on World Mission and Evangelism. London: Edinburgh House Press, 1965.

Hardy, Edward R. "Deacons in History and Practice." In *The Diaconate Now.* Edited by Richard T. Nolan. Washington, D. C.: Corpus Books, 1968.

Hatch, Edwin. "Archdeacon." *Dictionary of Christian Antiquities,* vol. 1. Edited by William Smith and Samuel Cheetham. Hartford: J. B. Burr Publishing Co., 1880.

Hatchett, Marion J. "The New Book: A Continuation of or a Departure from the Tradition?" *Open: The Newsletter of Associated Parishes,* June, 1977.

Hatchett, Marion J. "Rites of Ordination." Lectures at the School of Theology, University of the South, Sewanee, Tenn. Summer, 1975.

Hatchett, Marion J. *Sanctifying Life, Time and Space: An Introduction to Liturgical Study.* New York: Seabury Press, 1976.

Hatchett, Marion J. "Seven Pre-Reformation Eucharistic Liturgies." *St. Luke's Journal of Theology.* The School of Theology of the University of the South, Sewanee, Tenn. Vol. 16 (June, 1973): 13–115.

Hebert, A. G. *Apostle and Bishop: A Study of the Gospel, the Ministry and the Church-Community.* New York: Seabury Press, 1963.

Hefele, Charles Joseph. *A History of the Councils of the Church.*

Vol. 1. *A History of the Christian Councils, from the Original Documents to the Close of the Council of Nicaea,* A. D. *325.* Translated by William R. Clark, 2nd Ed., Rev. Edinburgh: T. & T. Clark, 1894.

Vo. 2. *A History of the Councils of the Church, from the Original Documents.* A. D. *326 to* A. D. *429.* Translated by Henry N. Oxenham. Edinburgh: T. & T. Clark, 1876.

Vol. 3. *A History of the Councils of the Church, from the Original Documents.* A. D. *431 to* A. D. *451.* Translated by the Editor of Haggenbach's *History of Doctrines.* Edinburgh: T. & T. Clark, 1883.

Vol. 4. *A History of the Councils of the Church, from the Original Documents. A.D. 451 to A.D. 680.* Translated by William R. Clark. Edinburgh: T. & T. Clark, 1895.

Henderson, Robert W. "Notes on the Diaconate in American Presbyterianism." *The Ministry of Deacons.* Geneva: World Council of Churches, 1965.

Hippolytus. *The Apostolic Tradition of Hippolytus.* Translated by Burton Scott Easton. Cambridge: University Press, 1934.

Hippolytus. *The Treatise on the Apostolic Tradition of St. Hippolytus of Rome.* Edited by Dom Gregory Dix. London: S. P. C. K., 1932. New York: Macmillan Co., 1937.

Holmes, Urban T., III. *The Future Shape of Ministry: A Theological Projection.* New York: Seabury Press, 1971.

Holmes, Urban T., III. *Ministry and Imagination.* New York: Seabury Press, 1976.

Ignatius. *The Apostolic Fathers.* Translated by J. B. Lightfoot, ed. and completed by J. R. Hunter. Grand Rapids: Baker Book House, 1956, reprint 1891 ed.

Ignatius. *The Apostolic Fathers,* vol. 1. Translated by Kirsopp Lake. Cambridge: Harvard University Press, 1912, reprint 1970.

Ignatius. "The Letters of Ignatius, Bishop of Antioch." Translated by Cyril C. Richardson. *Library of Christian Classics,* vol. 1: *Early Christian Fathers.* Philadelphia: Westminster Press, 1953.

Ignatius. "The Letters of St. Ignatius of Antioch." *The Fathers of the Church,* vol. 1: *The Apostolic Fathers.* Translated by Francis X. Glimm, Joseph M. F. Marique, and Gerald G. Walsh. New York: Cima Publishing Co., 1947.

Innocent I. *Epistle 37 to Felix.* In *Patrologiae Latinorum,* vol. 20. Edited by J. P. Migne. Paris: 1845.

Irenaeus. *Against Heresies. Library of Christian Classics,* vol. 1: *Early Christian Fathers.* Philadelphia: Westminster Press, 1953.

Jaffé, Philip. *Regesta Pontificum Romanorum,* vol. 1 (A S. Petro ad A. MCXLIII). Leipsig: Veit et Comp., 1885. Reprint, Graz: Akademische Druck-U. Verlagsanstalt, 1956.

Jalland, Trevor G. "The Doctrine of the Parity of Ministers." In *The Apostolic Ministry: Essays on the History and the Doctrine of Episcopacy,* pp. 305–350. Edited by Kenneth E. Kirk. London: Hodden & Stoughton, 1946.

Jalland, Trevor G. *The Life and Times of St. Leo the Great.* London: S. P. C. K., 1941.

Jasper, R. C. D. and Cuming, G. J. Trans. and ed. *Prayers of the Eucharist: Early and Reformed.* 2nd ed. New York: Oxford University Press, 1980.

Jerome. *The Dialogue Against the Luciferians. Nicene and Post-Nicene Fathers.* Second Series. Vol. 6.

Jerome. *Epistle XXVIII Ad Praesidium. De Cereo paschali. Patrologiae cursus completus. Series latina.* Edited by Jacques Paul Migne. Vol. 30. *S. Hieronymi, Tomus undecimus.* Paris: 1846. Published on Microcards, 1960. The Microcard Foundation, Washington, D. C. Fo-60 M359-2, Microcard V. 30—Card 1 (of 6).

Jerome. Letter 146. *Early Latin Theology.* Translated by S. L. Greenslade. *Library of Christian Classics.* vol. 5. Philadelphia: Westminster Press, 1956.

Justin. "The First Apology of Justin, the Martyr." Translated by Edward R. Hardy. *Library of Christian Classics,* vol. 1: *Early Christian Fathers.* Philadelphia: Westminster Press, 1953.

Käsemann, Ernst. *Essays on New Testament Themes.* Studies in Biblical Theology 41. London: S. C. M. Press, 1964.

Käsemann, Ernst. *New Testament Questions of Today.* London: S. C. M. Press, Ltd., 1969.

Kelly, J. N. D. *A Commentary on the Pastoral Epistles 1 Timothy, 2 Timothy, Titus.* New York: Harper & Brothers, 1963.

Kelly, J. N. D. *Jerome: His Life, Writings and Controversies.* New York: Harper & Row, 1975.

Klauser, Theodore. *A Short History of the Western Liturgy: An Account and Some Reflections.* Translated by John Halliburton. London: Oxford University Press, 1969.

Khodr, George. "The Diaconate in the Orthodox Church." *The Ministry of Deacons.* Geneva: World Council of Churches, 1965.

Knox, John. *The Early Church and the Coming Great Church.* New York and Nashville: Abingdon Press, 1955.

Krimm, Herbert. "The Diaconate in the Lutheran Church." *The Ministry of Deacons.* Geneva: World Council of Churches, 1965.

Küng, Hans. *The Church.* Translated by Ray and Rosaleen Ockenden. New York: Sheed and Ward, 1967.

Küng, Hans. *Structures of the Church.* Translated by Salvator Attanasio. New York: Thomas Nelson & Son, 1964.

Lake, Kirsopp. *The Apostolic Fathers,* vol. 1. Cambridge, Ma.: Harvard University Press, 1912 (Reprint 1970).

Lake, Kirsopp. Note 12: "The Communism of Acts 2 and 4–6 and the Appointment of the Seven." *The Beginning of Christianity,* vol. 5: Part 1, *The Acts of the Apostles.* Edited by F. J. Foakes Jackson and Kirsopp Lake. Grand Rapids, Mi.: Baker Book House. Paperback edition, 1979.

Lambert, J. C. and Johnston, George. "Deacon." "Ministry." *Dictionary of the Bible.* Edited by James Hastings. Rev. ed. by Frederick C. Grant and H. H. Rowley. New York: Charles Scribner's Sons, 1963.

The Lambeth Conference 1958. The Encyclical Letter from the Bishops together with the Resolutions and Reports. London: S. P. C. K. and Greenwich, Ct.: Seabury Press, 1958.

Lampe, G. W. H. "Acts." *Peake's Commentary on the Bible.* Edited by Matthew Black and H. H. Rowley. London: Thomas Nelson and Sons, 1962.

Lampe, G. W. H. *Some Aspects of the New Testament Ministry.* London: S. P. C. K., 1949.

Landon, Edward. *A Manual of Councils of the Holy Catholic Church,* vol. 1. London: Griffith Farrar & Co., n.d.

Latourette, Kenneth Scott. *A History of Christianity,* vol. 1: to A.D. 1500. New York: Harper & Row, Publishers, paperback, 1975.

Lawstuter, W. J. "The Pastoral Epistles: First and Second Timothy and Titus." *The Abingdon Bible Commentary.* Edited by Frederick Carl Eiselen, Edwin Lewis, and David G. Downey. New York: Abingdon, 1929.

Lea, Henry C. *The History of Sacerdotal Celibacy in the Christian Church.* New York: Russell & Russell, 1957. First published under the title *An Historical Sketch of Sacerdotal Celibacy in the Christian Church.* Philadelphia: J. B. Lippincott & Co., 1867.

Lemaire, André. "The Ministries in the N. T.: Recent Research." *Biblical Theology Bulletin* III:2 (June, 1973): 133–66.

Lemaire, André. "Pastoral Epistles: Redaction and Theology." *Biblical Theology Bulletin* II.1 (February 1972): 25–42.

Leo. *The Letters and Sermons of Leo the Great.* In *Nicene and Post-Nicene Fathers.* Second Series, vol. 12.

Lietzmann, Hans. *A History of the Early Church.* I: *The Beginnings of the Christian Church.* II: *The Founding of the Church Universal.* Translated by Bertram Lee Woolf. New York: The World Publishing Co. Meridian Books, 1961.

Lightfoot, J. B. *St. Paul's Epistle to the Philippians.* Grand Rapids, Mi.: Zondervan Publishing House, 1963, reprint of 1913 edition.

Lowrie, Walter. *The Church and Its Organization in Primitive and Catholic Times, An Interpretation of Rudolph Sohm's Kirchenrecht.* New York: Longmans, Green and Co., 1904.

Lupton, J. M. *Q. Septimi Florentis Tertulliani—De Baptismo.* Cambridge: The University Press, 1908.

Lutheran Church in America. *Bulletin of Reports, Eighth Biennial Convention of the Lutheran Church in America.* July 21–28, 1976.

Lutheran Church in America. *Minutes, Fifth Biennial Convention.* Minneapolis, Mn., June 15–July 2, 1970. Philadelphia: Board of Publication of the Lutheran Church in America.

Lutheran Church in America. "Report on the Ministry of Deacons." Mimeographed, n.d.

McBain, John M. "What On Earth Are Deacons For?" *The Deacon,* April, May, June, 1977. Nashville: The Sunday School Board of the Southern Baptist Convention, 127 Ninth Avenue, North 37234.

McCance, M. "Alb." "Dalmatic." "Stole." *New Catholic Encyclopedia,* vol. 1, 4, and 13, respectively. Prepared by an Editorial Staff at the Catholic University of America, Washington, D. C. New York: McGraw-Hill Co., 1967.

MacDonald, A. J. *Hildebrand: A Life of Gregory VII.* London: Methuen & Co., 1932.

Macgregor, G. H. C. "Exegesis." "The Acts of the Apostles." *The Interpreter's Bible,* vol. 9. New York: Abingdon Press, 1954.

Maclean, A. J. "Ministry (Early Christian)." *Encyclopedia of Religion and Ethics.* vol. 8. Edited by James Hastings. New York: Charles Scribner's Sons, 1916.

Mayer-Thurman, Christa C. *Raiment for the Lord's Service: A Thousand Years of Western Vestments.* Chicago: The Art Institute of Chicago, 1975.

Michael, J. Hugh. *The Epistle of Paul to the Philippians.* The Moffat New Testament Commentary. New York: Harper & Brothers, n.d.

Moorman, John R. H. *A History of the Church in England.* Second Edition. New York: Morehouse-Barlow Co., 1967.

Moorman, John R. H. *Saint Francis of Assisi.* London: S.P.C.K., 1963.

Moule, C. F. D. "Deacons in the New Testament." *Theology* 58. London: 1955: 405–407.

Müller, Jac. J. *The Epistles of Paul to the Philippians and to Philemon.* The International Commentary on the New Testament. Grand Rapids, Mi.: Wm. B. Eerdmans, 1955.

Neale, John Mason. *A History of the Holy Eastern Church.*
Vol. 2: *The Patriarchate of Alexandria.* London: Joseph Masters, 1847.
Vol. 3: *The Patriarchate of Antioch.* Edited by George Williams. London: Rivingtons, 1873.

Nicene and Post-Nicene Fathers of the Christian Church, A Selected Library of the.

First Series. 14 vols. Edited by Philip Schaff. Grand Rapids, Mi.: William B. Eerdmans Publishing Co., 1956.

Vol. 1. *St. Augustin: Prologomena, Confessions, Letters.*

Vol. 2. *St. Augustin's City of God and Christian Doctrine.*

Vol. 3. *St. Augustin: On the Holy Trinity, Doctrinal Treatises, Moral Treatises.*

Vol. 4. *St. Augustin: The Writings Against the Manichaeans and Against the Donatists.*

Vol. 7. *St. Augustin: Lectures or Tractates on the Gospel According to St. John.*

Vol. 11. *St. Chrysostom: Homilies on the Acts of the Apostles and the Epistle to the Romans.*

Vol. 13. *Saint Chrysostom: Homilies on Galatians, Ephesians, Philippians, Colossians, Thessalonians, Timothy, Titus, and Philemon.*

Nicene and Post-Nicene Fathers of the Christian Church, A Select Library of the. Second Series. 14 vols. Edited by Philip Schaff and Henry Wace. Grand Rapids, Mi.: William B. Eerdmans Publishing Co.

Vol. 1. *Eusebius: Church History, Life of Constantine the Great, and Oration in Praise of Constantine.* Translated and edited by Arthur Cushman McGiffert, 1952.

Vol. 2. *Socrates, Sozomenus: Church Histories,* 1952.

Vol. 3. *Theodoret, Jerome and Grennadius, Rufinius Historical Writings, etc.,* 1953.

Vol. 4. *St. Athanasius: Select Works and Letters.* Translated by Archibald Robertson, 1953.

Vol. 6. *St. Jerome: Letters and Select Works.* Translated by G. Lewis and W. G. Martley, 1954.

Vol. 7. *St. Cyril of Jerusalem. St. Gregory Nazianzen,* 1955.

Vol. 10. *St. Ambrose: Select Works and Letters.* Translated by H. de Romestin, 1955.

Vol. 12. *The Letters and Sermons of Leo the Great.* Translated by Charles Lett Feltoe. *The Book of Pastoral Rule and Selected Epistles of Gregory the Great.* Translated by James Barmby, 1956.

Vol. 14. *The Seven Ecumenical Councils.* Edited by Henry R. Percival, 1956.

Nicetas, David Paphlago. *Vita S. Ignatii.* In *Patrologiae sive Latinorum, sive Graecorum,* vol. 105. Edited by J. P. Migne. Belgium: Brepols, n.d.

Norris, Herbert. *Church Vestments: Their Origin and Development.* London: J. M. Dent & Sons, 1949.

Open. The Newsletter of Associated Parishes. 3606 Mt. Vernon Ave., Alexandria, Va. 22305. June, 1977.

Optatus. *The Work of St. Optatus, Bishop of Milevis, Against the Donatists.* Translated by O. R. Vassal-Phillips. London: Longmans, Green & Co., 1917.

The Ordination of Bishops, Priests, and Deacons: Prayer Book Studies 20. The Standing Liturgical Commission of The Episcopal Church. New York: The Church Hymnal Corporation, 1970.

O'Rourke, J. J. "Deacons—In the Bible." *New Catholic Encyclopedia,* vol. 4. Prepared by an editorial staff at the Catholic University of America. New York: McGraw-Hill, 1967.

O'Shea, W. J. "Easter Vigil." *New Catholic Encyclopedia,* vol. 5. New York: McGraw-Hill Book Co., 1967.

The Oxford Dictionary of the Christian Church. 2nd Edition, ed. by F. L. Cross and E. A. Livingstone. London: Oxford University Press, 1974.

Paredi, Angelo. *Saint Ambrose: His Life and Times.* Translated by Joseph Costelloe. Notre Dame: University of Notre Dame Press, 1964.

Parker, Pierson. "Violence in the Gospels." Lectures at The Graduate School of Theology, University of the South, Sewanee, Tn. Summer, 1972.

Patton, David M., ed. *New Forms of Ministry.* Research Pamphlets No. 12. World Council of Churches, Commission on World Mission and Evangelism. London: Edinburgh House Press, 1965.

Paul VI. *Approval of a New Rite for the Ordination of Deacons, Priests, and Bishops. Apostolic Constitution,* June 18, 1968.

Paul VI. *General Norms for Restoring the Permanent Diaconate in the Latin Church (Motu Proprio).* June 18, 1967. Washington, D.C.: United States Catholic Conference.

Paul VI. *Laying Down Certain Norms Regarding the Sacred Order of the Diaconate, (Ministario Quaedom).* Issued *motu proprio.* August 15, 1972. Printed in *The Deacon, Minister of Word and Sacrament* Washington, D. C.: United States Catholic Conference, 1979.

Paul, Robert S. "The Deacon in Protestantism." *The Diaconate Now.* Edited by Richard T. Nolan. Washington, D.C.: Corpus Books, 1968.

Paulinus. *Life of St. Ambrose.* Translated by John A. Lacy. *Early Christian Biographies.* In *The Fathers of the Church,* vol. 15. Edited by Roy J. Deferrari. New York: Fathers of the Church, Inc., 1952.

Phillips, Walter. "Dalmatic." *Encyclopaedia Britannica,* vol. 6. *A New Survey of Universal Knowledge.* Encyclopaedia Britannica, Inc. Chicago: William Benton, 1961.

Philostorgius *Ecclesiastical History. Patrologiae Cursus Completus Omnium SS. Patrum, Doctorum Scriptorumque Ecclesiasticorum Sive Latinorum, Sive Graecorum,* vol. 65. Edited by J. P. Migne. Turnhout, Belgium: Brepols, n.d.

Plater, Ormonde. *The Deacon in the Liturgy.* Boston: National Center for the Diaconate, 14 Beacon St. 02108, 1981.

Pocknee, Cyril E. *Liturgical Vesture: Its Origins and Development.* London: A. R. Mowbray & Co., 1960.

Polycarp. Massey H. Shepherd, Jr. "The Letters of Polycarp, Bishop of Smyrna, to the Philippians." In *Early Christian Fathers,* vol. 1. Edited by Cyril C. Richardson. Philadelphia: Westminster Press, 1953.

Porter, H. Boone, Jr. *Canons on New Forms of Ministry.* Kansas City: Roanridge, n.d.

Porter, H. Boone, Jr. "Modern Experience in Practice." *New Forms of Ministry.* Edited by David M. Patton. London: Edinburgh House Press, 1965.

Porter, H. Boone, Jr. "Ordained Ministers in Liturgy and Life." *The Living Church,* January 9, 1977.

Prayer Book Studies VIII: The Ordinal. The Standing Liturgical Commission of the Protestant Episcopal Church in the United States of America. New York: The Church Pension Fund, 1957.

The Proper for the Lesser Feasts and Fasts together with the Fixed Holy Days. 3rd edition. New York: The Church Hymnal Corporation, 1980.

Prosper of Aquitaine. *Chronicon,* in *Monumenta Germaniae Historica,* vol. 1. Edited by G. H. Pentz and others. Berlin & Hanover, 1826.

Quasten, Johannes. *Patrology.* Westminster, Md.: Newman Press, 1950.

Rackham, Richard B. *The Acts of the Apostles.* 13th ed. London: Methuen & Co., 1947.

Rahner, Karl. *Bishops: Their Status and Function.* Translated by Edward Quinn. Baltimore: Helicon Press, 1964.

Rahner, Karl. *Theological Investigations.* Vol. 5: *Later Writings.* Translated by Karl H. Kruger. Baltimore: Helicon Press, 1966.

Rashke, Richard L. *The Deacon in Search of Identity.* New York: Paulist Press, 1975.

Reicke, Bo. "Deacons in the New Testament and in the Early Church." *The Ministry of Deacons.* Edited by the Department of Faith and Order. World Council of Churches. Geneva, 1965.

A Religious Encyclopaedia or Dictionary of Biblical, Historical, Doctrinal, and Practical Theology, vol. 1. Edited by Philip Schaff. New York: Funk and Wagnalls, 1882.

"The Report of the Consultation." Part II of *The Ministry of Deacons.* Edited by the Department of Faith and Order. The World Council of Churches. Geneva: 1965.

"A Report on the Restoration of the Office of Deacon as a Lifetime State." By a Committee of the Catholic Theological Society of America, Edward Echlin, Chairman. Made at the request of the Bishops' Committee on the Permanent Diaconate (Roman Catholic). Published in *The American Ecclesiastical Review* 164:3 (March 1971), pp. 190–204.

Research Report, Women in Church and Society. Edited by Sara Butler. Bronx, N.Y.: The Catholic Theological Society of America, 1978.

Richardson, Cyril C. "The Letters of Ignatius." See entry under "Ignatius."

Richardson, Cyril C. "The Teaching of the Twelve Apostles, commonly called the Didache." *Library of Christian Classics.* Vol. 1: *Early Christian Fathers.* Philadelphia: Westminster Press, 1953.

Riley, T. J. "Deacons—In the Church." *New Catholic Encyclopaedia,* vol. 4. Prepared by an editorial staff at the Catholic University of America. New York: McGraw-Hill, 1967.

Robinson, John A. T. "Taking the Lid Off the Church's Ministry." *New Ways with the Ministry.* Edited by John Morris. London: Faith Press, 1960.

The Roman Missal, The Sacramentary. New York: Catholic Book Publishing Co., 1974.

Ross, J. M. "Deacons in Protestantism." *Theology* 58 (London: 1955): 429–436.

Sarapion. *Bishop Sarapion's Prayer Book: An Egyptian Sacramentary Dated probably about* A.D. *350–356.* 2nd edition. Translated by John Wordsworth. London: S. P. C. K., 1923.

Schaff, Philip. *History of the Christian Church,* vol. 2. *Ante-Nicene Christianity* A.D. *100–325.* New York: Charles Scribner's Sons, 1924.

Schamoni, Wilhelm. *Married Men as Ordained Deacons.* London: Burns & Oates, 1955.

Schillebeeckx, E. *Celibacy.* Translated by C. A. L. Jarrott. New York: Sheed and Ward, 1968.

Schweizer, Eduard. *Church Order in the New Testament.* Translated by Frank Clarke. London: S. C. M. Press Ltd., 1961.

Scott, Ernest F. "The Epistle to the Philippians." *The Interpreter's Bible,* vol. 11. New York: Abingdon, 1955.

A *Self-Supporting Ministry and the Mission of the Church.* By a Group of Sixty Bishops, Other Clergy and Lay People of the Episcopal Church. The Division of Christian Ministries of the National Council of the Episcopal Church, and the Overseas Missionaries Society, 1964.

Shepherd, Massey H., Jr. "The Church in the Fourth Century." Lectures at the Graduate School of Theology, University of the South, Sewanee, Tn., Summer, 1970.

Shepherd, Massey H., Jr. "Deacon." "Deaconess: KJV Servant." *The Interpreter's Dictionary of the Bible,* vol. 4. Edited by George A. Buttrick. New York: Abingdon Press, 1962.

Shepherd, Massey H. Jr. "Ministry, Christian." "Priests in the NT." *The Interpreter's Dictionary of the Bible,* vol. 3. Edited by George A. Buttrick. New York: Abingdon Press, 1962.

Shepherd, Massey H., Jr. *The Oxford American Prayer Book Commentary.* New York: Oxford University Press, 1950.

Shepherd, Massey H., Jr. "Prayer Book Revision." Lectures at The Graduate School of Theology, University of the South, Sewanee, Tn. Summer, 1970.

Shepherd, Massey H., Jr. "Smyrna in the Ignatian Letters: A Study in Church Order." *Journal of Religion* 20 (1940): 141–159.

Simpson, E. K. *The Pastoral Epistles: The Greek Text with Introduction and Commentary.* Grand Rapids, Mi.: William B. Eerdmans, 1954.

Siricius. *Epistle 1 to Himerius.* In *Patrologiae Latinorum,* vol. 13. Edited by J. P. Migne. Paris: 1845.

Socrates. *Ecclesiastical History. Nicene and Post-Nicene Fathers.* Second Series, vol. 2.

Sozomen. *Ecclesiastical History: A History of the Church in Nine Books from* A.D. *324 to* A.D. *440.* Translated (none given). *The Greek Ecclesiastical Historians of the First Six Centuries of the Christian Era.* London: Bagster & Sons, 1846.

Sozomen. *Ecclesiastical History. Nicene and Post-Nicene Fathers.* Second Series, vol. 2.

Stamm, Raymond T. "Exegesis." "The Epistle to the Galatians." *The Interpreter's Bible,* vol. 10. New York: Abingdon-Cokesbury, 1953.

Stevenson, J., ed. *Creeds, Councils and Controversies: Documents Illustrative of the History of the Church* A.D. *337–461.* London: S. P. C. K., 1966.

Stevenson, J., ed. *A New Eusebius: Documents Illustrative of the Church to* A.D. 337. New York: Macmillan, 1957.

"Stole," *Encyclopaedia Britannica—A New Summary of Universal Knowledge,* vol. 21. Encyclopaedia Britannica, Inc. Chicago: William Benton, 1961.

Symonds, R. P. "Deacons in the Early Church." *Theology* 58 (London: 1955): 404–414.

Teegarden, Kenneth L. *We Call Ourselves Disciples.* St. Louis: Bethany Press, 1975.

Tertullian. *Tertullian's Homily on Baptism.* The text edited with an introduction, translation, and commentary by Ernest Evans. London: S. P. C. K., 1964.

Thomas, Donald F. *The Deacons in a Changing Church.* Valley Forge, Pa.: Judson Press, 1969.

Thomas of Celano. *The First Life of St. Francis.* Translated in Marion A. Habig, *St. Francis of Assisi: Writings and Early Biographies: English Omnibus of the Sources for the Life of St. Francis.* Chicago: Franciscan Herald Press, 1972.

Titus, Eric Lane. "The First Letter to Timothy." *The Interpreter's One-Volume Commentary on the Bible.* Edited by Charles M. Laymon. Nashville: Abingdon, 1971.

Toynbee, Arnold J. *A Study of History.* Abridgement by D. C. Sommervell. New York: Oxford University Press, 1957.

Turner, C. H. "The Organization of the Church." *The Cambridge Medieval History,* vol. 1. Edited by H. M. Gwatkin. Cambridge: University Press, 1936.

Tyrer, John Walton. *Historical Survey of Holy Week: Its Services and Ceremonial.* London: Oxford University Press, 1932.

Tytler, Donald. "Each in His Own Order." *New Ways with the Ministry.* Edited by John Morris. London: Faith Press, 1960.

Vischer, Lukas. "The Problem of the Diaconate." *The Ministry of Deacons.* Edited by the Department of Faith and Order. World Council of Churches. Geneva: 1965.

Walker, Williston. *A History of the Christian Church.* New York: Charles Scribner's Sons, 1947.

Wallach, L. "Alcuin." *New Catholic Encyclopedia,* vol. 1. New York: McGraw-Hill, 1967.

Wallis, Ernest. "Introductory Notice to Cyprian." *Ante-Nicene Fathers,* vol. 5.

Walsh, Gerald G. "The Letters of St. Ignatius of Antioch." *The Apostolic Fathers,* vol. 1 of *The Fathers of the Church.* Translated by Francis X. Glimm, Joseph M. F. Marique, and Gerald G. Walsh. New York: Cima Publishing Co., 1947.

Wand, J. W. C. *A History of the Early Church to* A.D. *500.* Third Edition. London: Methuen & Co., 1949.

Ware, Timothy. *The Orthodox Church.* Baltimore: Penguin Books, 1964.

Webster's New World Dictionary of the American Language. College Edition. Cleveland: The World Publishing Co., 1966.

Williams, George H. "The Ministry of the Ante-Nicene Church (c. 125–325)," pp. 27–59, and "The Ministry in the Later Patristic Period (314–451)," pp. 60–81. In *The Ministry in Historical Perspective.* Edited by H. Richard Niebuhr and Daniel D. Williams. New York: Harper & Brothers, 1956.

Wilson, Frank E. *The Divine Commission: A Sketch of Church History.* New York: Morehouse-Gorman, 1946.

Winter, Gibson. *Elements for a Social Ethic: Scientific Perspectives on Social Process.* New York: Macmillan, 1966.

Wordsworth, John. *The Ministry of Grace: Studies in Early Church History with Reference to Present Problems.* London: Longmans, Green & Co., 1901.

Wright, J. Robert. "The Distinctive Diaconate in Historical Perspective." June, 1979. Available from The National Center for the Diaconate, 14 Beacon Street, Boston, Ma. 02108.

Wright, J. Robert. "Ministry in New York: The Non-Stipendiary Priesthood and the Permanent Diaconate." *The St. Luke's Journal of Theology* 19 (Dec., 1975): 18–50.

Zosimus. *Epistle 9 to Hesychius.* In *Patrologiae Latinorum,* vol. 20. Edited by J. P. Migne. Paris: 1845.

Index